JÙJÚ

JÙJÚ

A Social History and Ethnography
of an African Popular Music

CHRISTOPHER ALAN WATERMAN

The University of Chicago Press
Chicago and London

Christopher Waterman is assistant professor of music and adjunct assistant professor of anthropology at the University of Washington in Seattle. He has been a professional bassist since the age of fourteen and has performed with jùjú bands in Nigeria.

The University of Chicago Press, Chicago 60637
The University of Chicago Press, Ltd., London
© 1990 by The University of Chicago
All rights reserved. Published 1990
Printed in the United States of America

99 98 97 96 95 94 93 92 91 90   5432

Library of Congress Cataloging-in-Publication Data
Waterman, Christopher Alan, 1954–
Jùjú : a social history and ethnography of an African popular music / Christopher Alan Waterman.
        p.   cm.—(Chicago studies in ethnomusicology)
Includes bibliographical references (p.   ).
ISBN 0-226-87464-8 (cloth).—ISBN 0-226-87465-6 (paper)
1. Juju music—Nigeria—History and criticism. 2. Yoruba (African people)—Music—History and criticism. 3. Songs, Yoruba—Nigeria—History and criticism. 4. Nigeria—Social life and customs.
I. Title. II. Series.
ML3503.N6W4   1990
781.63′09669—dc20
89-28691
CIP
MN

This book is printed on acid-free paper.

For

Richard Alan Waterman
árábá ni bàbá

and

Maxfield Alan Waterman
èbùn pàtàkì

Contents

Illustrations following page 116

Acknowledgments

Although authors are notoriously possessive of them, all books are social things, the products of human relationships. It would be impossible to list here all of the people and institutions that have instructed, stimulated, supported, and nurtured me in ways that contributed to the completion of this book. Much that is good herein is theirs; egregious errors and interpretive excesses are the sole property of the author.

An initial summer of fieldwork in Nigeria (1979) was supported by the Department of Anthropology and the Center for International Comparative Studies at the University of Illinois. My dissertation research (1981–82) was generously supported by the Social Science Research Council and the Fulbright Program of the U.S. Department of Education. The Institute of African Studies at the University of Ibadan kindly offered me a research post and facilitated my visa. The School of Music at the University of Washington allowed me a year's leave (1987–88) to accept a fellowship in the Society for the Humanities at Cornell University, during which I began to turn my dissertation into a book. A subvention from the Graduate School Research Fund of the University of Washington supported preparation of the illustrations.

In Ibadan, Kọla Nicholas Ọlanrewaju Oyeṣiku ("Koli Bobo Around") kept me alive and honest, generously sharing his flat, his musical expertise, his beer, and his friendship. Kọla's family—Mama Yetunde, Yetunde, Funke, Wale, and Laide—provided a haven in times of need. Anjọla Abọdẹrin, the electronics wizard of Oke-Ado, provided technical support, advice, more beer, and many useful insights. Adebisi Adeleke, master drummer, taught me a great deal about the role of the "talking drum" in Yoruba music and helped with the interpretation of drum texts. Christine Purisch provided encouragement, moral support, and a tenacious sense of humor.

Julius O. Araba, Tunde King, the late Bobby Benson, and Chiefs David "Pa" Adeniyi, Adebayọ Faleti, John Ayọrinde, Adeboye Babalọla, and Janet Bọlarinwa kindly shared their rich memories of music and social life in the 1930s, 40s, and 50s. The jùjú musicians of Ibadan—especially Uncle Toye Ajagun, King Bayọ Owo-Ọla, The Honourable Joshua Olufemi, Captain Jide Ojo, Dele Ojo, and Lamina Oguns—put up with my insistent inquiries and helped me in ways too numerous to mention. Tunji Oyelana and the Benders—Tunde Daudu, Tony Akaile, Yọmi, Ṣegun, Jimmy Sato, and Tall Man—provided camaraderie. At the University of Ibadan, Professors Robert G. Armstrong, Saburi O. Biobaku, Afọlabi Ọlabọde, E. O. Olukoju, and Abiọla Irele were sources of collegial support and advice. Thanks are due also to Joe, Aubrey, Chris, and Nina.

Bruno Nettl has been a valued adviser, mentor, and friend. He trained me in ethnomusicology, supported my interest in African popular music, and alternately nurtured and prodded me when appropriate. I am grateful to the other members of my doctoral committee, Norman E. Whitten, Jr., Lawrence Gushee, and Mahir Saul; and to Donald W. Lathrap, John Stewart, Kris Lehman, Clark Cunningham, Claire Farrer, Victor Uchendu, Edward M. Bruner, and Anita Glaze, all gifted and generous teachers. Joseph B. Casagrande was a superb role model in the not wholly unrelated domains of anthropology, poker playing, and grace. I am also grateful to William Belzner, Richard Edging, Lorraine Aragon, Marcia Blaine, Bruce Miller, Cindy Ferre, Tunde Lawuyi, Clark Erickson, Jose Oliver, John Isaacson, Mary Weismantel, and Colin MacEwan for encouragement and friendship.

Charles Keil provided moral support, trenchant criticism, an indispensable collection of gramophone recordings, and his detailed fieldnotes on jùjú music in Ibadan, written exactly fifteen years before my research. The basic schema of jùjú history presented in chapters 3 and 4 owes much to a paper Charlie presented at the 1969 African Studies Association meetings in Los Angeles. John Chernoff has also been a steadfast source of support and advice. Discussions with Akin Euba and a reading of Afọlabi Alaja-Browne's excellent dissertation (1985) deepened my understanding of the early history of jùjú music. Gage Averill, Karin Barber, Phil Bohlman, John Chernoff, Andrew Frankel, Stuart Goosman, Charles Keil, Laurel Sercombe, Lauralee Smith, Philip Yampolsky, and Patricia Waterman read the manuscript at various stages and offered suggestions.

My deepest gratitude is reserved for the Watermans. Patricia has lovingly encouraged me to follow my path, taught me to listen to people's voices, and kept me in touch with my Boasian roots. Brother David's creativity has continually reminded me of the importance of joy in work. My wife Glennis has been a source of joy and comfort, and a writerly critic.

This book bears a double dedication: to Richard, who taught me what a ball it is to play the bass and, although he probably could not have foreseen it, inspired me to study ethnomusicology; and to Maxfield, whose recent arrival has brightened my world immeasurably.

Technical Notes

Linguistic Note

Yoruba is classified as a member of the Kwa subgroup of the Niger-Congo family of languages (Greenberg 1963). The term *Yorùbá* is used in this book to refer to modern Standard Yoruba (SY), the dialect most widely used in education and mass media. Standard Yoruba was developed from the Ọyọ dialect, one of numerous regional variants in southwestern Nigeria. These dialects, which continue to coexist alongside SY and play an important role in the expression of cultural identity, are referred to here by their specific names, for example, Ẹgba, Ijẹbu, Ekiti.

SY is a tonal language with three underlying levels: high (indicated by an acute accent), low (grave accent), and middle (unmarked). In this book tones are represented in all textual transcriptions and analyses of nomenclature, although not in proper names. Yoruba speech is characterized by pitch glides between tone levels, the use of timbral effects to indicate tone (e.g., the low-tone buzz), and down-drift.

The Yoruba orthography established by missionaries and linguists in the nineteenth century is followed, with ẹ for [ɛ], ọ for [ɔ], p for [kp], ṣ for [sh], and N representing nasalization except in initial position or between vowels. A, E, I, O and U have continental values. Elision (usually indicated by an apostrophe) is a common feature of Yoruba speech and is very frequent in sung texts.

Monetary Values

The main unit of Nigerian currency is the Naira (N), subdivided into 100 kobos (k). Dollar exchange rates and real value of the Naira are heavily dependent on the international market for oil and fluctuate wildly. During my 1981–82 fieldwork, the exchange rate of the Naira was about US$1.65.

The informal market value was lower, perhaps $.75. Since the reestablishment of military government and the creation of a second-tier foreign exchange market, the exchange rate of the Naira has declined steeply to about $.20. Monetary figures given in the second part of this book refer to the 1981–82 rates.

1

Introduction

This is a book about the relationship of music, identity, and power in a modernizing African society. I began graduate studies in anthropology after a year on the road with a Top 40 dance band, weary of bland music, gesellschaft bar relationships, and duplicitous club managers. Pursuing an avid interest in African-American culture history, I was struck by the prominence of Yoruba terminology and concepts in neo-African religious traditions of the Caribbean and South America. What, I wondered, might account for the apparent dominance of Yoruba patterns in the theology and practice of Cuban *santeria* and Bahian *candomblé?* Who were these people, anyway?

An initial summer of fieldwork in Lagos and Ibadan (1979) impressed upon me the notion, well-nigh universal among urban Yoruba, that anyone may achieve wealth and high status through the cultivation of patron-client networks. The economic inequities of late–Oil Boom Nigeria register now in my memory as a series of social tableaus: for example, the lavish neotraditional celebrations where lace-clad elites "sprayed" money onto the heads of praise musicians, while the urban dispossessed gathered round waiting for food, drink, and happiness (*idùnnún*, lit. "sweet-stomachedness") to trickle down; and the patio of the Eko Hotel (part of the Holiday Inn chain), from which dancing African and expatriate elites viewed driftwood shacks perched on a sandbar, a community of the poorest of Lagos's poor, shimmering in the equatorial sun.

When I returned to Nigeria in 1981, I wanted to explore the relationship of music and inequality in contemporary Yoruba society. Several factors led me to concentrate on jùjú music. First, I knew that jùjú had played an important role in the expression of Yoruba nationalism after World War II, although it was surely not the only genre of popular music to have done so. In addition, jùjú was the economically and stylistically preeminent Yoruba popular music during my stay and seemed an obvious choice for a

1

dissertation topic.[1] Other factors appear more serendipitous in retrospect. I was lucky to meet and become fast friends with Kọla Oyeṣiku, the son of J. O. Oyeṣiku, a well-known guitarist of the 1950s (see chapter 4). Kọla is an urban intellectual, an ex-prison guard, accountant, and versatile guitarist. Because he played on a temporary basis with most of the jùjú groups in Ibadan—a strategy of purposive self-marginalization rooted in a profound mistrust of bandleaders—Kọla was able to offer unique insights into the micropolitics of the local music scene. He helped me make connections, vouched for my character, and sheltered me in his one-room flat—along with his wife and four children—when several of my Fulbright checks temporarily disappeared into the maws of the Central Bank of Nigeria.

And, finally, I loved the music. I was fascinated by the melding of "deep" Yoruba praise singing and drumming, guitar techniques from soul music, Latin American dance rhythms, church hymns and country-and-western melodies, pedal steel guitar licks and Indian film music themes, and by the fact that this modernist bricolage could so effectively evoke traditional values. One jùjú bandleader made the point neatly: "You know, our Yoruba tradition is a very modern tradition."

As my work progressed—observing performances, interviewing musicians and patrons, and making music—I was increasingly drawn to historical problems, particularly the efflorescence of Yoruba popular culture during the 1920s and 1930s. The first part of this book (chapters 2–4) thus describes the development of jùjú and a number of its early twentieth-century stylistic antecedents. This social history is complemented in the second half of the book (chapters 5, 6, and 7) by an ethnography of jùjú music and musicians in the city of Ibadan during the period 1981–82.

The problem of combining ethnographic and historical approaches in the study of musical change has been addressed by John Blacking:

> From a purely practical point of view, there are conflicting needs to study a musical system both intensively in its social context and at various stages of its evolution. . . . The year or two that is normally allowed for fieldwork in ethnomusicology rarely provides opportunities for observing musical change and the sequences of decision-making that lead to it, and yet studies of music history can be misleading without the microscopic data that can only be obtained by intensive study of the cultural and social context of music-making (Blacking 1977:13, 14).

How well I have mediated the "conflicting needs" cited by Blacking is for the reader to judge. The first part of this book necessarily emphasizes broad stylistic patterns and institutional forces, while the second focuses more closely on the details of urban Yoruba musical practice and discourse about music. I have attempted to unify the account around a number of themes, including the relationship of continuity and change; the social construction of culture; the role of style in the enactment of identity; and the ideological role of popular culture. My aim is to illustrate how one aspect of Yoruba culture—that is, music—has both reflected and played a role in shaping patterns of social identity. I also attempt to show how large-scale economic and political structures articulate with and broadly condition the localized microprocesses of musical performance.[2]

This is also a tale of two Yoruba cities. The early chapters are situated predominantly in Lagos, cosmopolitan port town and capital of Nigeria since 1914. "Lagos," a popular Yoruba aphorism asserts, "is a bed of sin, a house of wisdom" (Èkó àkéte, ilé ọgbọ́n). The social life of precolonial Lagos was shaped by waves of immigration and two centuries under the hegemony of the hinterland polity of Benin. Thus, although the military conquest of Lagos Island by the British in 1851 marked the beginning of a new historical era, Lagosians already had long experience with social change, cultural and linguistic heterogeneity, and external political control.

The later chapters deal mostly with music and musicians in Ibadan, commercial center and political capital of the former Western Provinces (1939–51), Western Region (1951–76), and Ọyọ State (1976-present). Ibadan, the largest indigenous settlement in Africa south of the Sahara, was founded by refugees and freebooters during the internecine Yoruba wars of the nineteenth century. Yoruba stereotypes of Ibadan stress the excitement and unpredictability of life in the "black metropolis" (Lloyd, Mabogunje, and Awe 1967). "You know Ibadan," the old saw has it, "but you don't know its hidden places, its inner character" (ó mọ̀ Ìbàdàn, óò mọ̀ Láípo)!" Although they differ in many important historical and social-structural respects, both Lagos and Ibadan were "motors of development" (Gutkind 1974:34) of British colonialism in Nigeria, focal points for economic penetration, political control, and syncretic cultural construction.

The Study of African Popular Music

> Division of labor among various social sciences and between the social sciences and the humanities . . . have long worked like a conjuring trick: making vast and vigorous expressions of African experience de facto invisible, especially to expatriate researchers. African scholars have been slow to denounce this state of affairs, perhaps out of an elitist need to set themselves apart from the loud and colorful bursts of creativity in music, oral lore, and the visual arts emerging from the masses (Fabian 1978:315).

The history of African response to European colonialism encompasses nationalist movements, labor strikes, armed resistance, and an astonishing efflorescence of creativity in language, religion, theater, cuisine, visual arts, dress, dance, and music. There was, however, no serious scholarship on the syncretic forms of African popular culture before World War II. This lacuna was related to the colonial imperative to define traditional cultures, and to a fundamental anti-Creolization ideology expressed across a wide range of colonial discourse (Killam 1968; Asad 1973). As Collins and Richards (1982:121) have noted in regard to Anglophone West Africa; "It was supposed that 'savagery' had a certain natural nobility, the full heat of racist venom being reserved . . . for the creole trader families of Lagos and Freetown, who, it was presumed, aimed to thwart 'scientific' principle by disguising a 'natural' condition under a thin veneer of European dress, manners and culture."

The bulk of Africanist urban ethnography from the late 1930s through the 1960s was carried out by British anthropologists, most notably by members of the Rhodes-Livingstone Institute in Northern Rhodesia, now the Institute for Social Research of the University of Zambia (Kuper 1975:182–90; Hannerz 1980:119–62). Although the "Manchester School" produced what is arguably the most cohesive body of monographs in urban anthropology, their concentration on social institutions and networks relegated expressive culture to an ancillary role. Music and dance were generally deemed interesting only insofar as they elucidated patterns of social organization (e.g., Mitchell 1956). Nor did the impact of Marxist theory on African Studies in the 1960s and 1970s encourage the study of popular culture. Marxian analyses have often treated performance arts as superstructural epiphenomena, or assumed that mass cultural forms not explicitly involved in class struggle are counterrevolutionary and thus unworthy of explication.

Evidence of these attitudes is found in the writings of expatriate and African social scientists working within both the structural-functionalist and Marxian traditions. Thus, La Fontaine (1970:3) characterizes Leopoldville as "a city seething with unrest and criminal activity, yet hiding its problems behind a facade of music and bustle," while Ekekwe, in a discussion of the impact of the oil economy on Nigerian culture, asserts that

> one can easily and without exaggeration characterize contemporary urban culture in Nigeria as hostile and alienating. It is a culture of violence. If there is any one dominant note, it is discord and strife. It is very difficult to observe Nigerian urban culture and deduce from it any sense of the inhabitants' self-image and history. Dominant in it are corruption, confusion, bewilderment, and insecurity (Ekekwe 1983–84:21).

That the great majority of city dwellers in Nigeria live in densely populated, unhealthy environs under conditions of tremendous economic hard-
ship can scarcely be disputed. It does not, however, necessarily follow that
Nigerian popular culture is bereft of historical significance. As Karin Barber succinctly phrases the matter:

> the views that ordinary people express may be "false consciousness"
> (a concept not without its own problems) but they are also *their* con-
> sciousness: the "people's" arts represent what people do in fact think,
> believe and aspire to. Their ideology is forged in specific social-
> historical circumstances and takes specific forms (Barber 1987:8).

Ethnomusicological interest in African popular music has expanded
since the first articles appeared in the 1950s (e.g., Nketia 1955, 1957; Rycroft 1956, 1958). This trend, heralded by the appearance of journal issues
devoted to the subject (Kinney 1970; Mukuna 1980b), has been part of a
more general growth of ethnomusicological interest in urban musics worldwide (Nettl 1978c; Manuel 1988). A survey of the literature suggests that
some areas of the continent have received more attention than others; in
general, Southern and West Africa are best represented,[3] while the popular
musics of Central and East Africa[4] have been studied less intensively. Few
attempts have yet been made at systematic comparison; the pioneering
chapter by John Storm Roberts (1972:239–60); David Coplan's (1982) introduction to theoretical problems in the field; and recent popular accounts
by Bergman (1985), Collins (1985a), Stapleton and May (1987), and Graham (1988) provide a basic overview of the subject.

    Studies of African popular music have drawn heavily upon theories
of culture contact developed in the 1940s by Herskovits, Redfield, and
other American anthropologists.[5] Although it has been suggested that ethnomusicologists have too often relied upon "trite generalisations about
cultural 'syncretism' and stylistic 'diffusion'" (Collins and Richards
1982:111), the impact of acculturation theory on ethnomusicology did
have a salutary effect. For one thing, it encouraged the analysis of styles as
cultural structures, as learned, normatively patterned configurations of relationships. Thus, for example, Kauffman suggested that in the music of
the Shona of Zimbabwe

> the exact nature of the individual entities is of far less importance than
> the nature of the processual relationships of these entities. Therefore,
> the use of nontraditional musical products, such as guitars, a Western
> tuning system, I–IV–V harmonies, Western melodies, and 4/4 time
> do not destroy the basic nature of Shona music making, so long as the
> traditional relationships are maintained (Kauffman 1972:50).

Until the late 1970s, the scholar of music in urban Africa was confronted with an anthropological literature that paid little attention to expressive culture, and an ethnomusicological literature strong on acculturation theory but weak on the social and economic organization of performance. The last decade has seen a bridging of this gap, reflected in a surge of interdisciplinary interest in urban African performing arts. This is a movement to which I hope the present book will contribute. Works such as David Coplan's (1985) *In Township Tonight!*, a social history of black music and drama in South Africa; Sylvain Bemba's (1985) study of popular music history in Congo-Zaire; and Karin Barber's (1987) excellent survey of research on the African popular arts are exemplars of this trend. These studies, and others like them,[6] situate the humanistic analysis of performance within a broader perspective concerned with social organization, symbolic communication, and political economy. More important, they suggest that musical style may be more than icing on an infrastructural cake: that patterns of popular performance may not only mirror, but also shape, other social and historical processes.

Style, Identity, and Power in Urban Africa

It is one thing to describe a music, and quite another to explain why it perdures or changes under certain historical conditions. Musical style is grounded in values, "the bases of discrimination between what is music and what is not music, between what is proper music and what is improper music, between what is our music and what is someone else's music, between what is good and meaningful music, and what is bad and inept music" (R. Waterman 1963:85–86). From this perspective, it is clear that an adequate analysis of "the music itself"—a classic example of scholarly animism—must be informed by an equally detailed understanding of the historically situated human subjects that perceive, learn, interpret, evaluate, produce, and respond to musical patterns. Musics do not have selves; people do.

The social anthropological literature on urban Africa emphasizes human adaptation to changing circumstance, as reflected, for example, in the formation of social networks to replace or supplement kinship-based institutions. This emphasis upon adaptive strategy is rooted in the assumption that the heterogeneity and unpredictability of urban life creates unique possibilities, as well as liabilities, for the migrant. In short, life in the city is correlated with choice.

The [urban] migrant does not drop into a predetermined complex of culture patterns or institutions, in which each single factor seems to

> be logically entailed by the others. . . . Instead, he is confronted by
> an institutional diversity which imposes on him the constant need to
> pick and choose. He must build up his own synthesis of habits and
> institutions from a wide available variety, just as he must build up his
> own network of relations (Mayer 1961:14).

The total musical systems of African cities include dominant and counter styles and performance roles, some "surviving from the past and available to be re-worked to form new styles" (Szwed 1970:226). This heterogeneity offers urban residents a degree of latitude in their participation in various musical contexts and the adoption of particular styles as emblematic expressions of identity (Nettl 1985:19). Musical style "carries traces of the processes through which the performer has effected and realized his choices, has established his personal (and social) 'stance' or position" (Blum 1975:217). The total array of stylistic systems and relationships among them provides a "map" of shifting identity patterns in densely populated, culturally heterogeneous urban centers.

An appreciation of the role of individual volition in the construction of culture should not, however, lead us to ignore a broad conclusion of ethnomusicological research: that the values and psychomotor habits guiding musical practice are often subconscious and may prove extraordinarily conservative under conditions of social change (e.g., R. Waterman 1952; Merriam 1964:304–7; Keil and Keil 1977; Nettl 1983:172–86). My interpretation of modern Yoruba music history is based upon the assumption that adaptive strategies are always played out within the limitations of world view and material circumstance.

Culture and society are analytically distinct and mutually constituting aspects of human organization (Geertz 1973b:145; Giddens 1984; Sahlins 1976). Culture patterns are reproduced and transformed through social behavior within the constraints of particular historical situations, while human consociation is ineluctably guided by learned configurations of knowledge, value, and affect. Too often in ethnomusicological writing "culture" and "society" have been treated as interchangeable abstractions or blurred together to form a gray background called "sociocultural context." I want to suggest than an effective analysis of musical practice must concern itself at some level both with the analytical *distinction* between the cultural and the social and with their *necessary interdependence;* and, further, that this dialectic is essential to an understanding of musical history.

Music is both a species of culture pattern and a mode of human action in and upon the world. While it would surely be a mistake to underestimate the "iron hold of culture upon the average individual" (Boas 1932:613), it is also clear that human behavior can never be the "mere execution of the model" that guides it (Bourdieu 1977). Every realization of musical norms in performance carries the potential for purposive or unconscious change; every enactment of tradition opens tradition to transformation (see, for example, Katz 1970).[7]

In many sub-Saharan African cultures aurality and social experience are inextricably linked.[8] Under conditions of pervasive political and economic change, music continues to play a crucial role as a medium of symbolic transaction and a means of forging and defending communities.

> Music is essential to life in Africa because Africans use music to mediate their involvement within a community. . . . As a style of human conduct, [musical participation] characterizes a sensibility with which Africans relate to the world and commit themselves to its affairs. . . . In the midst of change [musical values] characterize a culture's continuity from generation to generation, suggesting the underlying strengths which vitalize the efforts of individuals and communities as they meet the realities of new situations (Chernoff 1979:154).

Musical style may articulate and define communal values in heterogeneous, rapidly transforming societies. The very act of naming a genre— *highlife, jùjú, makossa, tarabu, soukous, chimurenga, marabi,* or *mbaqanga*—may, as Keil (1985:126) suggests, be a declaration of cultural consolidation.

African popular musics have been broadly conditioned by competition for power within colonial and postcolonial political economies. In this book, I view power as a quality inherent in all social relationships, including those enabling and created through performance. Power enters into many aspects of musical production and meaning in urban Africa. Perhaps most obvious is the matter of technology, particularly the electronic reproduction and dissemination of sound. In West Africa, the first commercial recording of music occurred in the 1920s, more than twenty years after European firms began operating in Asia, the Middle East, and Latin America (Gronow 1981:252–53). The trade in mass-reproduced music was for the most part organized along emergent class lines, with performers drawn from the urban migrant wage force and consumers from a small population of African civil servants and merchants. Both the socioeconomic position of the musician and the dynamics of patronage were conditioned by the development of colonial structures of inequality.

One important outcome of the creation of colonial economies— whether predominantly mercantile as in West Africa, plantation based as in parts of Central Africa, or industrial as in South Africa—was the emergence of a mobile population of African workers. In Africa, popular styles have rarely trickled down from the Western-educated elites or bubbled up from an autochthonous wellspring; rather, they are often pioneered by members of an intermediate urban wage force that includes laborers, artisans, drivers, sailors, railway workers, clerks, and teachers (Roberts 1972:254). These cosmopolitan individuals are characteristically adept at interpreting multiple languages, cultural codes, and value systems, skills which enable them to construct styles that express shifting patterns of urban identity. They are the master syncretizers of modern Africa.

The anthropological concept of syncretism is often cited in ethnomusicology; unfortunately, it has commonly been used in ways that rob it of much of its original analytical subtlety. Melville Herskovits, who first used the term to describe the symbolic fusion of West African deities with Catholic saints in neo-African religion, defined syncretism as "the tendency to identify those elements in [a] new culture with similar elements in the old one, enabling the persons experiencing the contact to move from one to the other and back again, with psychological ease" (Herskovits [1945] 1966:57–58; see also Baron 1976). Herskovits knew that *people,* not musics or cultures, accept or reject new ideas and practices. It is ultimately tautological to explain musical dynamics in terms of the retrospective "compatibility" of reified musical structures. Syncretism is fundamentally grounded in human actors' interpretations of similarity and difference, and in their attempts to make sense of a changing world in terms of past experience. Indigenous discourse about musical structure and compatability is a crucial source of data for the study of syncretism.[9]

Cultural creativity and economic adaptation are intimately linked as migrants make a place for themselves in the city. In the process of consolidating patronage networks that complement or supplant their daily wages, African urban musicians may act as culture brokers (R. Adams 1975:50–51; Coplan 1982). Highly mobile and positioned at important interstices in heterogeneous urban societies, they forge new styles and communities of taste, negotiating cultural differences through the musical manipulation of symbolic associations. Proletarian experience is encoded—often ambiguously or ironically—in performance styles, "maps of meaning which obscurely re-present the very contradictions they are designed to resolve or conceal" (Hebdige 1979:18). I do not hold, however, that syncretism is of necessity inherently subversive or that it always serves the interests of the oppressed (cf. Comaroff 1985: 197–98). In the final chapter of this book, I argue that syncretic modes of expression may in fact uphold hegemonic ideological patterns. At the very least, analyses of cultural accommodation and resistance must take into account the specificity of particular social formations and historical moments (see Genovese 1976, who amply demonstrates this point with regard to African-American "slave culture").

Finally, African popular music provides a window on the experiences

and values of groups characteristically excluded from dominant institutionalized means of representing history. Terence Ranger emphasized this in
his pioneering study of the *Beni Ngoma,* a colonial performance tradition
of southern and eastern Africa:

> the "masses" did not control formal means of articulating their de-
> sires—the universities, the pulpit, the press, the theatre, the political
> pronouncement—and . . . when spokesmen did emerge they were at
> instant risk. For this reason, we have to look at the informal, the fes-
> tive, the apparently escapist, in order to see evidence of real experi-
> ence and real response (Ranger 1975:3).

The Popular and the Traditional in Yoruba Musical Culture

The Yoruba—some twenty million strong—live in southwestern Nigeria,
from the Guinea Coast west of the Niger Delta, two hundred miles inland
to the Niger River, and west into the Benin Republic (formerly Dahomey)
and Togo (see map 1). Yorubaland straddles two broad ecological zones:
the lagoons, swamps, and dense rain forest of the south, and drier grass-
lands and laterite hills in the north. The mainstays of traditional economy
are sedentary hoe farming, craft specialization, and trade. The major food
crops are tubers, grains, and plantains, and the Yoruba grow nearly all of
Nigeria's cocoa, the nation's major export product before the Oil Boom of
the 1970s.

Yoruba urbanism predates the first direct contact with Europeans in
the fifteenth century. "The reasons for the initial establishment of Yoruba
towns were probably similar to those elsewhere in West Africa: a complex
division of labour, craft specialisation giving rise to (and intensified by)
long-distance trade, and the need to control the major trade routes" (Eades
1980:43). Although the Yoruba are often cited as the most highly urbanized
of all sub-Saharan African peoples, the unusual size and number of their
towns dates only from the eighteenth and nineteenth century, when inter-
kingdom warfare over control of slave routes led to the expansion of indigenous population centers such as Ọyọ, and the founding of war camps and
refugee settlements such as Ibadan. The ethnographic literature suggests
that the social organization of Yoruba-speaking peoples varies, although
hieratic political systems supported by an ideology of sacred kingship, kinship systems focused on the mediation of bilateral and patrilineal principles, and the relative economic autonomy of market women are ubiquitous. Population centers of precolonial origin are surrounded by belts of
farms to which individuals commute from their residential compounds in
the town. Goods are sold in markets organized into zones occupied by

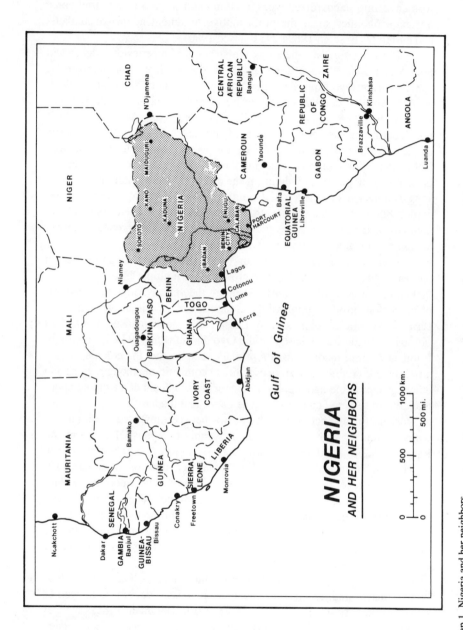

Map 1. Nigeria and her neighbors
Source: K. M. Barbour, J. S. Oguntoyinbo, J. O. C. Onyemelukwe, and J. C. Nwafor, *Nigeria in maps* (New York: Africana Publishing Co., 1982)

women selling standardized types of commodities. Accounts of traditional Yoruba economics stress the profit motive, middlemen, formal markets, and currency (Bascom 1969a:27; Belasco 1980).

The term *Yorùbá*—denoting the subjects of a series of independent precolonial political units (see map 2)—is derived from a name given the subjects of the Ọyọ Empire by their northern neighbors, the Hausa-Fulani. Modern Yoruba identity is crosscut by older kingdom-based ascriptions, such as *Ọ̀yọ́, Ẹ̀gbá, Ìjẹ̀bu, Ifẹ̀, Ìjẹ̀sà, Èkìtì,* and *Oǹdó.* Many individuals thus identify themselves first as Ẹgba, Ijẹbu, or Ekiti, and only secondarily as Yoruba. The notion of a unitary Yoruba people is grounded in mythological charters linking the various kingdoms to the sacred city of Ile-Ifẹ, and present-day monarchs to Oduduwa, the autochthonous culture hero whose sons established the precolonial polities. None of these myths were recorded before the mid-nineteenth century, and it has been convincingly demonstrated that each is the product of multiple reinterpretations linked to competition among kingdoms and factions (Law 1973).

The social construction of pan-Yoruba culture in the late nineteenth and early twentieth centuries was grounded in multiple historical forces, including centuries-old similarities among the various kingdoms; patterns of indigenous military-political hegemony established in the struggle over slave routes; the development by missionaries and linguists of Standard Yoruba, a lingua franca based on the Ọyọ dialect (Law 1977:5); the establishment of print media, mission primary schools, and the colonial wired-wireless radio rediffusion service; political competition among regions and ethnic groups at the national level; and the development of a syncretic popular culture centered on cities such as Lagos and Ibadan.

A useful distinction may be drawn between invented traditions, in which continuity with the past is demonstrably factitious (Hobsbawm and Ranger 1983:2), and normal processes of stereotypic reproduction, in which "the historical—supposedly factual accounts of what has happened—can never be entirely separated from the mythical-persuasive elaborations of what exists eternally and what might be" (Peel 1984:129). Although Yoruba traditions have been reworked with an eye to present and future interests, cultural memory, carried in oral traditions, constrains the play of strategic reinterpretation. Yoruba notions of tradition are neither etched in stone nor spun of thin air.

It is now frequently noted by ethnomusicologists that terms such as "art," "folk," "traditional," and "popular" represent ideological as well as musical categories (e.g., Nettl 1983:303–14; Bohlman 1988). Neither Standard Yoruba (Abrahams 1981) nor the many localized dialects related to it include a term mapping the semantic field of the English term "popular music." The literal translation *orin aráyé,* "songs of the people," is not

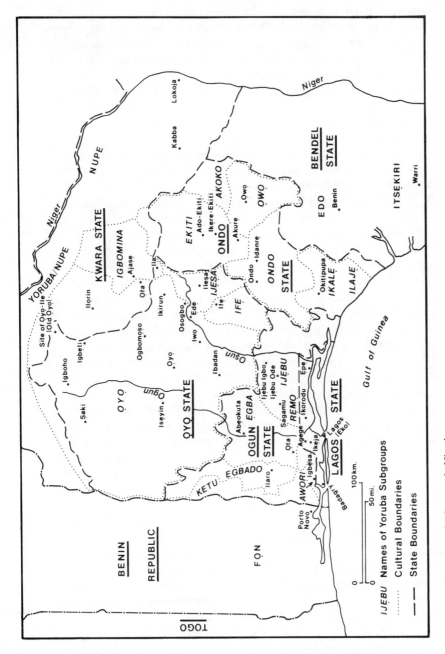

Map 2. Yoruba towns and subgroups in Nigeria
Source: J. S. Eades, *The Yoruba today* (Cambridge: Cambridge University Press, 1980)

commonly used. Innovations in musical practice, or any form of expression, are referred to as àrà, thus the term orin àrà, "a new [kind of] song." The term ìjìnlẹ̀ẹ̀, a fusion of the verb jìn ("to be deep") and the noun ilẹ̀ ("ground"), approximates the sense of the English term "traditional," and shares much of its ideological valence. Customs referred to as "authentic" or "original" by English-speaking Yoruba informants are àṣà ìjìnlẹ̀ẹ̀ Yorùbá, that is, "deeply grounded Yoruba practices." In this book I use the term ìjìnlẹ̀ẹ̀ Yorùbá to indicate traditions or expressive features that informants commonly viewed as deeply grounded in both a historical and affective sense. It is very difficult to draw a strict empirical boundary between the traditional and the popular in contemporary Yoruba culture, and the category of art music evaporates altogether, except in nationalist rhetoric, where the notion of "the traditional" as "art" may hold sway.

A tentative parallel may be drawn between the sociosymbolic organization of Yoruba foodways and music. In precolonial communities social rank was not clearly encoded in culinary distinctions. The meals of Yoruba kings, while exceptionally copious, were generally constructed from the same essential ingredients as the meals of commoner-farmers. In the late nineteenth century the most salient symbolic boundary was that drawn between ìjìnlẹ̀ẹ̀ Yorùbá food—the standard two-dish format of a starchy porridge or loaf and a stew of palm oil, pepper, and various meats and/or vegetables—and the bourgeois culinary practices of Western-educated African elites in Lagos—canned goods, salads, desserts (cf. Goody 1982.)[10]

The social symbolism of Yoruba musical style appears to have exhibited a broadly similar pattern. While a sacred king or powerful interest group (for example, a chieftaincy line, cult, or occupational guild) might exercise prerogatives over certain texts and sound-producing instruments, the core techniques and values of Yoruba musical performance—call-and-response patterns, complex aural configurations generated from the juxtaposition of multiple repetitive patterns, hierarchical structures and dense aural textures, the centrality of metaphor and panegyrics—were shared by commoners and royalty. An important symbolic distinction was drawn between the music of the town/sacred center, on the one hand, and music of the village or bush, on the other. Some notion of urbanity and bucolicity (the hip vs. the hick) thus predates the direct influence of European values. In the late nineteenth and early twentieth century literate African elites, centered in Lagos, patronized Western classical and ballroom music as a means of linking themselves to European prestige and power. This conceptual opposition was, as I hope to show, crucial grist for the mill of Yoruba cultural nationalism between the World Wars.

There is no satisfactory descriptive overview of musical styles in southwestern Nigeria. It is nonetheless clear that the study of Yoruba musical style involves at least two descriptive levels: features common to Yoruba music as a whole; and features or styles restricted to particular geographical areas, institutional settings, or segments of the population. It is possible to list a number of attributes that broadly characterize traditional Yoruba music: for example, unison and octave singing; relaxed, clear, and open vocal quality; call-and-response, verse and chorus forms; the use of rhythmic ostinatos; the technique of combining individual patterns to create complex rhythmic gestalts; the use of musical instruments to imitate speech; and the grouping of instruments into hierarchically organized families, usually with a "mother" as leader (Thieme 1967; Euba 1975).

Some of these features occur less consistently than others. Thus, although much traditional Yoruba singing is in unison or octaves, the polyphonic song styles of Ekiti and Ilẹṣa—which use major seconds and minor sevenths as points of resolution—and a large body of Western-influenced popular and religious music incorporating aspects of functional harmony are notable exceptions. While it is true that an open, relaxed quality is broadly characteristic of Yoruba singing, specialized types of praise and historical singing and styles influenced by Islamic practice are marked by vocal tension and nasalization.

The complex division of labor and cultural variation characteristic of Yoruba society is correlated with the existence of hundreds of named musical genres. In a survey undertaken in 1965, Darius Thieme compiled a tentative list of thirty-five types of music types recognized by his informants. He suggested that this roster represented only "a very small fraction of the styles now practiced by Yoruba musicians" (Thieme 1967:38).

Thieme also noted what he called general "tendency towards eclecticism, or borrowing, from other areas, Yoruba as well as non-Yoruba" (Thieme 1967:36). The incorporative nature of much Yoruba music is but one aspect of a more extensive culture pattern, what might be termed a utilitarian syncretic ideology (Baron 1976). The Yoruba have in general been willing to adopt new ideas and practices, provided that they prove efficacious. In the realm of religion, for example, many Yoruba see "nothing inconsistent about combining traditional rites at home with church or mosque attendance, though Christian and Muslim leaders preach against it" (Eades 1980:118). This relativistic stance is related to a well-developed conception of the interdependence of the social and the sacred.

The word *awo*, so fundamental a concept in Yoruba religion, as well as meaning 'secret' also means something like 'sacred mystery' or 'spiritual power'. It is by being made into a "secret" that a spiritual being gets its authority. It has been said "If something we call "*awo*" has nothing in it to frighten the uninitiated, let's stop calling it "*awo*":

but if we put a stone in the gourd and make a couple of taboos to stop
people looking into it, it's become an "*awo*". The face of a denizen of
heaven is "*awo*" for the very reason that if you removed its costume
you might find nothing there" (Barber 1981:739).

This pragmatic interpretation of the supernatural finds its parallel in Yoruba
categorizations of music, which demonstrate a keen appreciation of the
social uses of cultural forms. Yoruba genres vary significantly in terms of
instrumentation, rhythm, tempo, dynamics, text, dialect, use of harmony
or polyphony, and vocal technique (Thieme 1967:38–39). However, most
of my informants distinguished musical types primarily on social grounds:
who plays a type of music and patronizes the musician, what the music is
used for, and where and when it is played. While professional musicians
are more likely than nonspecialists to cite technical features when discussing genre boundaries, they also frequently invoke social criteria.

> [Yoruba] musical style is often associated with cultural practices
> which establish forms and not with the expressive forms per se, nor
> with the rigidity of their surface structures. . . . Diversities which re-
> sult from individual styles, cumulative time periods or from perform-
> ance frequencies of expressive forms are not necessarily regarded as
> changes of musical style so long as these diversities are in conformity
> with the cultural practices which established the musical genre. The
> tradition recognizes that no two performances are completely identi-
> cal; no two performers have exactly the same musical style; and of
> course not two time periods are completely the same. Hence musical
> style among the Yoruba has a broad definition and change in it seems
> to be defined in terms of a combined change in tradition, cultural prac-
> tices as well as expressive forms (Vidal 1977:82).

The most widely patronized Yoruba popular musics at the time of my
research were *jùjú,* a branch of the West African urban guitar band tradition; and a cluster of styles patronized and produced mostly by Muslims,
including *wákà, sákárà, àpàlà,* and *fújì.* Each of these genres is comprised
of hundreds of local variants, developed by urban musicians seeking to
secure productive niches in a precarious informal economy. The high value
placed on stylistic individuality is reflected in a jùjú bandleader's boast to
Charles Keil: "What you can study in my music, you can't study in another
man's music. The style I'm playing, no one else is playing in Western
Region" (Keil 1966–67:65).

Popular music is a public arena for the symbolic negotiation of
continuity and change. Several of my informants asserted that certain
bandleaders who coined new terms to describe their styles were simply

indulging in public relations, and that their "new" styles were often not distinguishable from their "old" styles on musical grounds. In discussing an elderly musician, two jùjú musicians said that they favored him because he played "the latest songs." Pressed for an explanation, one of them responded, "why we say he plays the latest music is that when he compose any new song now and then make record of it, well, we term that as the latest song. Maybe an olden song, that he just have some changes there. And then he turn it his own modern way" (Keil 1966–67:99).

Audiences take delight in neologistic terms for performance styles. Thus one jùjú bandleader calls his individual style *àdáwà*, "our independent creation," while another performs *àpọ́là*, a term used to describe a piece energetically separated from a homogeneous mass, for example, a chunk of wood chopped from a tree, a single lobe split from a kola nut, or a distinctive stylistic variant. Musicians regularly coin new terms as a means of boosting their public reputation for innovation: for example, *New Brian Fújì, Fújì Reggae, Bàtá Fújì, Talazo (Disco) Fújì, Syncro System, Mìlíkì System, Yo-pop,* and *Why Worry? Jùjú.* Technological "improvement" is also an omnipresent theme. Collins and Richards (1982:116) have discussed the "new instrument ethos" of much West African popular music.

> Musicians may attain prominence by claiming to be the first with a new instrument or style of playing. . . . A juju band of the 1980s is likely to have instruments, including synthesisers and amplification, worth many thousands of Naira. A recently re-equipped band will take space in the press to announce the launch of its equipment.

At the same time, Yoruba popular culture is often self-consciously traditional in form, function, and feeling. Ìjinlẹ̀ẹ̀ Yorùbá values often guide the use of imported technology. Thus, for example, photographs have sometimes come to replace *ère ibéjì*, small wooden statues in human form which embody the sacred power of twins.

> If the twins are of the same sex and one dies, the surviving twin is taken to the local photo studio and is photographed. The image is double printed so as to simulate the twins sitting together as they would have in life. This image is then framed under glass, placed on the family shrine and given the necessary food offerings. . . . One young high school teacher thought it was not a good idea because the photographs could not be washed or dressed and in any event were not as durable as wood carvings. On the other hand, an 80-year old traditional Yoruba king held the opposite view. He said that the only reason that wood carvings were made for twins in the first place was because

photography has not yet been invented when the practice first began. As he put it, "A carving is just a counterfeit of a human being. A photograph is better because it's a carbon copy of the person" (Houlberg 1983:14–15).

Even the most self-consciously traditional of Yoruba genres have been mass-reproduced and disseminated via electronic media. For example, *oríkì* chanters are expected to control a corpus of texts praising and recounting the histories of local kin groups and political institutions. When oríkì groups make commercial recordings or appear on radio or television, they rework their materials to appeal to a larger, more heterogeneous audience. It is impossible for even the most skilled performer to memorize the specialized mnemonic metaphors associated with lineages in the various villages and towns where his recordings are distributed. He must therefore develop a generic corpus of standardized filler texts. Although it is tempting to attribute this shift in performance practice solely to the impact of Western technology and commodification, the flexibility of contemporary oríkì is also clearly rooted in traditional performance norms and techniques.

> An oríkì performance is a string of units added on one after another. Since they are all periphrases for names, they are all in a sense equivalent to each other, and it does not make such difference where the performer cuts them off. There is no internal design which assigns each unit to a determinate position and which prepares for and culminates in the poem's ending. It is true that the singer will have a stock of formulas for opening, closing, and shifting from one theme to another, but these are more like indications of intent or signposts than structural features arising from the inner requirements of the poem's form. Indeed, the starting, stopping, and changes of direction in these long, homogeneous chants are as often as not governed by social rather than formal requirements (Barber 1984:508–9).

Other traditional verbal genres which have been commercially recorded include *ijalá*—hunters' chants for the *òrìṣà* (deity) Ogun, popularized by Alabi Ogundepọ—and *ìwì egúngún*—chants associated with the *Egúngún* ancestral cult, recorded by Mofoyeke Ajangila. The biggest contemporary stars are *ekéwì*, specialists in chanting *ewì*, a term which used to be synonymous with ìwì egúngún, but is now used to mean "poetry in general" (Euba 1975:473). The flexibility of ewì makes it a perfect candidate for wide dissemination via mass reproduction. As E. O. Olukoju, a scholar of the genre, puts it, "modern ewì suits anybody."

The two most popular ewì exponents are Lanrewaju Adepọju and Ọlatobọsun Ọladapọ, both residents of Ibadan. Adepọju was the first ekéwì to use musical backgrounds on his recordings and to establish his own record label. His 1982 album *Ọmọ Oduduwa* ("Children of Oduduwa"; Lanrad LALPS 117) recounted in poetic form the stereotypical characteristics of the Ifẹ, Ibadan, Ilọrin, Ọffa, Isẹyin, Ọwọ, Igbẹti, Ọyọ, Oro, Oṣogbo, Ekiti, Eko, and Ẹgba Yoruba sub-groups, while at the same time emphasizing their shared mythological origins and political interests. This hegemonic image of a heterogeneous yet fundamentally unified Yoruba world was rooted in a double agenda: to reinforce Yoruba unity as the 1983 national elections approached; and to sell the record over as wide a territory as possible.

Ọladapọ, who began his recording career after Adepọju, has further modernized ewì, emphasizing the musical component of performances in an attempt to compete with popular dance music genres such as jùjú and fújì. While Adepọju's recordings are primarily for listening, those of Ọladapọ are consciously designed to be suitable for dancing. Ọladapọ, unlike Adepọju, sometimes stops chanting entirely, foregrounding the accompanying instrumental ensemble. The musical backgrounds for commercially recorded ewì vary, generally relying on a variety of idiophones and drums, and sometimes aerophones such as flutes (*fèrè*).

Despite influence from Yoruba popular music, ewì continues to evolve along lines dictated in part by old genre distinctions. Ewì is chanted (kì), not sung (kọ), a distinction based both upon melodic contour and regularity of pulse. Unlike dance music genres, the rhythmic relationships between the background accompaniment and vocal performance is indeterminate. In a typical recording of ewì, the chant floats over a metric structure, and the distinction between poetic discourse and musical background is clearly maintained. Contemporary ekéwì have thus been able to incorporate the metric infrastructure of popular music without sacrificing the distinctive speech-based rhythms of their formerly more specialized genre.

Just as ìjinlẹ̀ẹ Yorùbá genres are mass-reproduced and electronically mediated, so a great deal of Yoruba popular music draws upon a repository of deeply grounded rhetorical techniques. Sandra Barnes quotes a song by jùjú superstar Sunny Ade, publicizing the switch from left-hand to right-hand driving in 1972. In this song Ade draws upon aspects of the genre ìjalá, dedicated to Ogun, patron god of warriors, hunters, metalsmiths, mechanics, surgeons, and drivers:

> You, motorcycle riders and bicycle riders,
> We should drive on the right-hand side of the road.
> Let's be careful, let's be careful.

Let's pay tribute to Ogun before we go out.
I hear the sound of iron rods when I pass the forge.
Blacksmith, I too will survive today.
We shall be taking the right-hand side of the road in Nigeria.
Let's be careful, let's be careful.
Let's pay tribute to Ogun before we go out. . . .
Hail, Ogun. Honor the visitor [i.e., the new system]
Hail, Ogun. Honor the visitor.

(Barnes 1980:50).

Current events, particularly political developments, are continually encoded in popular song texts. For example, the charismatic Ibadan Yoruba leader Adegoke Adelabu was killed in an automobile accident in 1958. It was widely believed that his death had been caused by supporters of his political rival, Ọbafẹmi Awolowo, a native of Ijẹbu. As rumors spread in Ibadan, many Ijẹbu Yoruba migrants were attacked, their houses burned, and property destroyed. Within six months of the vent, a dozen recordings appeared in a variety of genres discussing the incident. The following song by àpàlà star Haruna Iṣọla, from Ijẹbu-igbo, demonstrates the role of the popular musician as mediator.

Haruna Iṣọla and his Apala Group. "The Late Adelabu" Recorded in Lagos, 1958. Decca WA. 3034. [*Cassette example 1*].
> *Ẹja ńlá lọ nî' bú, àrìrà wọ' lè, erin ṣonù nî' gbó*
> *Èkó l' Adélabú lọ to ńpada bọ, agbègbè Òdè Rémọn l' ó ti ṣe*
> *gégé Ikú*
>> A big fish has gone into the ocean, something very good has
>> entered the ground, the elephant has got lost in the bush
>> Adelabu went to Lagos and was coming back, near Ode Remon
>> he met Death
> *Ód' ọla kón tó rojó-o, ekùn á gb' èbùrú ò lo m' éléjó*
> *Kò s' órìṣà tí ó ṣe bí Ogún, mo mọ̀-o*
> *Ẹ̀yin ará Ìbàdàn, taní ó gba' pò Adélabú?*
>> Tomorrow they will gossip, the lion will take a short cut to hold
>> the person responsible
>> There is no god that can do like Ogun, I know-o [i.e., that can
>> kill with metal]
>> People of Ibadan, who will replace Adelabu?

TALKING DRUM
> *Adélabú Adégòkè igídá!*
>> Adelabu Adegoke, a tree is fallen!

Aago mérin ìrọ̀lẹ́ kojá,
Máàrṣì tùéntì-fáífì, Naíntífífti-étì, l'ọ́jọ́ kẹta òsè tí ńṣe Tusde
Èkó l'ó ti ḿbò, Adé kò fẹ́ sinmi
Okìkí ayé

> Four o'clock in the morning has passed
> March 25, 1958, on the third day of the week Tuesday
> He is coming from Lagos, Ade doesn't want to rest
> Noise of the world [gossip]

Eṣé-o, gègé orí ọ̀gán lo
Ọkùnrin tí kì ìfọ̀yà, l'órítá méfà
Gbàdàmóṣí, penkelemési, ó lọ
Ògbójú alátakò tí ḿbá jọba t'ọpá iṣẹ́

> Thank you, it is the straw on top of the ant hill [that will indicate
> the killer].
> A man that is very brave, when he gets to a six-way cross-roads
> Gbadamosi, "peculiar mess" [popular nickname for
> Adelabu], he's gone.
> The courageous opposition leader that straightened the rod of
> work [accomplished many things]

Lórí ibojì Adélabú, àwọn ènìyàn jànkàn-jànkàn ni, nwọ́n ńsokún
Áwọn bíi Dennis Osadebey-o, Okotieboh, nwọ́n sokún fún lórí ité

> At the grave of Adelabu, important people, they are crying
> People like Dennis Osadebey and Okotieboh [political allies of
> Adelabu], they cried as he was laid to rest

Ikú Adélabú ba nkan jẹ́
Ilé tí wọ́n fọ́ n'Íbàdàn ólé lógójì,
Ayọ́kẹ́lẹ́ ọkọ uń lo bí ọgbọ̀n,
Ẹ̀mí ò l'óńkà,
Bí wọ́n ti tẹ̀l'Adélabú

> Adelabu's death has spoiled things
> They smashed more than forty houses in Ibadan
> As many as thirty comfortable cars were destroyed
> The lives [lost] are uncountable
> That is how they followed Adelabu

Ení kú ṣ'ọba tán
Enìyàn t'ó 'kú lẹ́hìn, ló tó kó rò'rí
Má f'ọrun yọ̀mí ọta, ṣo mọ̀-o?
Ìrìn àjò l'awà, gbogbo wá là dá agbádá Ikú

> The deceased behaved like a king
> People that Death has left behind [on earth] should use their
> heads to think.
> Don't make rash judgments, you know?

We are on a journey, all of us have cut the *agbada* [long formal gown] of Death

[CONTINUES PRAISING DIGNITARIES AT ADELABU'S FUNERAL]
Adégòkè, gbogbo Naijíríà ló mọ̀ p'ẹ́ja ńlá ti bómi lọ
Adegoke, all Nigeria knows that a big fish has entered the water and gone.

Mass-reproduced music, disseminated via cassettes, radio, and television, is an effective medium of social commentary. Hundreds of records in the gramophone library of Lagos State Radio—inherited from the old Nigerian Broadcasting Service—are marked NTBB (Not To Be Broadcast), their surfaces crossed with a wax pencil to prevent their being played on the air and offending one faction or another. The ideological content of Yoruba popular music ranges from the explicitly class-conscious critiques of Fẹla Anikulapọ-Kuti, whose Afro-beat style is most popular among urban youth in Lagos, to the tacit support for status quo values characteristic of jùjú and other forms of neotraditional praise music (see chapter 7). Even the claim that musicians should remain above the political fray, advanced by many upwardly mobile Yoruba bandleaders, has clear ideological implications. Those subjects that a musician avoids may reveal the limits of his social and ideological position (Macherey 1978; Barber 1982).

The social status of Yoruba popular musicians is ambivalent. The biggest stars are *gbajúmọ̀n* (big-shots), their electronically mediated aural and visual image appearing in the home, the marketplace, and on public transportation. The superstars of each genre are often arranged in oppositional pairs—for example, Sunny Ade and Ebenezer Obey in jùjí music, Sikiru Ayinde Barrister and Ayinla Kollington in fújì, Haruna Iṣọla and Ayinla Ọmọwura in àpàlà, and Yusuf Ọlatunji and S. Aka in sákárà. They may own expensive automobiles, have many wives and children, and rub shoulders publicly with powerful politicians and wealthy traders; yet they are still praise singers, a role widely associated with begging.

The Janus-faced relationship of praise and abuse—in order to praise a patron one must denigrate his enemies—is reflected in the competitive rhetoric of musicians. In some cases these disagreements are rooted in the struggle for control over scarce technological resources. In an interview with the tabloid *Variety Entertainment* (May 1982:13) published in Ibadan, jùjú star Shina Peters discussed his feelings about former co-bandleader Ṣegun Adewale:

"I love Segun greatly. My love for him transcends that of a woman to a man. In fact if he were a woman, I would woo him to marry me. I only do not like him but love him with all my heart, mind and soul."

"Segun is the type that is rare to be found. He has never been my enemy contrary to what the public thinks of our relationship."

"The relationship is fantastic, matured, and the best among friends. Tell the whole world that if Segun were a woman, I would definitely settle down with him and I am sure he would make a good husband," he remarked.

Shina however has an axe to grind with Segun on the question of some instruments alleged to be borrowed by Shina from Segun Adewale's band and which he has never returned.

Segun had alleged that Shina came to get the instruments under the pretext that he was going to do one advertisement for Nestle company. In a sharp reaction, the smiling face changed suddenly, and like somebody possessed, he (Shina) explained to me that his former boss, Mr. Kazzim, never knew Segun before and that all the instruments were solely owned by himself and the question of borrowing his instruments therefore did not arise.

He then advised him (Segun) to always watch his public utterances and reminded him that those who live in glass houses should never throw stones.

Feuds between stars are the subject of public gossip and are sometimes extended over a series of recordings. For example, fújì music star Ayinla Kollington and female wákà star Salawa Abẹni produced a notorious series of mutually abusive hit records in 1981 and 1982. After Abẹni married a wealthy Lagosian businessman, Kollington claimed that he was the biological father of her first child. His hit song, "Taní ó jọ?" ("Whom does it resemble?"), included the line "I was the first to eat her yam, it was very black".[11] The aggrieved Salawa Abẹni responded with the song "Bàbá rẹ ni ó jọ," ("It resembles its father!"), in which she describes Kollington as an "illiterate good-for-nothing" while praising his competitors Sikiru Ayinde Barrister, Sunny Ade, Ebenezer Obey, and Haruna Iṣọla. Another of her LPs features a cartoon strip depicting "The Rise and Fall of Baba Alatika," a disparaging reference to Kollington's nickname.[12] These exchanges harness traditional abusive rhetoric to the profit motive, since fans must buy the entire sequence of discs to keep up with the feud.

The private lives of musicians are dissected in a lively entertainment press, including both well-established offshoots of the major urban newspapers, such as *The Entertainer* and *Lagos Weekend,* and dozens of fly-by-night tabloids available on the streets and in the markets of Yoruba towns.[13] During the Kollington vs. Abẹni controversy, *The Entertainer* ran a front page article: "Stop It! Salawa's Child Is Mine, Husband Warns"

I can no longer keep quiet watching my people insulting my wife, Alhaj Lateef Adepọju, Salawa Abẹni's husband has declared. He told

'The Entertainer' at his office along Sipeolu Street, Lagos during the
month that arrangements had reached advanced stage with his firm of
solicitors to drag a fuji band leader to court . . . "You will agree with
me that music or no music, records or no records, my primary duty as
a husband is to protect my wife against unwarranted embarrassment
from whatever source," he explained (Adewoye 1982).

The competition between fújì superstars Barrister and Kollington has
also been a matter of great public interest. This excerpt from an interview
with Barrister in the tabloid *Variety Entertainment* (May 1982), published
in Ibadan, is typical:

Q: What is your present relationship with Ayinla Kollington like?
A: Two good friends.
Q: Don't pull any wool over my face, my dear bros. Trying to con-
vince me to the contrary when the whole world knows what goes
on. . . . If you are very good friends, how many times have you
and Kollington exchanged visits, apart from the verbal warfare that
is common knowledge. Can you eat in Kollington's house?
A: No. I can't, why should I eat in his house.
Q: Then my point is vindicated that you are not friends.
A: If Kollington invites me to eat in his house then I have no fear but
how can I eat in his house if he doesn't invite me.
Q: Why don't you invite him to your house instead.
A: If he will come.
Q: Why won't he come.
A: I don't know.
Q: And you say you are friends.
A: Yes.
Q: Then why the abusive songs against each other in records and live-
plays.
A: I have not abused anybody in my records.
Q: And he has not abused you too?
A: If Kollington thinks the only way for him to rise and make a name
is to abuse me so as to sell his records, let him continue. If God
had so wished that the only way for him to get recognition and followers is by abusing me, then he is on the path of his own chosen
destiny. There is no need to stop him. It is a sign of progress on my
own part for my music to be copied. There is nothing wrong for
any struggling Fuji musician to use my name to get recognition
through abusive songs for the purpose of creating markets for his
records and getting his own type of fans. It only shows their ac-

ceptance of my music as the superior one. Why then should I not
be grateful to God for putting me at the top, to be copied and en-
vied by those desperately struggling to make a name at all costs,
crude or fowl [*sic*] (p. 14).

The resolution of feuds is equally well publicized. For example, after
Kollington's fújì rival Barrister produced an album entitled *No More War*,[14]
a photograph of the two competitors sitting together, with a wealthy patron/
mediator's arms around them, appeared in all of the tabloids. Ayinla Kollington eventually won his public dispute with Salawa Abẹni. She divorced
her husband and married Kollington, began recording for his label, and, at
a concert in Ibadan in 1987, knelt before him in a gesture of supplication.

In Yoruba popular culture the technology of mass communications is
enmeshed in a broad discourse about ethics, power, and the relationship of
the new and the old. Even the wealthiest superstar cannot avoid the traditional redistributive responsibilities of the Yoruba king or chief. In a column entitled "Immaturity of Nigerian Musicians," one Lagosian journalist
complained about the flawed character of a fújì bandleader in terms that
might be applied to a self-centered, greedy ọba (king):

> Disappointingly enough, some of them are naive and stereo-typed, in
> particular, bandleaders in juju . . . and fuji brands of music. . . . A
> case in point is the typical example of a once crowd-pulling fuji band-
> leader among the lot. He takes pride and delight in being intractable
> and unnecessarily elusive. For his close friends and fans, to even talk
> to him on the telephone in his abode is problematic. He just can't be
> bothered. When you do buzz his telephone to speak to him, you are
> treated to the sonorous sound from his latest disc, blaring out from the
> answering tape-recorded telephone. Briefly, after that, another taped-
> talking voice takes over from the singing telephone and promptly, mo-
> mentarily interrupt itself followed by: "Sorry I am presently out.
> Please record and leave your name and telephone number for me to
> call you back after my own message stops. I will phone you back."
> You can be sure that after you've gone through all the rituals of leav-
> ing your name, telephone number and address, you will never hear
> from the superstar for months to call you back.
>
> On the other hand, the superstar surely had two wives and three
> security men who are normally left behind in the house. What is also
> most despicable in the man's habit is his constantly rude, bullish and
> threatening behaviour and the approach of one of his security men, a
> mallam, to visitors to the said superstar's house, even when on ap-
> pointment.
>
> Put bluntly, most of these talented artistes are living in a world
> of their own and at the same time, they must come to appreciate that

the acceptance of genuine criticisms is in their own best interests. It would be ironic and a disservice for them to expect praise-singing of their works all the time by review editors and critics, where it is uncalled for (Ajala 1988; 5,14).

While Ajala explicitly rejects the traditional role of praise singer, the rhetorical techniques he uses in exposing the superstar's flawed character are rooted in deep Yoruba values concerning the redistributive responsibility of the wealthy.

I will later return to the argument that the products and imagery of mass-mediated popular culture are continually reinterpreted in terms of ìjinlẹ̀ Yorùbá communal values, a process which plays a role in the social reproduction of those values. However, I want to begin by examining the broad sociohistorical forces that conditioned the emergence of modern Yoruba popular music in the early twentieth century.

2

Sákárà, Aṣíkò, Highlife, and Palmwine: Lagosian Popular Music between the World Wars

Our understanding of the emergence of jùjú music in Lagos between the World Wars should be built upon some knowledge of the history and social makeup of Lagos, and of the genres of popular music which preceded jùjú and played a role in its genesis. The earliest commercial gramophone discs bearing the designation "Yoruba" were recorded in England in the mid-1920s by the Zonophone label (part of the West African EZ series). The first commercial recordings made in Lagos were the work of a field agent of the German Odeon Company, who visited Nigeria 1929 or 1930. While these were surely watershed events in the history of Yoruba popular music, most of the features that characterize popular music worldwide—urban-centeredness, professionalism, mass appeal, the combination of features from diverse sources (Nettl 1978c; Marre 1985; Manuel 1988)—were established in Lagosian musical culture well before the advent of Western recorded technology and mass reproduction.

Music and Social Identity in Early Twentieth-Century Lagos

Lagos, a "sandy and insignificant island, far removed from the centers of power in the Nigerian interior" (Aderibigbe 1975:1), was first inhabited in the fifteenth century by Awori fishermen from the adjacent mainland and nearby coastal islands (Mabogunje 1969:238). The island was involved in a system of periodic markets linking it to communities on the mainland, and its population had, by the middle of the eighteenth century, come to include Ijẹbu traders, Edo-speaking peoples from the kingdom of Benin, and refugees from the Dahomey Kingdom. Major transformations in Lagosian social and political institutions were precipitated by the Atlantic slave trade, which shifted the economic focus of powerful savannah kingdoms, such as the Yoruba megastate of Ọyọ, away from Saharan trade and toward the Atlantic coast. French (1791) and British (1807) laws against

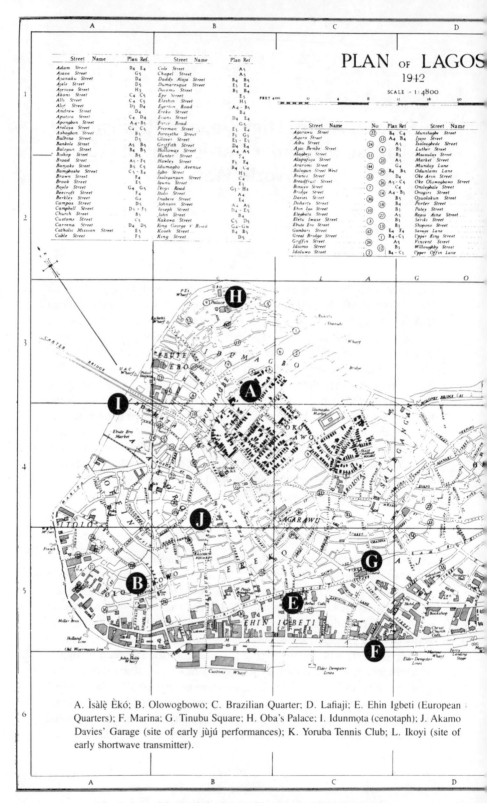

A. Ìsàlẹ̀ Èkó; B. Olowogbowo; C. Brazilian Quarter; D. Lafiaji; E. Ehin Igbeti (European Quarters); F. Marina; G. Tinubu Square; H. Oba's Palace; I. Idunmọta (cenotaph); J. Akamo Davies' Garage (site of early jùjú performances); K. Yoruba Tennis Club; L. Ikoyi (site of early shortwave transmitter).

Map 3. Lagos Island, 1942 Source: Photograph of British colonial survey map, reprinted

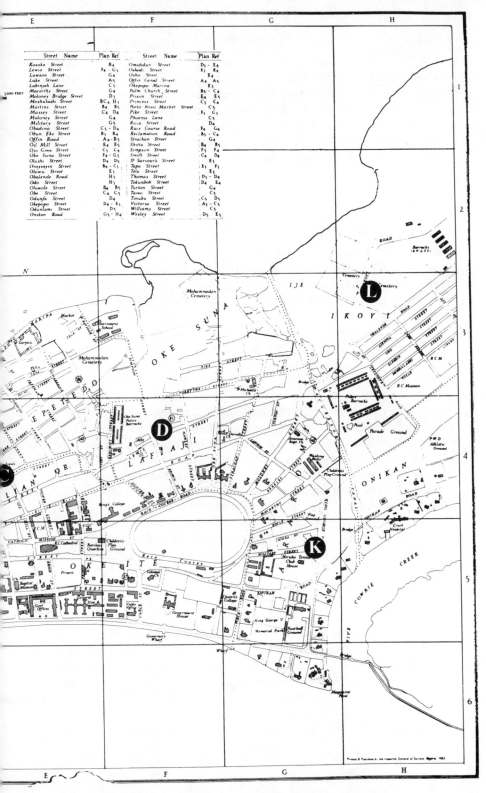

Street Name	Plan Ref	Street Name	Plan Ref
Kosoko Street	B4	Omididun Street	D3 - E4
Lewis Street	F4 - G5	Oshodi Street	E5 E4
Lawson Street	G4	Osho Street	E4
Lake Street	A5	Oftin Canal Street	A4 A5
Labinjoh Lane	C5	Okepopo Marina	E5
Macarthy Street	G4	Palm Church Street	B5 - C4
Moloney Bridge Street	D5	Prison Street	E4 E5
Moshalashi Street	BC4, H3	Princess Street	C3 C4
Martins Street	B4 B5	Porto Novo Market Street	C5
Massey Street	C4 D4	Pike Street	F3 G5
Moloney Street	G4	Phoenix Lane	C5
Military Street	G5	Ricca Street	D4
Obadina Street	C5 - D4	Race Course Road	F4 G4
Obun Eko Street	B3 B4	Reclamation Road	B5 - C4
Offin Road	A4 - B5	Strachan Street	G4
Oil Mill Street	E4 E5	Shitta Street	B4 B5
Ojo Giwa Street	C5 C4	Simpson Street	F3 F4
Oke Suna Street	F4 - G5	Smith Street	C4 D4
Olushi Street	D4 D5	St Saviour's Street	E5
Oroyinyin Street	B4 - C5	Tapa Street	E3 F5
Olowu Street	E5	Tela Street	E5
Obalende Road	H3	Thomas Street	D5 - D4
Odo Street	H5	Tokunboh Street	D4 E4
Oluwole Street	B4 B5	Turton Street	G4
Obe Street	C4 C5	Taiwo Street	G4
Odunfa Street	D4	Tinubu Street	C5 D5
Okepopo Street	D4 - E5	Victoria Street	A5 - C5
Odunlami Street	D5	Williams Street	C5
Onikan Road	G5 - H4	Wesley Street	D5 E5

slave trading reinforced Lagos' share in the trade, as slaving ships found the creeks and lagoons around the island advantageous for avoiding the antislavery squadrons that patrolled the Bight of Benin. The British seized Lagos Island in 1851, and ten years later the town was officially ceded to the British Crown. By 1914, Lagos was capital of the Crown Colony of Nigeria—an amalgamation of the former Southern and Northern Protectorates—and a bustling port town with over 70,000 inhabitants. The population of Lagos was made up of culturally distinctive communities, centered in neighborhoods on the island and adjacent mainland.

The indigenous Lagosian community (Ọmọ Èkó, "children of Lagos"), governed by a sacred king and several specialized lines of chiefs, lived in the crowded northwest corner of Lagos Island (Ìsàlè Èkó or "Old Town"). "Of all the Yoruba kingdoms, Lagos has always been the most remote from the mainstream of traditional Yoruba culture. Lagosians consider themselves to have a unique legendary origin, a distinct corporate identity, and a separate development" (Baker 1974:202).

The traditional royalty's control over political and economic resources was undermined by the British invasion, and rituals associated with kingship and chieftaincy took on added importance as a means of reinforcing the Ọmọ Eko community's sense of cohesion. Ọmọ Eko identity was enacted in performances that symbolized the demographic and cultural layers that made up precolonial Lagos. The royal song genres *igbè* and *karajagba* are, for example, attributed in local traditions to the original Awori Yoruba settlers of the island; the *gbèdu* drum is said to have been introduced by seventeenth century Edo diplomats as a symbol of the hegemony of Benin; the ritual dance and music genre *hunwe* is associated with early migrants from Dahomey; and instruments such as *abèbè* (leather fans) and *dùrù* (plucked idiochord) are attributed to Ijẹbu Yoruba migrants. Isalẹ Eko was home to three types of *bàtá,* the two-headed conical drum of Ṣàngó, the Yoruba God of Thunder, one associated with the Awori, another with the Ijẹbu, and a third with the Ọyọ (Aig-Imoukhuede 1975:209, 210; Vidal 1977:67, 70).

Although reliable data are limited, it is clear that there was a close relationship between musical performance and the portrayal of Lagosian social history and identity. The juxtaposition of genres within a single context was an important feature of performances linked to political authority. Thus, the *Adámú-Orisà* festival, a multimedia dramatic genre first staged in 1854 for the funeral of Ọba Akintoye, utilized materials and techniques associated with the Awori, Ijẹbu, and Ẹgba Yoruba, the Edo, Dahomeans, and other groups involved in the growth of Lagos. Adámú-Orisà performances wove the heterogeneous strands of Lagosian culture history into a hegemonic fabric, providing the Ọmọ Eko with a "cross-sectional view of the many musical and dance traditions of Lagos" (Vidal 1977:71) and an aesthetically satisfying representation of their corporate unity vis-à-vis various groups of immigrants.

Extensive Islamic conversion led to the development of musical genres performed during Muslim holidays (e.g., Ramadan, Id-El-Fitr) and ceremonies marking the return of pilgrims from Mecca (àláji, m.; àlájà, f.). One of the earliest of these genres was *wákà*, sung by women and accompanied by beaten *sẹ́lí* or *pẹ́rẹ̀ṣẹ̀kẹ́*, pounded tin discs with metal rings attached.[1] Another popular genre, *wẹ́rẹ̀* or *ajísáàri*, was performed by groups of young men during the Ramadan fast to wake the faithful for their early meal. Both of these genres incorporated aspects of Islamic cantillation—nasalized, tense vocal quality, melismatic text settings, microtonal melodic embellishments, and Qur'anic texts—into performances guided by Yoruba musical values and techniques. Wákà and wẹ́rẹ̀ were associated with the high status of Islam in traditional Lagos and the continued vitality of economic networks linking the Yoruba to Muslim societies in the northern hinterland.

Professional players of hourglass-shaped "talking drums" such as *dùndún* and *gángan* were members of, or apprentices to, specialized drummers' patrilineages. They performed in a variety of situations and provided a highly effective medium for social criticism and political rhetoric. The importance of these performers in the Isalẹ Eko community is suggested by vociferous protests following British attempts to impose taxation upon drummers' craft guilds. Songs also provided a public channel for praise, derision, and enforcement of social norms. The bawdy satirical song genre *kẹ́rikẹ́ri*, used to ridicule social deviants and non-Yoruba ethnic groups, was periodically banned by colonial authorities (Aig-Imoukhuede 1975: 211).[2]

During the nineteenth century two groups of repatriated Yoruba slaves migrated to Lagos. The *Àgùdà* (also referred to as *Amaro* or Brazilians) were emancipated slaves of Yoruba descent from Brazil and Cuba, who, "having succeeded by industry, frugality or conduct in purchasing their freedom and that of their wives and children, later returned to Lagos" (Mabogunjẹ 1969:243). They settled in the middle of Lagos island, in an area which became known as Popo Aguda or the Brazilian Quarter. The Latin American *emancipados,* including such prominent families as Campos, Da Silva, Fernandes, Gomez, and Pereira, were mostly Roman Catholics familiar with syncretic transformations of traditional Yoruba religious practice. They introduced distinctive styles of architecture, dress, and cuisine; and dominated such skilled crafts as tailoring, carpentry, masonry, and baking (Laotan 1943; Da Cunha 1985).

The Aguda introduced Catholic sacred music, Portuguese and Spanish song forms and guitar techniques, and neo-African music and dance genres such as the *samba da roda,* "a round-dance involving soloists" (Behague 1980:241). Tambourines, guitars, flutes, clarinets, and concertinas were used to perform *serenatas, fados,* and polkas at weddings and wakes in the Brazilian Quarter. The most distinctive Aguda performance traditions were the *burrinha,* an adaptation of the Afro-Brazilian *bumba-meu-boi* carnival tradition with elaborate masquerades called *calungas,* and the *caretta* or Fancy Dance, a syncretic fusion of West African ring dance and European country dance patterns which involved dancers gesturing with a handkerchief in their hand. The *caretta* was eventually adopted by other black immigrant groups in Lagos, and became a mode of competition between various quarters of the city (Akinṣemoyin 1969; Alaja-Browne 1985:18). Although the Aguda constituted only a small part of the total population of Lagos by the outbreak of World War I, their syncretic musical styles profoundly influenced popular music in Lagos. The Brazilians and Cubans, along with other Afro-American migrants from the United States and British West Indies,[3] introduced a range of mature syncretic styles, providing local musicians with aesthetic and symbolic paradigms that could be adapted to African urban tastes.

Many Aguda initially considered themselves socially distinct from and culturally superior to the indigenes. In *The Water House,* Antonio Olinto's novel about late nineteenth and early twentieth century Lagos, an elderly woman cautions a recent immigrant from Bahia:

> We are Brazilians. You have just arrived and you don't know what things are like here. We are civilized people, different from these others. It was us who taught the people here joinery, we taught them how to build big houses, and churches, we brought cassava, cashews, cocoa, dried meat, coconuts. They stare at you with big round eyes and don't know how to enjoy themselves. The only thing they do know is how to cause trouble at our parties. It only needs a good bumba-meu-boi to come out and there's a fight (Olinto 1970:76–77).

The other major black immigrant community in Lagos was the *Sàró.* They were Africans, for the most part Yoruba, freed en route to the New World by the British antislavery patrols and deposited in Freetown, Sierra Leone, where most were educated by British missionaries (Kopytoff 1965). They migrated to towns along the West African coast, settling in Olowogbowo quarter in the southwestern corner of Lagos Island. Predominantly Protestant, they adopted British surnames such as Blaize, Carr, Cole, Davies, Crowther, Johnson, King, Macaulay, and Savage; and emulated petty bourgeois culture, including such indices of civilization as tophats and handlebar moustaches. In the late nineteenth century many of the Sierra Leonean repatriates were upper-level civil servants, missionaries, doctors, lawyers, or merchants representing European interests. Though frequently involved in hinterland political disputes and possessed of romantic notions regarding "authentic" Yoruba tradition, they often adopted a supercilious attitude toward the Ọmọ Eko, who in turn derisively referred to them as *òyìnbó dúdú*, "Black Europeans."

Descriptions of the musical culture of the repatriate elites suggest ideological contradictions stemming from their intermediate position in the colonial political economy. On the one hand, many of the black bourgeoisie emulated British middle-class practices, including "numerous 'conversaziones,' 'soirees,' 'levees', 'at homes,' 'tea fights,' and concerts of the work of Bach, Beethoven, Handel, and so on" (Cole 1975:45–46). By the early twentieth century there were a number of venues in Lagos for such performances, and ballroom dance demonstrations and recitals preceded motion picture showings up until the late 1940s, well into the era of modern Nigerian nationalism (Aig-Imoukhuede 1975:222). Prominent elite musicians performed, conducted, and composed within the stylistic and formal bounds of European concert and popular music traditions. The works of R. A. Coker, the first Nigerian musician formally trained in Europe, and Ekundayọ Phillips, born in Lagos in 1884, who received a certificate in organ and piano performance from Trinity College, were predominantly European in character (Aig-Imoukhuede 1975:216; Echeruo 1977:67–79).

However, the Saro also played a crucial part in the emergence of modern pan-Yoruba culture. They "introduced European technology, institutions and beliefs, but not without participating in transforming some of them to suit African conditions and interests" (Brown 1964:164). The process of cultural syncretism was often ideologically charged. Black elites were increasingly frustrated from the 1890s on by institutionalized racism in the colonial civil service and government favoritism toward European trading concerns and merchants. Their experience of economic and political discrimination by the British colonial administration was exacerbated by the scorn frequently shown by white colonists toward African emulation of European social behavior. Members of the literate African elite, some seventy-two percent of whom in 1915 were Saro, Aguda, or other repatriates (Mann 1985:28), were regarded by many Europeans and traditionalist Yoruba as inferior cultural hybrids who had incompletely adopted aspects of Western civilization and severed themselves from indigenous traditions.

Despite a history of conflict between the indigenous Lagosian community and the Victorian black elite, leaders of the two groups began to forge a political coalition around the turn of the century. This early nationalist movement was a response to British segregation of hospitals, schools, and cemeteries; reorganization of land tenure; and exclusion of blacks, regardless of education level and skills, from administrative positions they had previously dominated.[4] This movement split after World war I into nationalist and collaborationist camps, each including members of the repatriate and Ọmọ Eko elites (Cole 1975).

Nationalist leaders such as Herbert Macaulay were, despite their attachment to British bourgeois culture, keenly appreciative of the rhetorical efficacy of traditional Yoruba musical idioms. The professional drummers' association of Lagos, with an active membership of 108, was an important asset for Macaulay's Nigerian National Democratic Party (NNDP). "Their influence lay in the fact that the drums and songs were in effect the local newspapers and propaganda 'leaflets'—most of the songs were political in nature" (Cole 1975:138). The following passage from Macaulay's *Lagos Daily News* complains about advantages given to drummers supporting the collaborationist faction by the British authorities:

> They ["hooligans," hired by the collaborationists] had drums and drummers; and although the supporters of Prince Eshugbayi Eleko [Macaulay's choice for the Lagosian Ọbaship] have never once obtained a pass or permit to drum in the streets, these men had, each one on him, a ticket on which the following is printed:
>> This permit authorizes a drummer under the control of CHIEF OB-ANIKORO [a collaborationist leader] to beat drums in the streets of Lagos, off the main thoroughfares, on condition that no objection is made by members of the public. No drumming is allowed between the hours of 8 p.m. and 8 a.m. Lagos, January 1931.
> These cards bear the stamp of "Commr. of Police, Lagos, initialed by the A. C. P. on their faces, and they have not been withdrawn since the 4th July 1931, to equalize the withdrawal of the privilege of drumming in the Streets "off the main thoroughfares" from the 150 or more drummers of the people [i.e., the nationalists] (18 Aug. 1931, p. 2).

Papers in the Commissioner of the Colony's office document other disputes over drummers' licenses. One report cites a complaint from Sanni Adewale, Alli Balogun, Wahabi Shitta, Belo Alfa, Saka Maiyẹgun, and Lawani Alore about insulting songs sung between 10:30 P.M. and 3 A.M. on 24 September 1923 by members of the Democratic Party (Cole 1975:256). In 1931, the *Lagos Daily News* satirically quoted an indignant commentary from the *Nigerian Daily Times,* a collaborationist newspaper founded in 1926 with the backing of European commercial concerns:

> "Free reins have been given to the composition of vulgar Songs and Ballads into which the names of well-known persons . . . have been

introduced not excluding high officials who have retired from the [colonial Civil] Service. It was not because Sir Kitoyi, Mr. Henry Carr, Chief Obanikoro and the invalid Dr. Orisadipe Obasa have not sufficiently strong supporters who could retort with deadly effect that the miscreants have escaped scot free but because rustic frivolity and practices of the sharp tongues are the exclusive weapons of the mob and the illiterate masses who have been let loose on the community" (18 Aug. 1931, p. 2).

Although the interwar colonial economy was, as elsewhere in Africa, relatively stagnant, the population of Lagos continued to grow, from about 100,000 in 1921 to over 126,000 in 1931. This demographic expansion reflects the immigration of thousands of Yoruba "settlers" raised in hinterland towns and villages. During the 1920s, Yoruba migrants began to settle in the immigrant quarters of Lagos Island and new urban neighborhoods on the adjacent mainland. By 1931, the first year in which the official census distinguishes between Ọmọ Eko and immigrant Yoruba, about 36 percent of the total population of 126,108 Lagosians (45,811) were Yoruba settlers, predominantly Ọyọ, Ẹgba, Ilọrin, and Ijẹbu. The population of Lagos was also augmented by over 20,000 non-Yoruba Nigerian (e.g., Igbo, Hausa, Edo, Ijaw, Kalabari) and non-Nigerian (Akan, Ga, Ewe, Kru, Sierra Leonean Krio) migrant wageworkers. These groups were associated with particular areas of the city: the Kru, for example, frequented the Lagos Marina and the Elegbata area of Olowogbowo quarter; while Gold Coast immigrants held dances near Oil Mill street; and many West Indians lived in Ebute-Metta on the adjacent mainland.

The social and economic stratification of the African population of Lagos between the World Wars had much to do with differential access to Western education, which, until World War II, was largely in the hands of missionaries. Christian curricula emphasized conversion over secular education, and mission grammar schools in Lagos and the interior of Nigeria produced many semiliterate individuals, who worked as clerks and artisans, but were not able to move into better paying administrative positions. During the interwar period many of these individuals migrated to Lagos, forming the core of an emergent African working class. In 1926, the colonial Blue Book reported 5,800 permanent government employees, 5,533 skilled craftsmen working for the government, and 32,728 unskilled laborers in public employment (Hughes and Cohen 1979:32–33). These figures do not include thousands of clerks and other employees of mercantile interests in Lagos.

It should be stressed that African working-class consciousness in the 1920s and 1930s was highly evanescent, and that perceived cultural origins and language were often more salient bases for identity and collective action. "The social universe that was comprehended was often the workplace for a localized employer-employee relationship; rarely did [Lagosian] workers express, in the early period of colonial rule, a national, let alone an international, solidarity" (Cohen 1976:163). Nonetheless, the culturally and linguistically heterogeneous population of African migrant wage earners was crucial in the emergence of popular culture in Lagos.

Sákárà and Aṣíkò: Popular Religion and Popular Music between the World Wars

Sákárà and aṣíkò were among the various styles included in the first Lagosian commercial recordings, made by agents of the German Odeon Company and released through the Witt and Busch Company on 21 August 1931 (*The Lagos Daily News* 21 Aug, 1931, p. 2). Both of these genres emerged soon after the onset of World War I and the colonial unification of Nigeria in 1914. Both were local variants of a type of music widespread in West Africa, "group or communal music made . . . by the basic complement of three drummers plus other percussion" (Roberts 1972:241). They provide an instructive contrast, conditioned by the colonial urban environment, yet highly distinctive in terms of style and social symbolism.

Sákárà is a praise song and dance music performed exclusively and patronized primarily by Yoruba Muslims (Mustapha 1975; O. Ojo 1978). Oral traditions attribute the origins of sákárà to Yoruba migrants in Bida, a Nupe town (O. Ojo 1978:1–4); or to Ilọrin, the northernmost major Yoruba town and a prominent center of Islamic proselytization in Yorubaland (Euba 1971:179; Delano 1973:153). The style diffused to Ibadan, some ninety miles north of Lagos, sometime between 1914 and 1925 (Euba 1971:179), and was being performed in Lagos by a part-time laborer named Bello Tapa, probably a Nupe migrant, by 1916 (personal communication, David Adeniyi). Many influential sákárà musicians have come from the town of Abẹokuta, an important center for both Islamic and Christian proselytization.

The term *sákárà* refers to an instrument, a musical genre, and a dance style. The etymology of the term is by no means clear. Akin Euba (personal communication) has suggested that it might be derived from an Arabic word, and the following passage from Westermarck's description of Ramadan observances in *Ritual and Belief in Morocco* (1926) is suggestive:

> [A meal] called *shor* is eaten two hours before dawn, being preceded by public warnings in order that people shall rise in time; a *daqqaq* or a *sahhar* walks about in every *hauma,* or quarter of the town, beat-

ing or knocking at the doors, and there may be a *tabbal*, or drummer, besides, or in country villages a *tabbal* only (Westermarck
1926:2:95).

The possibility of an etymological link between the Arabic *sahhar*
and the Yoruba *sákárà* is lent credence by the customary use of the sákárà
drum in ajisáàrì music, performed in Yoruba towns during Ramadan to
wake the faithful for their early morning meal (*sáàrì*).

The drum—also referred to as ọrùn'ṣà (pot-neck)—is a circular,
single-headed, peg-fastened frame drum, made of clay.[5] The typical sákárà
group of the 1920s consisted of male performers, led by a praise singer
who played a plucked two- or three-stringed lute called *mólò*. Lagosian
author Issac Delano, writing in the mid-1930s, provides the earliest detailed description of a sákárà ensemble:

> The drum is the major instrument, the diameter of which is not more
> than nine inches. The opposite side is open, and a variety of tunes is
> obtained by pressing the face of the leather with the left-hand fingers
> while beating the drum with the right. Other important instruments
> are calabashes [*igba*], used face downwards, and beaten with the
> hands, and various tunes are obtained by constant opening and closing
> as required. In the band also are three calabashes and three beaters,
> and the string instrument [*mólò*]. . . . The drummer sits on a raised
> seat or chair, and others sit close together behind him on a mat. The
> man playing the stringed instrument occupies the middle position, and
> the others on either side. About six to ten chorus boys sit round the
> band, and the middle man with the stringed instrument starts all the
> songs in which the other join. The chorus boys sing continuously
> whilst the drumming goes on, and both drummers and singers sit close
> together and move their heads together so that the song is unanimous
> and impressive. It is also to enable the words of the songs to be heard
> by each of them, as the middle man who starts the song often intro-
> duces strange words that have never been practised. The names of a
> man, his wife, his friends and children, in fact everyone the singers
> know (and they know many people), are always mentioned in the
> songs. That is the way the drummers collect money. When they call
> one's name, it is generally understood that they want something from
> that person (Delano [1937] 1973:153–54).

The mólò plucked lute [*cassette example 2*] was gradually replaced
by the *gòjé* bowed single-string fiddle, symbolically associated with the
Hausa of northern Nigeria, important agents in the introduction of Islam to
Lagos. The gòjé's greater volume and penetrating timbre allowed it to cut
through the dense ensemble texture and made it easier to record [*cassette

example 3]. The mólò or gòjé provided thematic introductions and bridges and heterophonic accompaniment for the vocal lines. The sákárà drum ful-filled the traditional role of lead or "mother drum" (ìyá ilù), foregrounding rhythms produced by the supporting instruments signaling changes in tempo and style to the ensemble, and playing surrogate speech formulas such as praise names and proverbs. Gramophone recordings suggest that tempos were generally in the neighborhood of 80–100 beats per minutes, typical of many traditional Yoruba dance music styles. Sákárà style is to-day characterized as "solemn" by older Yoruba informants, a term denoting stateliness of tempo and demeanor and philosophical depth of song lyrics. "In a place like Lagos, which had the largest concentration of Western-educated Yoruba, it was usually the Muslims who wore traditional clothes and patronized traditional music. Many people therefore came to look upon traditional clothes and traditional music as belonging to Muslims" (Euba 1971:175).

Sákárà style was grounded in traditional Yoruba norms and tech-niques, including call-and-response singing, the generation of complex rhythmic structures through juxtaposition of multiple repetitive patterns, a preference for dense ensemble textures and buzzing timbres, and the pre-dominance of praise lyrics. Although associated by urban Yoruba with Muslim contexts, performers, and patrons, sákárà came to be regarded as an ìjinlè̩ Yorùbá genre. The syncretism of Muslim and traditional Yoruba styles may have been facilitated by preexistent similarities: for example, unison responsorial singing, characteristic of many Middle Eastern and North African traditions, is, with few exceptions, also a pervasive fea-ture of non-Islamicized traditional Yoruba musical performance (Thieme 1967:34).

The efflorescence of sákárà after 1914 was linked to patterns of Afri-can Muslim identity. Many O̩mo̩ Eko were converts to Islam, and the Mus-lim population of Lagos was continually augmented by migrants from the Nigerian hinterland, who also tended to maintain traditional values and patterns of behavior to a greater degree than their Christian counterparts. However, the dynamics of social identity and religion in Lagos went be-yond the simple association of Islam with Yoruba tradition, and of Chris-tianity with European influence and change. The 1920s saw the emergence of modern Islamic voluntary societies (*Ansar-Ud-Din, Nawar-Ud-Din*), devoted to the provision of grammar school education for Muslim children, and historically related to O̩mo̩ Eko organizations which supported Herbert Macaulay's nationalist coalition.[6] These associations, which included Western-educated Muslims from the Saro and Brazilian communities, pro-vided an institutional framework for interaction among African Muslims of varied backgrounds. They were in addition a source of patronage for sákárà musicians, who performed at associated outings, *Hajj* celebrations, Islamic festivals, naming ceremonies, weddings, and wakes.

Sákárà style was grounded in the self-image and values of a diverse Yoruba-speaking Muslim population, including Ọmọ Eko, minorities within the Sierra Leonean and Brazilian communities, and migrants from centers of proselytization in the hinterland. Sákárà musicians such as Abibus Oluwa, popularly known as *oniwáàsì* (The Preacher), were able to construct patronage networks by incorporating techniques and instruments associated with Islamic practice into a syncretic style evoking continuities in deep Yoruba values.

Aṣíkò was the Christian counterpart of sákárà, a music performed at weddings, wakes, mission schools, church socials, and outings of voluntary associations. A local variant of a type of syncretic street drumming found in port towns throughout Anglophone West Africa, aṣíkò had diffused to hinterland Yoruba towns such as Abẹokuta and Ibadan by the early 1920s. The most detailed description of an aṣíkò ensemble in Lagos between the World Wars was provided in the mid-1930s by Issac Delano:

> Another popular native dance is the "Ashiko". It is not a Yoruba dance in its origin, but was imported from Sierra Leone or somewhere that way. The "Ashiko" dance is chiefly performed by Christian people, and has only one kind of music, rather quicker than the "Sakara" . . . and resembles a fox-trot. No stringed instruments are employed, only drums and a carpenter's saw, used occasionally to make a kind of noise on its sharp edge, as an embellishment to "Ashiko" drum music. Sometimes a bottle is also used, a nail beating time on it, for the same purpose. The drummers, five in number, all beat similar drums, and produce a continuous volume of music. The dancing is done by pairs, two ladies and two gentlemen facing each other. The drummers sing as in the"Sakara" dance with chorus boys, but no one else sings with them (Delano [1937] 1973:157).

Aṣíkò tempos are often described as much faster than sákárà or most traditional Yoruba dance drumming. Some accounts refer to male-female couple dancing, with partners being chosen by the movement of a handkerchief, in the manner of the Brazilian caretta. Alaja-Browne (1985:16) reports that a musician's cap might be dropped in one's lap as an invitation to leap into the center of a circle for a "free-for-all" display.

Aṣíkò was symbolically associated with various predominantly Christian black immigrant groups in Lagos. While Delano suggests that the style originated in "Sierra Leone or somewhere that way", elderly Lagosian informants point to a relationship between aṣíkò rhythms and the Afro-Brazilian samba. The instruments used in aṣíkò, the wooden frame drum and the carpenter's saw, were associated with the Aguda, credited with introducing modern carpentry techniques to Yoruba artisans.[7] Elderly informants sometimes uses the terms aṣíkò and sámbà interchangeably. Alaja-Browne (1985:15) asserts that aṣíkò was "an adaptation of an indigenous music . . . introduced to Lagos during the late nineteenth century from the waterside—Atijere, Ilaje, Ikale areas of eastern Yorubaland—in present day Ondo state." John Collins writes that a social dance genre called ashiko was popular in Accra, the capital of the Gold Coast Colony, before World War I (Collins 1977:54). Similar neotraditional dance musics using wooden frame drums (*kpanlogo, gombe, konkomba*) were also found in towns along the West African coast from Fernando Poo to Bathhurst. Influence from cognate traditions maintained by Dahomean, Liberian, and West Indian immigrants is also possible.

According to veteran Lagosian guitarist Julius "Speedy" Araba, aṣíkò groups were initially formed by groups of young Christian men from particular neighborhoods or quarters of the city:

> That area will have its own *aṣíkò* band. We will have our own. You compose your own song, they compose their own. So on festival days, like Christmas Day, you come out with your *aṣíkò*. So we will be competing, you know, so that the elderly people will be listening to us. If you sing well, oh yeah, yeah, they will give you a penny.

This description is reminiscent of a wide variety of New World black traditions, including the samba "schools" of Brazil and the carnival bands of Trinidad. The role distinction between performers and audience—reflected in Delano's observation that aṣíkò "drummers sing as in the 'Sakara' dance with chorus boys, but no one else sings with them"—evinces the influence of European values on African musical practice.

The success of amateur aṣíkò groups allowed a few musicians to become professional, a means of augmenting their daily wages. The first gramophone recordings of aṣíkò music [Odeon A 24007–9] featured A. B. O. Mabinuori. One of the best-known aṣíkò bandleaders in Lagos was "Amusa (otherwise known as 'Captain'), accompanied by Jero and Bamgbose—Daniel and Dawodu of Mabinuori's family" (Alaja-Browne 1985:15). Elderly informants cite Jero as the most popular aṣíkò musician of the 1920s and 1930s. Other groups cited by Alaja-Brown's informants include those led by Tesilimi, Samu Egbo ("Samu Esu"), Ajayi Williams (alias "Ajayi Koboko") and Alabi Labilu (Alaja-Browne 1985:22, n. 9).

Aṣíkò song texts were predominantly in Yoruba and Pidgin English. Call-and-response forms predominated, the leader's phrases being composed of loosely-fitted poetic texts (*àwọn àṣàyọn ọ̀rọ̀*) [lit., "choice

words"], strung together to make a meaningful whole (*esa*), and . . . punc-
tuated by intermittent refrains by both the leader and chorus" (Alaja-
Browne 1985:15–16).[8] Chief John Ayọrinde (personal communication;
Ibadan, 1982) recalled an aṣíkò song popular in the 1920s:

> *B' ó ńfò má bái lọ*
> *Si London, ilú Ọba.*
>> If you are flying, I will go with you
>> To London, the King's land.

The Christian associations of aṣíkò are clear in another popular text:

> *Ikú l' ábá bo*
>> It is Death we should worship
> *Abá fi òrìṣà s' ílẹ̀*
>> We should put the òrìṣà (Yoruba deities) down
> *Ìgbàtí kú ńpa' ni*
>> When Death kills one
> *Kini òrìṣà ńwò?*
>> What are the òrìṣà looking at (i.e., what are they going to do
>> about it)?
> (Delano [1937] 1973:158)

Other aṣíkò texts commemorated important social events: for example, the arrival of the first airplane in Lagos in 1928; a song about a Saro
doctor (Adeniyi-Jones) attempting to collect rent from a poor tenant, who
responds by brandishing a machete; the story of Delfonso and Abayomi, in
which a former client shoots the lawyer who betrayed him at Tinubu
Square Courthouse, and then takes his own life; and a song about lighten-
ing striking a popular individual. Some songs derided low-status occupa-
tions (the song "Ṣáwá-ṣáwá" described the prostitutes in bars and hotels
along the Lagos Marina as "minnows," and included the phrase, "If you
didn't sleep there, how do you come about gonorrhea?") or non-Yoruba
immigrant groups such as Ashanti and Hausa (personal communication,
Julius Araba; Lagos, 27 May 1982).

The development of aṣíkò was linked to the growth of syncretic
Christian movements in Lagos and hinterland Yoruba towns. Elite African
offshoots of the established foreign missions, such as the United Native
African Church (founded in 1891), provided a forum for nationalist doc-
trines of racial equality, and the development of hymnody incorporating
Yoruba melodies and translations of Biblical verses. In addition to these
mainstream African churches, a variety of syncretic Christian sects sprang

up during the 1920s and 1930s in Lagos and hinterland towns, including Cherubim and Seraphim (founded about 1925), Church of the Lord (1930), and the Christ Apostolic Church (1931) (Gbadamọṣi 1975:191–92). Such independent prayer houses, frequently led by visionary prophets, provided opportunities for the formation of socioeconomic networks, offered protection against the magical attacks of competitors, and nurtured syncretic forms of cultural expression (Turner 1967; Peel 1968). Certain drums—for example, the *bàtá,* drum of Ṣàngó, the god of Thunder—were too explicitly associated with traditional religion to be used in syncretic Christian services. The sámbà frame drum and tambourine, free of associations with "paganism," became the predominant percussion instruments used in Aladura churches.

Like the practitioners of sákárà music, aṣíkò musicians arranged diverse features—for example, Christian hymns, Yoruba proverbs, urban slang, Latin American rhythms—into a performance style that symbolically linked the old and the new, the indigenous and the imported. This enabled them to attract the patronage of Christian converts, who made up a large segment of the Yoruba-speaking migrant work force.

Africanized Brass Band and Ballroom Dance Music

Another colonial musical tradition with numerous local variants was the Africanized marching band style, ambulatory predecessor of the dance band highlife tradition (Roberts 1972:247; Collins 1977; Coplan 1978). In Lagos this style was popularized during the 1920s and 1930s by the Calabar Brass Band, renowned for "steaming" from one end of Lagos Island to the other with jubilant crowds in tow. Bobby Benson, widely regarded as the father of highlife music in Nigeria, heard the Calabar Brass Band during the early 1930s:

> The Calabar Brass Band, they played mostly brass instruments for weddings and public parties. People would follow the band, all over in the streets. That is during Christmas and Easter. Then they have traditional Yoruba masquerades, and the Calabar Brass Band used to play, and we followed. I was one of the followers, of course, in those days, as I was very young. That band was led by the late Bassey (personal communication, Bobby Benson; Lagos, 25 Oct. 1982).

Several informants recalled having been so carried away as young children by the marching brass band that they found themselves wandering at parade's end in an unfamiliar neighborhood (personal communication, Bobby Benson, Frank Aig-Imoukhuede).

Commercial recordings of the Calabar Brass Band (who recorded for the Parlophone label under the pseudonym "Lagos Mozart Orchestra") suggest that it was modelled upon the European military band tradition, represented in Lagos by institutional groups such as the Hausa-staffed Police Band, the bands of the West African Frontier Force and the West Indian Regiment, and the Salvation Army Band. The Calabar Band, so named because its leader and a number of members were migrants from the eastern Nigerian port town of Calabar, included trumpets, trombones, tubas, and parade drums (snares, "side drums," and bass drum). The leader, Azukwo Bassey, distributed the main melody and counterlines orally, and arrangements were developed through a semi-improvised style of ensemble playing.

The sonic impact of the Calabar Band was, judging by the reminiscences of elderly Lagosians, highly impressive. Commercial recordings suggest that the upper and middle brass texture alternated between concerted harmonized statements of the melody—sometimes bordering on heterophony—and melody vs. one or two less active counterlines, a technique derived from Salvation Army band arrangements. Two general rhythmic schemes are evident on these recordings. The first is clearly derived from European martial music, with the tuba playing roots and fifths on the first and third beats of each 4/4 measure, and the parade drums playing a syncopated cadence influenced by the Brazilian caretta. The second was more strongly influenced by West African rhythms, with the tuba alternating between duple and triple meter, and the percussion playing a rolling 12/8 pattern [*cassette example 4*].

The Africanized brass band music of the CBB differed markedly from sákárà and aṣíkò in terms of style and social symbolism. Practitioners of the latter two genres melded elements of Yoruba, non-Yoruba African, Middle Eastern, European, and Afro-American styles into relationships which appealed to Yoruba performance norms. The Calabar Brass Band, on the other hand, utilized Western instruments to perform a music essentially modelled on European military band tradition, and spiced with African and Afro-American features. These three genres, sákárà and aṣíkò on the one hand, and brass band music on the other, may be seen as stemming from analytically distinguishable processes of modernization and indigenization (cf. Nettl 1978a:134). Sákárà and aṣíkò were modernized African musics; the Calabar Brass Band performed Africanized Western music.

The Calabar Band was a forerunner of dance band highlife groups such as Ezekiel Akpata's Lishabi Mills Orchestra and Bobby Benson's Jam Session Orchestra. Another important influence in the development of a Lagosian variant of the highlife tradition was ballroom dance bands staffed with African musicians, which performed at occasions attended by African and, more rarely, European elites. Their membership was drawn from the Police or Regimental Brass Bands. These musicians were frequently able to read musical notation, including the imported stock dance music arrangements which, according to informants, made up the bulk of the African ballroom orchestra repertoire (personal communication, Christopher Oyẹṣiku; Lagos, 1982). Some of the most popular dance bands of the 1930s were The Nigerian Police Band, the Triumph Club Dance Orchestra, The Chocolate Dandies, and The Lagos City Orchestra. These bands performed a variety of materials, including fox-trots, quicksteps, waltzes, lancers, rumbas, and, particularly from the late 1930s on, highlife numbers.

The repertoire of these groups was influenced by visiting dance bands from the Gold Coast.

> There was another big band which came from Accra, I've forgotten the name. They came to Lagos with a bigger musical instrument. This was before the War. . . . They played in the West Indian Quarters . . . opposite Clifford Street, now called Muritala Muhammed Way. A big band that came from Accra, they really hit it. They were the best, when they came down. I was very young, and we had to peek through the fence to see them . . . The Gold Coast something Dance Band. A big band. They were almost fourteen or seventeen pieces, big band (personal communication, Bobby Benson; Lagos, 25 Oct. 1982).

The highlife band heard by Benson might have been the twenty-seven piece Cape Coast Sugar Babies, who visited Lagos in 1935 (Alaja-Browne 1985:85).

Advertisements in Lagos newspapers suggest that the primary patrons of dance orchestras during the early 1930s were educated African elites. For example, an advertisement for a "Fancy Dress Dance" to celebrate the return and reinstatement of the exiled Ọba Eshugbayi Eleko lists the patrons of the event, including such Saro, Aguda, and Ọmọ Eko nationalist leaders as Herbert Macaulay, Dr. C. C. Adeniyi-Jones, Hon. E. O. Moore, Chief Oluwa, Esq. A. J. Marinho, and Alhaji Sanni Giwa. Tickets were three shillings for "gents" and two shillings for "ladies," which was within the means of elites and upper-level wageworkers, and were sold through a number of outlets, including African merchants. The venue was Glover Memorial Hall, and ballroom dance music was to be provided by the Triumph Club Dance Orchestra (*The Lagos Daily News,* 26 Aug. 1931).

On 31 July 1931 the following announcement appeared in Macaulay's *Daily News:*

THE MONTE CARLO CLUB

There will be a dance this evening at the Glover Memorial Hall at 8:30 o'clock by the members of the newly inaugurated Monte Carlo Club.

Admission will be by tickets at five shillings for a gentleman. Free
invitations have been issued out to several Ladies. The Nigerian Police Band will play the dance music.

By World War II, the confluence of three streams—the Calabar
Band's steaming marching band style; the African ballroom bands; and the
influential Accra-based highlife bands—led to the development of groups
performing a more extensive repertoire of highlife arrangements, as well
as rumbas, sambas, merengues, and swing numbers made popular by the
importation of gramophone records from Europe and the United States.

By the early 1940s a number of dance bands were working in Lagos,
including the Calabar Brass Band, the Police Orchestra, the Lagos City
Dance Band, the Chocolate Dandies, and new arrivals such as the Rhythm
Brothers, the Colonial Swing Orchestra, the Deluxe Swing Rascals, the
Eastern Progressive Swing Band, the M. O. Z. Swing Orchestra, and the
Harlem Dynamites. These groups performed at dances sponsored by literate African voluntary and occupational organizations—for example, the
Lagos Town Council Staff Union, the Young Aurora Club, the A Circle
Club, the Calabar Improvement League, and the Merry Band Circle—and
at New Year's and Christmas Eve Balls sponsored by the elite. Performance
venues included the Palladium Hotel (62 Bamgbose Street), the Hotel Way-
farers (on Campbell Street), the Island Club (King George V Park), and
the Yoruba Tennis Club (3 Onikan Road). Admission prices ranged from
two shillings to five shillings, with frequent discounts for women and
members of the Armed Forces, and public announcements emphasized
"cold beer in quantum," "superb arrangements," and a chance to "meet
Lagos socialites."[9]

Lagosian Guitar Music: Palmwine and "Native Blues"

The acoustic guitar, disseminated along mercantile networks linking West
African port towns and hinterland centers to Europe and the Americas, was
popular among Lagosian musicians by World War I. In the late 1920s and
early 1930s a "box" guitar could be obtained for one pound, a price within
the reach of many regularly employed wage-earning Africans. Guitar
strings were three shillings six pence a set, two or three pence per string,
and a number of European, Saro, and Yoruba merchants sold Western instruments and accessories.

Some members of the African entrepreneurial elite, such as Tunde
("Scottie") Scott, a Saro pharmacist, and Vidal Cole, who sold musical
instruments and supplies from his shop on Broad Street, were skilled guitarists. These men were amateur performers, playing for friends and rela-

tions at informal gatherings, club meetings, and picnics. They played styles such as "Spanish" (also the name of a tuning system, possibly related to the tuning scheme of the same name used by early rural blues musicians in the southern United States; see Titon 1977:46–47), "Maringa" (related to the Dominican *merengue,* also popular among the Sierra Leonean Krios; Collins 1977:54), "ragtime" (including tunes such as "Alexander's Ragtime Band"), and European fox-trots and waltzes. Such guitarists were appreciated by the African elite community as skilled amateurs.[10] Elite guitarists did not become professional musicians; the guitar, as in British bourgeois society, was not considered a serious instrument, and professional musicianship, particularly in the realm of popular music, was considered an insecure low-status occupation.

Most of the African guitarists performing in Lagos after the First World War were migrant wageworkers, members of the diverse intermediate sector of the colonial political economy that supported aṣíkò music. These men generally performed a musical genre known in port towns throughout Anglophone West Africa as palmwine music. This eclectic and loosely defined genre corresponds to a type of traditional African music described by Roberts (1972:241)

> personal music, in which one or maybe two people play largely for their own self-expression and amusement. An example . . . might be a man singing about his troubles with his wife to an audience of two or three fellow husbands and accompanying himself on a hand-piano. One of his listeners might be tapping a couple of sticks, and another clapping gently.

Palmwine songs were accompanied with lamellaphone—mólò, a term also applied to the lute used in sákárà music (Thieme 1967)—or imported instruments such as guitar, mandolin, or concertina. Palmwine accompaniment might also include rhythmic patterns played on a sámbà drum, beer bottles, or palmwine calabashes (kèrègbè) struck with a nail or stick, and a matchbox, rapped with the fingernails. The palmwine tradition was associated with semi-literate immigrants by members of the African elite, and was conceptually and contextually segregated from the more "refined" music performed in salons and parlors. As one informant put it, these bodies of music were produced and patronized by "different social circles" (personal communication, Mrs. Ṣodẹinde; Lagos, 17 Oct. 1982).

Gramophone discs imported by European firms such as the United Africa Company, Witt and Busch, and the Compagnie Francaise d'Afrique Occidental expanded the repertories of Lagosian guitarists. American country music star Jimmie Rodgers was very popular during the 1920s and

1930s. The most influential recordings were the Latin American G. V. series released by The Gramophone Company, Ltd. on the His Master's Voice label, including recordings of Cuban groups such as Septeto Habanero and Trio Matamoros. Hawaiian guitar records are also cited as a source of influence on local performers. Common Hawaiian slack-key tunings in C, G, and F—for example, "taro patch" (5–1–5–1–3–5, ascending)—are identical to tunings used by Lagosian guitarists (see Kanahele 1979:353). The international distribution of such tuning systems along trade routes has yet to be adequately investigated.

Music appears to have played some role in the construction of social networks among African workers in Lagos. As one elderly guitarist in Lagos described it:

> It is from all this sort of music that people got the idea of developing one tune to another. You know, when you hear a record and it's nice, it's likely you'll begin to sing it alone, in the bed or in the bathroom. That is how this thing happens, you know. If you have a G. V. record, and I'm living very near you, I'll be expecting you to play that record in the morning, and I can because of that become your friend. I'll be visiting you, "Mo like record-ẹ" [I like your record], and we'll drink beer and palmwine.

The earliest recordings known to me of Yoruba songs with guitar accompaniment were made in England in the late 1920s by the Zonophone Company. The *Catalogue of Zonophone West African Records by Native Artists,* published in Hayes, Middlesex in 1929, includes a number of songs in Yoruba with guitar and tambourine accompaniment, performed by Domingo Justus. None of my older informants mentioned Justus, and I have not been able to locate any of these discs for analysis. The first recordings of palmwine music with guitar accompaniment made in Lagos, performed by Irewolede Denge and Dickson Oludaiye, were part of the Odeon series previously mentioned. The masters of these recordings were likely kept in Germany and lost during the Second World War, and I have not managed to find any of the discs.

Guitar patterns and songs learned from gramophone records were adapted by palmwine performers for use in informal social gatherings. This process involved a schematization of patterns, much in the manner of a pidgin language. Palmwine guitar techniques were organized around a pool of basic harmonic-rhythmic grounds, and a two-fingered style of playing reputedly spread by Kru sailors from Liberia (Collins 1976:62), and known by Lagos musicians as *Krusbass.*[11] Some patterns were verbally labeled, their names deriving from the song they originally accompanied. Among the most popular patterns played in "Standard" tuning were *Ya-*

ponsa, derived from the Akan highlife tune "Yaa Amponsah"; "Tal'o Ri?" ("Who did you see?"), also derived from a popular song; *Johnnie Walker,* played in G position; and a pattern called "C Natural." All of these harmonic/melodic schemes could be played at different tempos and used to accompany a variety of texts. The open-ended nature of the genre is indicated in performers' definitions, which focus upon context rather than style: "When we say palmwine, we mean music that is played in palmwine bars. With guitar. No specialty, you know" (personal communication, Julius Araba: Lagos, 27 May 1982).

The colonial census of 1931 suggests that Lagos was both an immigrant city (fifty-nine percent) and a city dominated by individuals identifying as Yoruba (seventy-seven percent). The heterogeneous African labor force that migrated to Lagos after World War I contributed a variety of local guitar styles to the reservoir of expressive materials available to Lagosian musicians. Frank Aig-Imoukheude, whose uncle was a guitarist in the Yoruba town of Akure during the 1920s, offered the following description of the emergence of localized guitar styles in hinterland towns and villages: "The more interior you are, the less familiar you are with the new music you heard from the city. You form your own style, that sounds good to you, simplifying the music heard in the city. Of course, it sounds weird to visitors from the city" (personal communication, Frank Aig-Imoukhuede; Lagos, 3 Nov. 1982).

Feedback between rural and urban guitar styles, rooted in the cyclical migration of workers between Lagos and their home communities, was a continual source of influence upon Lagosian palmwine music. The Ilaje, for example, were a coastal Yoruba subgroup known in the city for their mellifluous singing and lamellophone-derived guitar techniques. The Ijẹbu Yoruba community contributed the first palmwine musician to be recorded in Lagos, Irewọlede Denge. His guitar accompanist on early recordings was Dickson Oludaiye, a migrant from Abẹokuta (personal communication, Wọle Ṣọyinka; 20 May 1988). Bands made up of non-Yoruba migrants also found niches in the Lagosian musical economy: for example, the Ishie Brothers, who sang in Kalabari and what one informant called "funny Yoruba," and S. S. Peters and His Group, a band of Ijaw migrants who accompanied their singing with guitar and tambourine, and were recorded in the mid-1930s by Parlophone.

The growth of pan-West African urban musical traditions was grounded in the demographic flow linking colonial entrepôts. Traders attempting to extend their networks, sailors manning the large vessels operated by European lines such as Elder Dempster, Ltd., and other Africans in search of employment as clerks or wage laborers moved from Freetown to Monrovia to Accra to Lagos and back during the interwar period. The transient population of sailors and stevedores who frequented the Lagos Marina and port areas on the adjacent mainland were important agents in the diffusion of guitar styles.

The most popular palmwine music group in bars along the Marina was the Jolly Orchestra, popularly known as Àtàrí Àjànàkú, "Occiput of the Elephant," a name derived from a Yoruba proverb and the title of their first hit record (Parlophone PO 502, recorded in Lagos ca. 1936). The band's personnel included Yoruba (Tommy Motajo, Akanbi Bale), Saro (Ambrose Campbell, Abiodun Oke [Brewster Hughes]), Kru (Sunday "Harbour Giant"), and Ashanti (Kofi "Mando") working-class immigrants. The instrumentation consisted of three guitars, mandolin, pennywhistle, and various percussion instruments, including the sámbà frame drum and the European triangle, derived from the military band tradition.

The Jolly Orchestra was a relatively large, formally organized and rehearsed ensemble. Yoruba guitarist Joseph Oyeṣiku, who heard the group perform in Lagos during the 1930s, recounted that they were widely regarded as skilled, cosmopolitan musicians. All of the guitarists played in different positions on the neck, using capos to bring all parts to the same pitch, so that the tone color of each instrument was distinctive. The guitarists and mandolinist played complementary, interlocking melodic-rhythmic patterns. The Jolly Orchestra spent a great deal of time at performance events tuning their instruments; the leader would establish the pitch, and each player walked off to a corner to tune his instrument. The act of tuning is associated with Western musical "literacy," and is sometimes used by professional Yoruba guitarists as a means of asserting technical and, in a broader sense, cultural mastery vis-à-vis competitors.

Though most of their songs were in Lagosian Yoruba, Jolly Orchestra's repertoire included "Yaa Amponsah" ("Abonsa," Parlophone PO 531 [cassette example 5]) and other pan-urban West African melodies and song texts identified by Lagosian musicians as originating in the Gold Coast and Liberia. "Àtàrí Àjànàkú," the group's signature song, beings with a traditional proverb, followed by an exegesis in English and plain (ṣákálá), denotative Yoruba, an interpretation of a deep metaphor for the benefit of immigrants not yet fluent in Yoruba:

àtàrí àjànàkú	The occiput of an elephant
kìí ṣerú ọmọdé	Is no load for a child
Dat mean to say	That is to say,
eré wa ṣòro ṣé	Our music is hard to play

(Alaja-Browne 1985:44; translation emended by C. W.)

The B side of this disc is a song in Yoruba and pidgin English called "Kò sí'bi tí a o fi Èkó wé" ("There is no place that compares with Lagos"), a tribute to the glamor and excitement of Lagosian life. Another early recording (Parlophone PO.511), entitled "Olówó lo obìrin mò" ("It is the rich man that women know"), features the refrain, "If-a money go a woman go," a terse expression of male perceptions regarding the instability of relationships in an economically precarious urban environment. The obverse side of this disc contains the song "Adusa Adufe," with a non-Yoruba African text.

Various of Jolly Orchestra's early recordings suggest strong identification with the interests of African wage-workers. Although complete biographical data are lacking, it is known that various members worked as clerks, drivers and sailors. For example, leader and pennywhistle player Sunday "Harbour Giant" was a Kru sailor (Alaja-Browne 1985:43) who later became a lorry driver in the eastern region of Nigeria (Ojogẹ Daniel, in Keil 1966–67:76–81). The song "Wallace Johnson" (Parlophone PO.570 [cassette example 6]) praises prominent Sierra Leonean journalist and labor leader I. T. A. Wallace-Johnson, the driving force behind the formation of the African Workers' Union in 1931. When the AWU ran into trouble with colonial authorities, despite the support of a few members of the educated elite, Wallace-Johnson's house was raided by the police. His departure one month later left an organizational vacuum in the worker's movement that was not filled until World War II (Hughes and Cohen 1979; Denzer 1982).

Palmwine song lyrics gave voice to the experiences of urban migrants. The following palmwine text is transcribed from a 1937 recording by Irewọlede Denge, a Yoruba immigrant from Ijẹbu-Ode.

Irewọlede Denge. *"Orin Asapẹ Eko"* ("Song of Prostitution in Lagos"). Recorded in Lagos, 1937. His Master's Voice J. Z. 3/OAB.5. [*Cassette example 7*]

> *M' báti l' áya, kèrègbè ní ó jẹ-o-a*
> *M' báti l' áya, kèrègbè ní ó jẹ-o*
> *Ọjọ́ itọ́rọ́, ọjọ́ isísì, ẹmu*
> *Ọjọ́ itọ́rọ́, ọjọ́ isísì, ẹm' báti l' áya, kèrègbè ní ó jẹ-o*
>> If I have a wife, it's palmwine calabash she will eat, oh
>> If I have a wife, it's palmwine calabash she will eat, oh
>> On the day of three-pence, the day of six-pence, palmwine
>> On the day of three-pence, the day of six-pence, palmwine, if I
>> have a wife, it's palmwine calabash she will eat, oh
> *M' báti l' áya, kèrègbè ní ó jẹ-o-a*
> *M' báti l' áya, kèrègbè ní ó jẹ-o*
> *Ọjọ́ itọ́rọ́, ọjọ́ isísì, ẹmu*
> *Ọjọ́ itọ́rọ́, ọjọ́ isísì, ẹm' báti l' áya, kèrègbè ní ó jẹ-o*
>> If I have a wife, it's palmwine calabash she will eat, oh
>> If I have a wife, it's palmwine calabash she will eat, oh

On the day of three-pence, the day of six-pence, palmwine
On the day of three-pence, the day of six-pence, palmwine, if I
have a wife, it's palmwine calabash she will eat, oh
Pírí-pérẹ mọ̀nọ̀n-mọ̀nọ̀n
Ọmọdé-o, bi bi bi [inaudible]
Eni máa pá, ọlá máa pá-o
Ẹnu l'a fi ún pá' kùró' jú ọ̀nà [inaudible]
Quickly-quickly, brightly-brightly
Child, oh, *bi, bi, bi* [to give birth]
Today I will crack it, tomorrow I will crack it, oh
We use our mouth to crack palm-kernels on the surface of the
road [inaudible]
Èyí ó wun á wí t'Èdùma' l'àṣẹ-o, he, he
Èyí ó wun á wí t'Èdùma' l'àṣẹ-o, he, he
Èyí ó wun á wí t'Èdùma' l'àṣẹ-o, he, he
Whatever we may say, God has the life-force
Whatever we may say, God has the life-force
Whatever we may say, God has the life-force
Ibí ní to ìbí
Pẹ̀lẹ́-pẹ̀lẹ́ l'a s'àgbà
Má pẹ̀ẹ́ à ìyá bá mi kọrin
Birth follows birth
Gently, gently, we say, elders
Don't wait too long before you join me in singing
Èdùmarè máà jẹ́ k'á kú k'á tó kú-o, dada ni
Alaura máà jẹ́ k'á kú k'á tó kú-o, dada ni
God, don't let us die, oh, before we are dead, oh, it is good
God [Islamic term], don't let us die before we are dead, oh, it is
good
Ó d'àràbà, Ọláníyọnu d'àràbà
D'àràbà, Ladagba mi d'àràbà
D'àràbà, Ọláníyọnu d'àràbà
Ladagba mi d'ènìyàn, inú dùn ọlá
He has become the silk-cotton tree [*Ceiba Pentandra*, the
"father of trees" in Yoruba mythology], Ọlaniyọnu has become
the silk-cotton tree [has become a father].
Has become a silk-cotton tree, my Ladagba has become a silk-
cotton tree
Has become a silk-cotton tree, Ọlaniyọnu has become a silk
cotton tree
My Ladagba has become a person, the belly is sweet ("happy")
with the honor
D'ènìyàn, Ladagba mi d'ènìyàn

D'àràbà, Ǫlánìyǫnu d'àràbà

D'àràbà, Ǫlánìyǫnu d'àràbà

D'àràbà, Ǫlánìyǫnu d'àràbà, inú dùn ǫlá

> Has become a person, my Ladagba has become a person [i.e., has been born]
>
> Has become a silk-cotton tree, Ǫlaniyǫnu has become a silk-cotton tree
>
> Has become a silk-cotton tree, Ǫlaniyǫnu has become a silk-cotton tree
>
> Has become a silk-cotton tree, Ǫlaniyǫnu has become a silk-cotton tree, the belly is happy ("sweet") with the honor

Mo gbǫ́ "koo koo e"

Èní l' èní

I di di di di d'àràb'ę̀ę̀-o

> I hear "koo koo e!" [cry of the rooster, *akukǫ*]
>
> Today is today [Lagosian Yoruba dialect]
>
> Become, become, become, become silk-cotton tree, so it is, oh

Denge begins this performance with his signature phrase, a highly compact image of the life of the itinerant urban musician, his love for drink, and the conflict between immoderate palmwine consumption and matrimony. Informants recalling this phrase often render it as "But for palmwine, I would have taken a wife." The use of strings of vocables to achieve impressionistic effects is typical of Denge's performance style. In this performance, the use of the vocable *bi*, which in one of its possible tonemic manifestations denotes "birth," helps to establish the theme of following lines, that is, renewal, fertility, and birth. The vocable *di* at the end of the song suggests the verb "to become," used just previously in the elided terms *d'àràbà* and *d'ènìyàn*. The use of aural imagery is exemplified by the phrase *pírí-péré mǫ̀nǫ̀n-mǫ̀nǫ̀n*, evoking qualities of lightness, brightness, and as one informant put it, "something pleasing to the senses," and by the first-person phrase *mo gbǫ́ kóò-kóò-e*, evoking the immediate sensation of the early morning cry of the cock, a traditional symbol of beginning.

Denge's performance also makes use of traditional Yoruba metaphors, proverbs (*òwe*), and praise names. The latter part of the above example is a song in honor of O. K. Laniyǫnu, one of two Yoruba entrepreneurs who arranged the singer's recording session with HMV. Other items in his early recorded corpus are praise songs for well-known Yoruba personages, including traditional sacred kings of hinterland towns.[12] The phrase referring to the cracking of palm kernels on the surface of a road is, for instance, a traditional Yoruba idiom for the difficulties encountered in the course of every human life, derived from the base metaphor "Life is a Road." It is also a continuation of the "palmwine" theme of the first lines: the palm kernel (*òkùrọ́*) is to the palm tree (*ọ̀pẹ*) as the germinating essence is to the living whole; the palm tree is in turn both a symbol of fertility and the source of palmwine (*ẹmu*). The image of the palm kernel is a fertile metaphoric nexus, a point of linkage between the opening theme of the palmwine drunkard musician, unable to sustain a wife and raise children, and the subsequent theme of birth, culminating in a praise song honoring the entrance of a child into the world. Denge's appeal to the elders and God, and his references to the ineffectiveness of human will in the face of supernatural forces, are also rooted in traditional Yoruba rhetoric.

Denge's song encapsulates the ambiguities of Yoruba immigrant working-class identity. Two sets of images predominate. He first presents himself as low-status itinerant urban entertainer economically unable to maintain a wife, yet a free man, hardheaded and unrecalcitrant in the face of social criticism. Denge than takes the role of the traditional Yoruba bard, drawing upon a store of ìjinlẹ̀ Yorùbá metaphors to praise the honorable, abuse the irresponsible, and give aesthetic form to eternal truths: the continuity of generations; the wisdom of the ancestors; the unpredictability of human destiny; and the life-giving power of Elédùmarè, the Yoruba creator deity. His role-switching represents, in aesthetic form, the cultural dilemma faced by migrants from the Yoruba hinterland: to survive and exploit urban social transformations, while adhering to traditional moral values.[13]

Conclusion

Two factors appear to have been particularly important in the development of the musical genres examined in this chapter: the development of hierarchical economic networks linking Lagos to Europe and the Americas, to other African ports, and to the West African hinterland; and the role of musicians as culture brokers in a heterogeneous urban environment. The continual dissemination of musical ideas and practices by civil servants, sailors, railroad workers, militiamen, and traders[14] was an crucial factor in the evolution of popular music in Lagos. As Collins and Richards (1982:132) have noted, "an important part of the appeal of 'popular' music in West Africa is the range of references upon which it is based, and the delight an audience takes in decoding these influences and quotations. Listeners are reminded of the way they have come and the route they may hope to travel."

While sákárà style was embedded in tenacious cultural and economic links with the Islamic north, aṣíkò, highlife, and palmwine were musics of the coastal entrepôts that linked Nigeria to Europe and the Americas. One style configuration pointed north, to the Hausa kingdoms, Saharan trade, and Mecca; the others south, toward the European metropole, transatlantic trade, and a complex network of port towns reaching from Goa to Cape Town, from Bristol to Port of Spain. In addition, the numerous substyles of palmwine music practiced in Lagos were rooted in the movement of migrants to and from their communities of origin, a continual transfer enriching styles in both the coastal capital and hinterland towns.

The sámbà drum, probably introduced to West Africa by nineteenth century Afro-Brazilian repatriates, symbolized the identity of musicians who utilized it and individuals involved in social events in which it was employed. Originally associated with the Aguda community, and thus, by analogy, with Roman Catholicism, sawyer-carpentry, the burrinha masquerade, and Brazilian dress, architecture, and cuisine, the sámbà drum became an index of Christianity at a more general level, a pattern linking the repatriate communities and a majority of immigrant Yoruba. The relationship between Islam and Christianity was signified in musical contexts by two forms of imported frame drum: the sámbà, angular, wooden, and Christian; and the sákárà, circular, ceramic, and Muslim.

A range of forms were involved in the negotiation of relations between Yorubas and non-Yorubas, Christians and Muslims, and the old Victorian black elite and a growing African immigrant work force. Although they differed in symbolic orientation and perceived historical derivation, sákárà, aṣíkò, highlife, and palmwine music all heralded the coalescence of a modern Yoruba urban culture centered on Lagos. The strong link between musical style and identity was grounded in the strategic attempts of migrant musicians to construct patronage networks in a heterogeneous urban setting. Although we have little biographical information concerning such master syncretizers as Abibus Oluwa, Jero, Azukwo Bassey, Sunday "Harbour Giant," and Denge, it is clear that their skill at manipulating diverse musical techniques and modes of discourse was grounded in their mobility and expertise at crossing social boundaries.

3

Early Jùjú Music (1932–1948)

Jùjú music, a local variant of the urban West African palmwine guitar tradition, emerged as a defined genre in the Nigerian colonial capital of Lagos around 1932. As I suggested in chapter 2, Yoruba palmwine ensembles varied in size and instrumentation. The core of palmwine music was a singer, accompanying himself on lamellaphone or an imported instrument such as guitar, mandolin, or concertina. These performances were a form of small group interaction, relying upon the creative deployment of musical and textual materials appropriate to particular social situations. The musical infrastructure of palmwine consisted of cyclical harmonic/melodic grounds derived from a corpus of standard patterns. The genre was defined more by ethos and social context than by a delimited set of stylistic features.

The initial popularizer of jùjú was a Lagosian guitarist named Tunde King. He incorporated elements of syncretic Christian hymnody, aṣíkò drumming, and ìjinlèẹ Yorùbá poetic rhetoric into the labile palmwine framework. Although musicians in Lagos were already performing similar styles, "T. K." was the first jùjú practitioner to develop a following among the colonial black elite, and the first to be commercially recorded. His contemporaries thus generally regard him as the man who "brought jùjú music out." Early jùjú style remained remarkably stable from 1932 through the Second World War. As veteran jùjú musician Ojogẹ Daniel expresses it, the style's trajectory may be broadly characterized as an initial burst of innovation followed by a long period of "small-small shifts" in performance practice (Keil 1966–67:77).

Early Jùjú Style and Instrumentation

The typical early jùjú group was a trio: a leader, who played banjo and sang; a tambourine player; and a ṣẹ̀kẹ̀rẹ̀ (netted bottle-gourd rattle) player.

In some cases a fourth member, a supporting vocalist, was added. By World War II, most jùjú bands were quartets; Alaja-Browne (1985:46) records the slogan oníjùjú kìí pò, àwa mérin péré ni, ("the jùjú band is not large, it is only we four"), popular in Lagos in the mid-1940s.

Jùjú performances characteristically alternated concerted choral singing and call-and-response patterns. Vocal melodies were strongly influenced by Christian hymns, and organized around a schematic tonic–subdominant–dominant-seventh (I–IV–V⁷) relationship. While traditional Yoruba songs are most often pentatonic or hexatonic, early jùjú melodies were diatonic. Overall melodic range was generally between an octave and a tenth. In the sections characterized by concerted leader-and-chorus singing, short melodic units descended from an initial pitch or began with a rise and then a conjunct descent to a final held tone, usually a pitch in the tonic triad. Textual patterns often occurred in pairs, the second finishing on a lower pitch than the first. A third, related phrase often answered the paired phrase. Call-and-response sections allowed the leader to improvise between the fixed choral refrains. Harmonization of the melody in thirds was common, a feature derived from Christian musical practice, and rare in traditional Yoruba choral singing, which is predominantly unison.[1] An excerpt of jùjú singing, transcribed from a recording by Tunde King [cassette example 8], is given in figure 3.1.

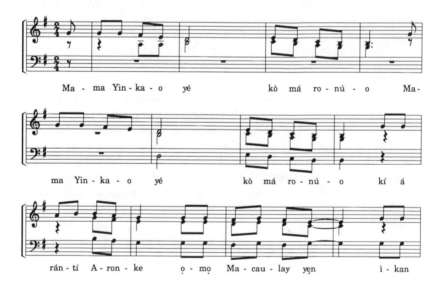

so-so ná - à l'ó - wó   dó - kí - tà ni   t'ó - wá

d'o - ló - ò - gbe   l'É - kó - o

d'o - ló - ò - gbe   l'É - kó - o   kò s'é - ni t'í - kú

ò   lè   pa   l'É - kó - o   k'á rán - tí ni Ká -

yò - dé   ni Ká - yò - dé - o   o - ní - dà - jó

to   tun   d'o - ló - ò - gbe   so - se - e   l'É - kó - o

Mother of Yinka, Please	Who slumbered (died) in Lagos, oh
Do not brood, do not brood	There is no one that Death cannot kill
Let us remember Aronke	Let us (also) remember Kayode, Kayode, oh
The only child of Doctor (Herbert) Macaulay	The magistrate who died unexpectedly
	not long ago, in Lagos

Figure 3.1. Vocal parts, "Aronke Macaulay"
Tunde King and His Group, 1936 (PO.508)

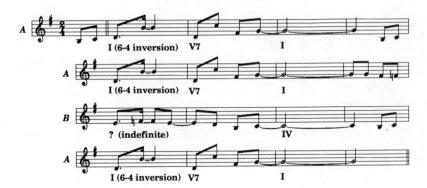

Figure 3.2. "Johnnie Walker" Pattern

The harmonic structure of early jùjú music was based upon a schematic pattern referred to as "Johnnie Walker." The essential Johnnie Walker harmonic-melodic scheme is shown in figure 3.2.

The core of the pattern is a pitch sequence which outlines the dominant-tonic cadence (see fig 3.3). A–B–A and A–A–B–A patterns are found at a number of levels in early jùjú performance, and may be related to the rhetorical structure of Yoruba proverbs as they are traditionally performed on surrogate speech instruments. In such performances the core idea is often stated first, then repeated for emphasis and clarity. A contrastive phrase follows, and the initial phrase is repeated to close the sequence. While this structural pattern is clearly linked to the practical problem of comprehension—giving the listener a chance to identify a sequence of pitches as a particular verbal formula—it is also a generative aesthetic principle.

On the basis of recordings and informant accounts, I believe that the tempo of early jùjú music ranged from around 130 to 150 beats per minute, described by informants as "sharp" (intense), faster than most traditional

Figure 3.3.

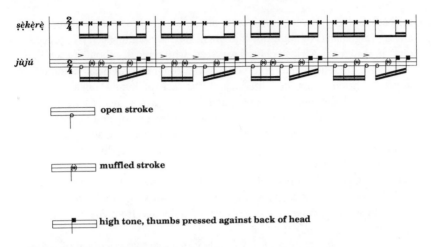

Figure 3.4. Early jùjú percussion patterns

Yoruba social dance drumming, and similar to the European quickstep. Jùjú rhythm patterns were organized around a duple equal-pulse base, derived from aṣíkò music. Some early jùjú bandleaders started their careers playing aṣíkò, and both styles were patronized by African Christians, particularly members of the numerous syncretic churches and prayer bands. A typical supporting pattern played by the jùjú and ṣèkèrè in a jùjú band is illustrated in figure 3.4. During breaks in the singing the tambourine and rattle were allowed to vary their patterns, setting up cross-rhythms.

Early jùjú singing, as represented on gramophone records and in performances by elderly practitioners, used the upper portion of the male full-voice register, and was moderately tense, with slight nasality and little or no vibrato. This vocal quality was evidently popularized by Tunde King, who was described by admiring patrons as *olóhùn ęyę,* "one who has the voice of a bird" or *olóhùn gooro,* "one who has the voice of a ringing bell." Yoruba musical and heightened speech traditions make use of a variety of voice qualities, ranging from the tense, highly nasal sound associated with genres such as ìjalá (poetry for Ògún, god of hunters, war and iron) and *rárà* (praise poetry) to a more relaxed, open quality often used in secular entertainment and dance music. The use of the upper male full-voice range in early jùjú may represent continuity in traditional norms, which place a positive value on high-register voices.

The vocal quality on early recordings of Lagosian palmwine music is also high in tessitura, moderately tense, and slightly nasalized. There are indications that a mannered, nasalized mode of speaking (sometimes described as "guy") was considered an emblem of urban sophistication among Lagosians. In addition, jùjú vocal style was influenced by "precentors" in syncretist African church services, who typically shouted each line of a hymn "in a high and rapid voice as the congregation [was] commencing it, to provide for the illiterates or the lack of hymn-books" (Turner 1967:113). Although Christianity and Islam are regarded as distinctive bodies of belief and practice, there is a long history of mutual tolerance and interchange between the religions in Yorubaland (Gbadamọṣi 1978; Laitin 1986). It is therefore possible that the vocal quality of syncretic Christian preaching was influenced by the Qu'ranic chanting (kéwú) of àl-ùfá, peripatetic Muslim teachers. In addition, the fact that "throughout Sierra Leone, male soloists and choruses tend to sing in a high register" (Oven 1980:302), raises the possibility of influence from Sierra Leonean migrants.

The instrumentation of jùjú bands was a creative bricolage of indigenous and imported resources. The banjo, including such variants such as the six-string banjo-guitar and the banjo-mandolin, was originally disseminated in West Africa by sailors and migrant workers. It was regarded as a cosmopolitan replacement for the acoustic guitar, an innovation well within the range of palmwine music performance practice. The jùjú drum, purchased by King at the Lagos Salvation Army Store, was symbolically linked with the spiritual power of syncretic Christianity, and could also be used as a surrogate speech instrument. King gave it to his drummer and "right-hand man," Lamidi, as a replacement for the square wooden sámbà drum used by palmwine and aṣíkò musicians. The ṣèkèrè netted bottle-gourd rattle was used in a wide range of traditional Yoruba praise song and social dance styles.

The banjoist generally played single-pitch melodic lines introducing or bridging between segments of a song, tonic pedal pitches or triads during sung sections, and, less frequently, heterophonic accompaniment for the vocal melody. King and other early jùjú musicians used the generic "two-fingered" (thumb-and-forefinger) palmwine guitar technique. This method, which also involved use of the thumb of the left hand to hold down bass notes, is often attributed to Kru sailors from Liberia, and referred to by Lagosian musicians as "Krusbass." The A–A–B–A Johnnie Walker scheme was also used as the basis of many banjo introductions, and was generally played in G major position. Three variants of the Johnnie Walker pattern, played by popular jùjú musicians, are given in figure 3.5, 3.6, and 3.7 (all examples are transposed to G for comparison)[2] [cassette examples 8, 9, and 10].

In the course of a performance, the banjo often foreshadowed the melody of the following vocal section. Jùjú bandleaders sometimes also

Figure 3.5. Guitar-banjo introduction/Tunde King
"Aronke Macaulay" (Parlophone PO.508)

struck the skin head on the banjo with the nails of their right hand. This
technique allowed the leader to function as an additional percussionist,
playing patterns which interlocked with those of the tambourine and rattle.

The adoption of the tambourine by Yoruba palmwine musicians
evinces both the diffusion of musical technology along trade networks and
pragmatic innovation on the part of Lagosian musicians. It was used by the
Salvation Army band and syncretic churches and was thus broadly associated with Christianity. The tambourine was also a popular instrument
among the Aguda, who used it and the sámbà frame drum in their burrinha
(meu boi) street carnival tradition and the caretta. Tambourines could be
purchased from a number of local outlets, including European trading com-

Figure 3.6 Introduction (guitar?)/Ayinde Bakare
"Ojo Davies" (HMV JZ.17)

panies and African merchants; and, most important, they could produce the complex "buzzing" or "burred" tone colors highly valued by the Yoruba and traditionally associated with supernatural manifestations. Alaja-Browne (1985:29–30) reports that the sizzling sound of the jingles was associated with the spiritual potency of Christianity.

One popular etymology for the term jùjú argues that it was a phonaesthetic neologism coined to describe a feature of tambourine technique. Yoruba is a tonal language, rich in sound imagery and metaphor, and sociolinguistic norms encourage wordplay and verbal improvisation. Tunde

Figure 3.7. Banjo introduction/Ojo Babajide
"Abasi Olubadan" (Parlophone PO.501)

King reports that his drummer, Lamidi George, developed a virtuosic style of playing the tambourine, tossing it high into the air and catching it at a rhythmically appropriate moment. Onlookers and potential patrons attracted by this technique described the rising, whirling motion of the tambourine with the phonaesthetic term *jù-jú* (pronounced with a low tone-high tone pitch glide), a reduplication of the term *jù*, "to throw" (Abrahams 1981:354). This term, applied first to the technique, and then to the tambourine itself, was extended to include the musical genre and associated dance movements.

Context, Patronage, and Performance Practice

Jùjú musicians worked in three major contexts during the 1930s and 1940s: (1) "parlor parties" held by descendants of the black bourgeoisie of nineteenth century Lagos, composed mainly of Saros; (2) urban bars, frequented by a heterogeneous audience of African migrant workers; and (3) neotraditional ceremonies held by wealthy merchants, including Lagosian Yorubas, Yoruba settlers, and descendants of the Sierra Leonean and Brazilian repatriates, who increasingly sought to forge ties with Yoruba lineages. The last type of event, including naming, wedding, funeral, and housewarming celebrations, became the dominant source of income for jùjú musicians after World War II, with the rise of a new Yoruba elite composed largely of individuals born in hinterland towns and villages (see chapter 4).

The musical and textual patterns of early jùjú performance were grounded in the efforts of musicians to consolidate patronage networks within a stagnant urban economy, strongly affected by the world depression of the 1930s. Only a handful of individuals were able to move from part-time musicianship—a supplement to other forms of wagework—to fully professional musical practice, a shift dependent upon elite patronage. Tunde King was the first jùjú musician to construct these patronage links, and it is appropriate to take a closer look at his life and position in Lagos society.

Abdulrafiu Babatunde King was born on Lagos Island, in the Saro-dominated quarter of Olowogbowo, on August 24, 1910. His father, Ibrahim Sanni King, was a chief Native Court clerk at Ilaro and had lived for some time at Fourah Bay in Sierra Leone. A member of the minority Muslim segment of the Saro community, Tunde attended Olowogbowo Methodist Primary School and Eko Boy's High School, where he became acquainted with the Anglican "Hymnal Companion."[3] He was taught guitar by a schoolmate named Ariyo and polished his skills as a member of an informal neighborhood-based group of "area boys" or "rascals" who gathered at the mechanic's shop of "Akamo" Davies on West Balogun Street, next door to a syncretic church headed by Ezekiel Davies, Akamo's father (Alaja-Browne 1985:23). These cosmopolitan young men held their parties in the evening, drinking, gossiping, telling stories, and singing.

In 1929, King was working as a clerk at the United Africa Company and as a part-time professional guitarist and singer. His band started as an informal trio, including King on guitar, Ahmeed Lamidi George on sámbà, and Iṣọla Caxton-Martins on maracas, with a fourth member, "Snake" Johnson added later as supporting vocalist. In the early 1930s the tambourine, guitar-banjo, and ṣèkèrè were substituted, the last two instruments given to King by "area boy" and patron Esumbo Jibowu (Alaja-Browne 1985:37; Aig-Imoukhuede 1975:226). By the mid-1930s his patronage network had expanded to include a number of wealthy and well-known residents of Olowogbowo quarter. A public performance at the church burial service for Dr. Oguntọla Ṣapara in 1935, another at the Yoruba Tennis Club in 1936, and a series of gramophone recordings and broadcasts on the colonial radio rediffusion service helped to boost his reputation and generate still more elite contacts.[4] As Alaja-Browne describes it, King's success was centered on a

> "salon culture," which meant quiet entertainment during the late evenings in family compounds and drawing rooms, but never in the streets of Lagos, and with "T. K.", as Tunde King was affectionately known, supplying the desired music . . . while they (the hosts) enjoyed themselves with their women friends over the game of cards or billiards (Alaja-Browne 1985:31).

As Tunde King himself put the matter:

> Going around with friends, I started to sing, to enjoy all these things. Then it began to spread, spread, spread, spread, and people told me, "Well, this thing is no more a joke! You must try and realize something as fees. If they want to call you, they should give you fees, say five shillings or ten, it's alright. This one likes you, that one likes you, this one likes you!" I said, "Alright!" (Tunde King; Lagos, 7 Nov. 1982).

King suggested that his "cool" small-group style was more appropriate for indoor performance than competing styles, such as the Africanized brass band music of the Calabar Brass Band, performed at outdoor ceremonies, picnics, and parades, or the palmwine music of the Jolly Orchestra, played at sailors' bars along the Marina.

By the late 1930s and early 1940s a number of bands were performing jùjú music. Alabi Labilu of Lafiaji, a neighborhood next to the Brazilian Quarter and populated by a mix of Agudas and Yorubas, formed a jùjú band in 1934, after some success as an aṣíkò musician. According to Alaja-Browne, Labilu still claimed in 1984 that jùjú had originated in Popo Aguda rather than Olowogbowo quarter. Ogunrombi, an Olowogbowo area boy, led a group that played at palmwine depots. Another band was run by Theophilus Iwalokun, a migrant from Abereke village in Okitipupa, who played guitar and sang in his local dialect (Alaja-Browne 1985:41, 43, 47).

King's major competitor by the late 1930s appears to have been Ayinde Bakare, the song of Yoruba "settlers" from Ilọrin and Ijẹbu. He began his career as a sámbà drummer in Alabi Labilu's band, formed his own group in 1937, and was recorded the same year by His Master's Voice. Just as King's performances were initially supported by his mates from Olowogbowo, Bakare played for and represented the area boys of Lafiaji. Although Bakare was indeed popular, King was regarded as the quintessential elite jùjú singer; the relative status of these two stars broadly paralleled that of their respective neighborhoods. Other groups, including those of Ladipo Eṣugbayi of the indigenous Yoruba quarter of Isalẹ Eko, Tunji Banjo of Ebute Metta on the adjacent mainland (Alaja-Browne 1985:62), Akanbi Wright of Olowogbowo quarter, and Ojo Babajide and Mutairu of Ibadan, some ninety miles northeast of Lagos, were also associated with their communities of residence and primary support. Competition between jùjú groups was regarded as an aspect of the competitive social discourse between quarters in Lagos.

Patterns of class and ethnic identity in 1930s Lagos were complicated and evanescent. Both the Saro and Brazilian communities, which continued to dominate the African elite until World War II, also included

> Muslims as well as Christians, illiterates as well as literates, and merchants and traders as well as members of other occupations. . . . some Saro and Amaro forged ties with other groups in the population through intermarriage, patron-client relationships and participation in religious or other voluntary associations. The distinctions between these repatriates and the rest of the population began to blur, and religious, educational, and economic differences among Saro and Amaro became more important than their shared origins (Mann 1985:18).

In addition, the Lagosian Yoruba community of Isalẹ Eko quarter, ruled by a hereditary sacred king and council of chiefs, included a number of wealthy merchants and literate lower-level civil servants.

The symbolism of musical style in 1930s Lagos was embedded in crosscutting patterns of social interaction and cultural identity. According to Alaja-Browne (1985:31), King's primary patronage network included "men such as Messrs. E. Oladipo Moore, Peter Abisogun Wright, J. I. C. Taylor, Lawyer Odunsi, Agbabiaka (Assistant Superintendent of Police), Tesilimi Fuja, Raji Etti, Olaseinde Oshodi, Asogbon, the Ariyos, the Jibowus, J. K. Randle, and M. S. Adewale." While the fathers of many of these men had been lawyers, doctors, or held civil service posts and lucrative brokerage positions, their own upward mobility had been increasingly restricted by regulations designed to keep blacks out of the upper reaches of the colonial hierarchy. They were, in a sense, sandwiched between the British colonial elite and the indigenous Yoruba community.

Although many British civil servants left the colony to serve in World War I, these posts were again filled by whites after the war, stirring resentment among qualified Africans. In addition, the war encouraged economic discontent, since the British seized "the assets of the German firms, which many African businessmen preferred to English firms since they offered better credit facilities" (Cole 1975:100). Disputes over land, tax rates, salaries and promotions, and leadership of the indigenous Yoruba community exacerbated ideological divisions among literate Africans. The association of "civilization" and upward mobility with bourgeois British practices was tenacious, but perceptions of a structural opposition between whites and blacks—including, in theory, African repatriates, wage-labor migrants, and the indigenous Yoruba community—encouraged the growth of political nationalism and the development of Yoruba neotraditional cultural forms during the 1920s and 1930s. It should, however, be noted that criticism of British policies was rarely if ever explicitly revolutionary, and that many literate Africans expressed a cultural ambivalence born of their position in colonial society.

This ambivalence is reflected in the repertoire of Tunde King, who both composed songs implicitly criticizing the colonial administration and praise songs for British royalty. The song "Ọba Oyinbo" ("European King," Parlophone PO.567) employs traditional idioms to commemorate the 1936 ascension of King George VI. The performance begins with the following responsorial pattern:

> *Tani p'awaà ní bàbá?*
>> Who says we have no father?
>> *Kàí!! A ní bàbá!!*
>> Ha!! We have a father!!
> *Tani p'awaà ní bàbá?*
>> *Kàí!! A ní bàbá!*
> *King George, bàbá wa!*
>> King George is our father!
>> *Kàí, a ní bàbá!*
>> Ha!! We have a father!!
> *Òyìnbó Kaiyero, bàbá wa!*
>> White man Cameron [Governor of Nigeria 1921–1935] is our father!
>> *Kàí, a ní bàbá!*
>> Ha!! We have a father!!

The traditional phrase k'ádé pẹ́ l'órí, kí bàtà pẹ́ l'ẹ́sẹ̀ ("let the crown stay on the head, let the shoe stay on the foot") is also used by King to laud the new monarch.

Afọlabi Alaja-Brown (1985) collected a number of songs performed by Tunde King in the 1930s, but never commercially recorded. In this repertoire, African resentment of British racism is more frequent and explicit. The song "Sọja Idunmọta" ("Soldier at Idunmọta"), for example, commemorates the completion of a cenotaph built by the colonial administration in honor of British and Nigerian servicemen killed in World War I.

> *Òyìnbó ṣe kísà méjì, kí a tó' gun afárá*
> The whites have made two wonderful things at the approach to
> the (Carter) bridge
> *Mo rí sójà kan tó lé làálì, tó gbé ìbọn dání*
> I see a (statue of a) soldier with its feet painted, carrying a gun
> *Aláàárù ó mú òṣùká ẹ̀, ó wá sori kọ́*
> His native carrier holds his headpad, with his head hung
> downward
> *Ìkórítà mẹ́ta, ìkórítà mẹ́ta, la máa sìnkú àwọn alágbára sí*
> At the crossroads, at the crossroads, is where those of great
> strength are usually buried
> *Tí ọmọ kékeré bá débẹ̀, á foríbalẹ̀*
> If a small child arrives there, he will prostrate himself [a
> traditional sign of respect]
> *Tí àwọn àgbàgbà Èkó bá débẹ̀, wọ́n á foríbalẹ̀*
> If the Lagosian elders arrive there, they will prostrate
> themselves
> *Wọ́n á fi oríbalẹ̀ fún oní Bourdillon, Ọba òyìnbó*
> They will prostrate themselves for Bourdillon [Governor of
> Lagos 1935–1942], white king
> *Màsì ma wòye, màsì máa wòye*
> Looking [at the statues] I cannot but ponder
> *Ṣìkàṣìká wọ́n gbàgbé àjọbí*
> Cruelly, they forget the common descent of man
> *Ó dára, ó dára, adánilóró ò gbàgbé òla*
> It is good, it is good, oppressor, that you not forget tomorrow
> [i.e., that you foresee the inevitability of retribution].
> (Alaja Browne 1985:142–44; translation emended by C. W.).

Alaja-Browne also collected the song "Eti Joluwe," in which King criticizes the terms of government employment for Africans. This text expresses a value held by many Yoruba wageworkers: that it is better to work for oneself than for the government.

> *Iṣé ìjọba kò láyòlé, iṣé ìjọba kò láyòlé*
> Government work does not make the home happy,
> Government work does not make the home happy
> *Ẹ̀dá tó ṣiṣé títí tí ò rere jẹ*
> The person that works a great deal and doesn't eat well

Ambọ̀sìbọ̀sí eni tí ò ṣe
The one who comes every day, person that doesn't make [good wages]
Ẹ fi'ti Jólúwè kó ọgbọ́n, l'Èkó-o, ẹ fi'ti Jólúwè kó ọgbọ́n, l'Èkó
Ponder Joluwe, people of Lagos, ponder Joluwe, people of Lagos
Bàbá Wisikí, Jolúwè, Bàbá Gódìnì yé-e, Jolúwè
Father of Wisiki, Joluwe, father of Gordon, please, Joluwe[5]
Nínu pátákó irélùwé-o, nínu pátákó irélùwé-o
Carpenters of the railway-o, carpenters of the railway-o
Gbogbo yín ni oní kakí ní rélùwé-o, nínu pátákó irélùwé-o
All of you who wear khaki uniforms for the railway, carpenters of the railway, oh!
(Alaja-Browne 1985:159–60; translation emended by C. W.).

Tunde King's ability to gain the patronage of Western-educated Africans was rooted in his creative juxtaposition of aspects of Christian hymnody, Yoruba praise song, and preexistent popular styles such as palmwine guitar music and aṣíkò. King fused the roles of bourgeois parlor entertainer and Yoruba praise singer and constructed a syncretic cultural code that could be "read" by participants as both cosmopolitan and autochthonous. He symbolically enacted and mitigated the ambiguities of modern African identity, through performances melding Yoruba, European, and Afro-American musical and textual features.

> Tunde's music was not all that too slow or too fast. Medium, you know. We called it *fájì* [pleasure], Because in those days, Tunde played like a preacher. He'd philosophize, you know, tell you about life . . . people who tried to do more than themselves and ended their life by committing suicide. Or wives that are ferocious to the extent that they kill their husband. And when he sings, this is not an amplified something like that. No! It used to be cool!
>
> And it is not meant for just every Dick and Harry to dance. Because by sitting and listening like that, we used to call it *wáàsí*. *Wáàsí* means you want to go to listen to sermon, like you are going to church. From his songs you will get some understanding of life, you know. He plays for aristocrats, people who matter. And when he plays, it must be for people who command respect. It's not for riff-raffs (Julius Araba; Lagos, 7 Nov. 1982).

Successful Yoruba entrepreneurs, including both indigenous Lagosians and immigrant settlers from the hinterland kingdoms, were also important patrons of early jùjú bands. These merchants, middle-level brokers for the large European trading concerns, were often wealthier than the highest-paid African civil servants. Strongly oriented toward their natal communities, they tended to observe the rights and responsibilities traditionally incumbent upon them as successful individuals. Neotraditional ceremonies celebrating the naming of children, marriage, death, or the acquisition of property served as an idiom for demonstrating wealth, urban sophistication, and generosity—expressed by the provision of food, drink, and entertainment—toward less fortunate kin and acquaintances. These occasions also provided a context for establishing social relationships among Ọmọ Eko, Yoruba settlers, and African repatriates.

Jùjú performances typically lasted several hours without a break. Tunde King, for example, states that he was sometimes engaged to play all night long, and that he could play for four hours in a row without stopping. Songs were constructed from the individual musician's memorized repertoire of melodic and verbal patterns. It was the responsibility of the jùjú bandleader to evaluate the course of interaction at a given social event and adjust the musical performance to comment effectively upon it. Various sorts of signals were used to effect changes in ensemble performance. Changes in melodic pattern were often introduced on the banjo, and subsequently picked up by accompanying singers. Onomatopoeic verbal phrases were sometimes used to signal rhythmic changes to the tambourinist. King, for example, used the verbal phrase *pagidarì* ("Fancy that!"; Abrahams 1981:540) to instruct his tambourinist to take a more active role during segments of a performance. The jùjú drummer could, in turn, use his instrument to articulate surrogate speech patterns, imitating the tones of Yoruba speech in order to comment upon the performance and the ongoing interaction of participants.

In performing at house parties, naming ceremonies, weddings, and wakes, jùjú bandleaders drew upon a stock of verbal formulas, fashioning song texts relevant to the social occasion. The lyrics performed by early jùjú singers were derived from deep Yoruba rhetorical techniques used to praise patrons, abuse competitors and enemies. offer philosophical insights, commemorate important events, and communicate thanks and pleas for success to God. King, for example, composed the following song text to praise an elite social group composed of wealthy Saros and Yoruba merchants.

Tunde King and his Group. "Association." Recorded in Lagos, 1936. Parlophone PO. 500. [*cassette example 11*]

> *Ke máà kelẹ̀sù lọ́nà*
> *Kéyin máà pàdé àgbákò láyé*

Yé jòwó-o-e-e, Baba máà dójútì mi-o láyé
  May you not meet *Eṣu* [the trickster deity] on the road
  May you not meet misfortune in life
  Please, Father, don't disgrace me in life
K'árìrà máà mà jé ẹ ráhùn owó
K'árìrà máà mà jé ẹ ráhùn ọmọ
  Good fortune, don't let us complain for lack of money
  Good fortune, don't let us complain for lack of children
Agbe ló l'áró, kìí ráhùn áró
Àlùkò ló l'ósùn, kìí ráhùn osùn
Lékéléké, kìí ráhùn ẹfun
Ìyàwó àkọ́fé, kìí ráhùn ajé
Òkèlè ẹbà, kìí ráhùn ọbẹ̀
  The blue Touraco parrot is the owner of indigo dye, it doesn't
  usually complain for lack of indigo
  The red Aluko bird is the owner of rosewood
  [*Pterocarpus Erinaceous*, used to make red dye], it doesn't
  usually complain for lack of rosewood
  Cattle egret [a white bird], it doesn't usually complain for lack
  of chalk
  The first wife one marries, she doesn't usually complain for lack
  of money
  The first morsel of cassava porridge, it doesn't complain for lack
  of soup
Ẹ jẹ ká dúpẹ́ l'ọ́wọ́ Jìófà
Ọdún tó wọlé ṣojú ẹmí wa
  Let us give thanks to Jehovah
  The new year enters in the presence of our life spirit.
Nwọ́n mí kọ́lé, nwọ́n mí ra mọ́tọ̀
Èwo ńt'ádárípọ̀n tó mí wòye-o
  They [the celebrants] are building houses, they are buying
  automobiles
  What business does the red-headed male lizard [the hosts' rivals]
  have looking at the future?

Orí fún wa ní tìtí pẹ̀lú boy yìí-o
Ke r'ọmọ ránṣẹ́ léhìn wá ọ̀la-o
  Head [destiny], give us a boy and a girl, oh
  So that we have children to send on an errand after tomorrow [in
  the future]
Ẹ k'áràbà, ẹ k'áràbà-o
Olórí ẹgbẹ, ẹ k'áràbà-o

Greet Araba, greet Araba, oh
Head of the club/association, greet Araba, oh!
Nwǫn ni, "Bonzo pana daba-o, bonzo pana daba-o"
    They say, "Bonzo pana daba, oh" [Kru phrase, to signal end of performance].

The affective potency of early jùjú texts was grounded in Yoruba conceptions of the immanent power of speech framed by musical sound, and in the rhetorical deployment of metaphor (Sapir and Crocker 1977). In this text, King forges a correspondence between the natural relationship of birds and bright colors, on the one hand, and the cultural relationship between beginnings—of lives, marriages and meals—and richness of experience, on the other. In another line, he likens the precariousness of urban life to meeting the trickster deity at a crossroads. Yet another sequence transforms the patrons' competitors into red-headed lizards, bobbing their heads up and down inquisitively and uselessly. King, like other competent jùjú singers, was valued for his ability to generate novel and socially appropriate combinations of standardized materials, and to convey biographical information about important participants in a ceremony in an aesthetically satisfying manner.

The final customary context for jùjú performance was the urban palmwine bar, patronized by sailors, railway workers, and manual laborers. According to Aig-Imoukhuede (1975:213), an alternative, "more perjorative" term for jùjú was *tombo bar* music, the term *tombo* referring to the calabash in which palmwine (*ǫmu*) is stored. Alaja-Browne (1985:43) notes that a clear distinction was drawn between patrons who drank at palmwine bars and elites who "could afford to drink 'schnapps' and 'cased beer,' not 'palmwine'." This symbolic opposition was fluidly mediated by African workers who consumed the syncretic drink *kakaji*, a mixture of Guiness Stout and palmwine. A 1947 painting by a Lagosian schoolboy (Onimole 1949, Plate 4) shows a banjo player accompanied by jùjú and ṣèkèrè, with an uncorked calabash of palmwine given prominent place, sitting on the ground directly in front of the musicians. The musicians are seated on a wooden bench facing a Lagos street, and participants are dressed in a variety of styles, ranging from Western/Brazilian trousers and shirt to Yoruba gowns and Muslim caps.

Performances at neighborhood bars were less profitable for musicians than the ceremonies or parties held by wealthy Yoruba and repatriate elites. Nevertheless, it is in such contexts that the versatility of musicians appears to have been most rigorously tested. Thus, for example, phrases from African languages other than Yoruba were incorporated in the process of constructing song texts. The phrase *bonzo pana daba ye,* reported by

Yoruba informants to be in the Kru language, appears at the end of all of Tunde King's earliest gramophone recordings. Although it was first incorporated in live performances in the Lagos night spots frequented by Liberian seamen, this phrase was used to signal accompanists that the performance had reached the three minute mark, a temporal limitation of early recording.

> Finishing touch. Kru language. You see, this one, when I want to close, I play it, because I heard them playing it and it's alright in my ear, so I used to use it. They [the Kru] know the meaning, and I says it out, when I play this thing, their people would know the meaning. 'This man! How do you manage to know our language?' I say, 'Well, I cannot just explain, I just put it inside, *gba!* That's all.' And when I go to that line, the people will start to dance again, like to say I know the in and out of their language. They used to throw money (personal communication, Tunde King; Lagos, 7 Nov. 1982).

Jùjú musicians incorporated non-Yoruba African (for example, Kru, Ashanti, Ewe, Fanti) songs in order to satisfy their mobile audience of urban migrants, a creative response to the demands of "stranger" patrons.

Such innovations were, in addition, a source of novelty highly valued by Yoruba settlers, a group which by the early 1930s comprised over a third of Lagos' total population and eventually came to constitute the largest segment of the jùjú audience. Many of these individuals were semiliterate (that is, they had a few years of mission school education) and viewed wagework as a stepping-stone to becoming a merchant or entrepreneur. Often regarded as *ará oko* ("farm people," rubes) by long-term Lagosians, they were concerned with projecting a sophisticated, non-bush identity. The demonstration of taste through patronage of particular sartorial, culinary, dance, and musical styles was one means of publicly negotiating a cosmopolitan image. Jùjú musicians who did not have elite patrons were able to augment their daily wages by producing music that satisfied the desire of Yoruba migrants for forms of expression governed by ìjinlèé ("deep," traditional) values, yet heterogeneous in content and modern in orientation.

Although jùjú was broadly associated with syncretic Christianity, some bandleaders attempted to solicit the patronage of modernizing Muslims, including Yoruba, Saro, and Brazilian members of progressive movements such as Nawar-Ud-Din and Ansar-Ud-Din. Several recordings by Tunde King evidence the influence of sákárà, a popular music patronized by Muslims in Lagos and hinterland Yoruba towns. These recordings, which bear the designation jùjú, are clearly distinguishable from the rest of King's corpus. Stylistic characteristics derived from sákárà include unison singing, nasality, melismata, microtonal melodic embellishments, and markedly slower tempos. These features were associated both with Islam and deep Yoruba tradition, part of a more general identification of Muslims as guardians of Yoruba culture (Euba 1971:175) [*cassette example 12;* Tunde King. "Faji" (Parlophone PO.576)].

The values and self-images of jùjú's varied patrons had a crucial impact upon the performance practice of the musicians they hired to entertain and praise them. Yoruba sound imagery and metaphor, Christian instruments and harmonies, the songs of perpetually mobile sailors and their inland counterparts on the railroad, and pan–West African palmwine songs and guitar techniques were combined in the production of a style symbolically grounded in local traditions, yet oriented toward the world economic and political system into which Nigerians were ineluctably drawn.

The Social Status of Early Jùjú Musicians

The diversity of jùjú's audience, including civil servants, artisans, and daily paid laborers, was reflected in the existence of higher and lower status ensembles. As already described, most groups remained semiprofessional, providing a secondary source of income for immigrant workers attempting to gain a foothold in a competitive urban environment. Even the most successful musicians were forced to return to part-time wagework during the Second World War, when a strict curfew was enforced in Lagos (Alaja-Browne 1985:42).

One pioneer jùjú performer has stated that the difference between *onígángan* ("talking drummers") and jùjú musicians was that the gángan players were illiterate, while jùjú players were generally "half-educated," that is, had received two to four years of grammar school education. "In the old days people don't recognize jùjú. Jùjú musicians were Class 2 or 3, not getting jobs, doing jùjú. People didn't like it, but we continue until we succeed" (Ojoge Daniel; in Keil 1966–67:76–81).

Jùjú practitioners were derided both by conservative bourgeois Africans and staunchly traditionalist Lagosian Yoruba. Even Tunde King, who had the highest status among jùjú practitioners, expressed an essential ambiguity born of singing praises for money in bourgeois sitting rooms. When asked about lower-status jùjú musicians who played in bars along the Lagos Marina, he stated: "You see, I saw them, I heard them, but they are not connected with me, I don't connect with them. I didn't move [associate regularly] with them."

In another context, responding to a question about the attitude of Christians toward jùjú musicians, King asserted: "In those days we were ashamed, because when you play they would tell you off! 'You are a drummer, you are this, you are that, you are unpopular!' They don't listen. They used to abuse us, *gǫnǫn* [a lot]!!" (Tunde King; Lagos, 7 Nov. 1982).

I have already mentioned that ideological divisions within the African repatriate communities were pronounced by the 1930s. Descendants of the nineteenth century literate black elite had split into two major political groups: cultural nationalists, who supported Macaulay's Nigerian National Democratic Party and the exiled Prince Eshugbayi Eleko, and sought to associate themselves with hypostatized Yoruba traditions; and a collaborationist faction—including Saros such as Henry Carr and Ǫmǫ Eko leaders such as Chief Ǫbanikoro—which aligned itself with the British administration. The former group provided a crucial source of support for jùjú music, while the latter generally regarded jùjú practitioners as insincere or incomplete converts performing an aesthetically displeasing hodgepodge of European and African musical elements. Conservative elite evaluations of the relative worth of musical traditions by and large replicated those of the British colonialists: "pure" European music and "pure" African music were noble traditions, equally to be respected on their own terms, but attempts to mix the two were generally viewed as "bastardizations." This separate-but-equal aesthetic, which imposed negative evaluations upon the syncretic expressive forms performed and patronized primarily by the modernizing urban African work force, was essentially a variant of the anti-Creolization ideology that justified British attempts to exclude literate Africans from positions of administrative responsibility.

Although I was able to ascertain less about Ǫmǫ Eko perceptions of jùjú style and its practitioners, two factors stand out in informants' accounts: first, the low social status traditionally accorded to itinerant musicians, particularly praise singers and drummers; and second, the symbolic association of elements of jùjú style (for example, the tambourine, hymn-derived melodies, harmony) with Christianity, Western culture, and British hegemony. According to one popular etymology, the term jùjú, applied by Europeans and Christian Africans to traditional Yoruba religion and magical-medical practices, was satirically applied by the indigenous Yoruba themselves to Western elements of the new genre, derived in large part from Christian musical practice. With characteristic alacrity, Yoruba wits inverted and subverted the insulting term: "It was jùjú; **their** [the Christians'] jùjú!"

The ambiguous status of even the most successful jùjú musicians was linked to the development of a nocturnal subculture in Lagos. In Yoruba tradition, the night (*òru*) is regarded as a primary locus of uncertainty and danger, when spirits and witches are most active. Respectable families retire soon after nightfall, shuttering their houses tightly; individuals who roam the streets at night are inherently suspect. Urban musicians tell stories

of strange occurrences while on their way to or from nocturnal performances. The opening of the night, a sociotemporal correlate of urbanization
and the organization of proletarian leisure time, exposed humans to supernatural forces constrained during the day. Tunde King composed lyrics
commenting upon this aspect of his professional life:

> Màmá ti bá mi wí ké mi má rìnru,
> Pàpá ti bá mi wí ké mi má rìnru,
> Èmi ò lè ṣe kin má ṣeré òru
> Olúwa ńbẹ lẹ́hìn a rìnru
> Lẹ́hin a rìnru, sito-o.
>> Mother has warned me against walking about at night,
>> Father has warned me against walking about at night,
>> I cannot do but play at night,
>> God supports the one who walks about at night,
>> sito-o [Kru word, used at cadence]
> (Alaja-Browne 1985:34).

The association of magical potency and menace with aspects of jùjú
performance—the radiant efficacy of sound, the imbibing of spirits, the
wearing of hats with visors, the use of cigarette smoke to create a protective aura—reinforced the ambiguity and the power of nocturnal performers. Competition among bandleaders was intense and involved gossip and
supernatural attacks. After the imposition of the military curfew in 1939,
Tunde King joined the Merchant Marines, returning to Lagos in 1941, and
then disappearing for the next eleven years. Friends discovered him playing in Francophone port towns such as Conakry and Dakar; he returned to
Lagos in 1954 (Alaja-Browne 1985:42). King has suggested that his pro-
longed absence was caused by a spell placed on him by a jealous competitor, who nailed an oògùn (magical power object) to the dock on the Lagos
Marina from which he embarked. The oògùn caused him to forget his
home, despite many letters from friends and admirers in Lagos. When the
nail disintegrated and the power object sank beneath the waves, King came
home (Andrew Frankel, personal communication).

Mass Reproduction and Jùjú Performance

The mass reproduction and dissemination of jùjú on 78-rpm shellac gramophone discs began in the mid-1930s. Tunde King and his group were first
recorded by Parlophone in 1936, and Bakare by His Master's Voice in
1937. The former discs were distributed by the Compagnie Francaise

d'Afrique Occidental, and the latter by the British United Africa Company. Broadcasts originating from a 300-watt shortwave station on Ikoyi began in the late 1930s (Mackay 1964), and also helped to disseminate the style.

The relationship between live performance practice and the selective aural paradigms of jùjú style provided by commercial recordings was complex, with the live and recorded traditions continually influencing one another, yet remaining autonomous in a number of important respects. Jùjú style was not wholly created by the processes of electronic recording and commercialization, but its developmental trajectory was strongly conditioned by the attempts of European recording firms and the trading companies that distributed their products to exploit and generate sociomusical needs.

Only a few of the numerous jùjú groups working in Lagos had access to recording opportunities. Those groups with strong ties to the African elites, particularly merchants, had an advantage in this regard. King, for example, has stated that he was recommended to the Parlophone company by influential patrons, and his first recording was in fact a praise song in honor of two of the major African distributors of gramophone discs and supplies in Lagos, Yoruba entrepreneurs O. A. L. Araba and Ẹnigbọkọn. The earliest recordings of Lagosian musicians issued on the His Master's Voice label of the Gramophone Co., Ltd., bear the acknowledgement "By arrangement with A. S. Lawal and O. K. Laniyọnu." These two individuals were Yoruba entrepreneurs who positioned themselves as middlemen, linking the recording company and the trading oligopoly which imported and distributed HMV discs (United Africa Company) with local musicians and retail outlets.

The immediate profits realized by jùjú practitioners from sales of "their" recordings were minimal. King, for example, was paid five shillings (about $1.20) by Parlophone for each side, plus one pence ha'penny royalty per disc sold. Although sales figures are not available, King has indicated that his earnings from recording were minuscule compared to what he earned in live performance during the height of his popularity. The profits accrued by jùjú musicians as a result of the recording and commercial dissemination of their music on gramophone discs were primarily realized in live performance contexts. Their popularity among the elites resulted in opportunities to record; the distribution of their recordings, particularly among the African elites who could afford to purchase gramophones, in turn increased their popularity and resulted in a greater demand for their services at ceremonies and parties. On the other hand, musicians who did not have access to the means of musical reproduction were caught in a negative cycle: no elite contacts, no recordings, and no chance for upward mobility. As Lagosian guitarist "Speedy" Araba expresses it:

The dealers, it was between the dealer and the company. They don't regard the artist who made the music. It is the dealer who can afford to buy and sell. Because the dealer is making money for the company and the company is making money for the dealer, but the artists are not being reckoned upon. We are used as a tool, even in those days (Julius Araba; Lagos, 7 Nov. 1982).

Mechanical reproduction reduced performances of neotraditional praise music adapted to particular social contexts to three-minute segments of sound. It also intensified the influence of a few groups, thereby exercising a selective effect on the establishment of performance paradigms. Only a few of the substyles of jùjú were recorded, and only certain elements were selected from the diverse repertoire of materials utilized in live performance.

However, the stylistic autonomy of live jùjú performance was ensured by several factors. First, it is clear that even "stars" like Tunde King were primarily dependent upon the direct patronage of their audiences. Commercial recordings, made in Lagos, shipped to Europe for pressing, and imported and marketed in West African coastal urban centers by European and African merchants were never more than an ancillary source of direct income for early jùjú musicians. In addition, jùjú's role as praise music guaranteed that recapitulations of popular songs copied from recordings would, in live performance, be adapted to the unique flow of any particular social event. Finally, continuity in traditional aesthetic norms among Yoruba settlers in Lagos limited the possibilities for radical change in performance practice. Innovations introduced on commercial recordings, and regarded by a significant segment of jùjú musicians and patrons as inappropriate or impractical, appear to have been rejected in live performance contexts.[6]

Jùjú Music and the Second World War

Although jùjú style did not change substantially until the late 1940s and early 1950s, various social and economic processes that were to play a role in this transformation were encouraged by the Second World War. The closure of Mediterranean sea routes and Japanese capture of British East Asian colonies made Lagos a crucial supply station for Allied forces in North Africa. Construction of ports, airfields, roads, and railroads stimulated wage-labor migration from the hinterland to Lagos and other cities. Despite the imposition of a curfew in the capital city, the swelling population of migrants provided new patrons for musicians.

British wartime policy in Nigeria focused on the production of raw materials, particularly palm products, leather, and tin. Though the total value of Nigerian exports more than doubled during the war, from £10,300,000 to £24,000,000 (Crowder 1978:246), strict limits were set on the wages paid to African urban workers, including civil servants, artisans, and manual laborers. The deprivations suffered by urban Africans were exacerbated by rapid increases in the cost of living, some forty-seven percent over the first three years of the war. In 1945, a delegation representing the trade union movement in Lagos testified before a colonial commission of inquiry that the price of rooms for workers had more than quadrupled during the war, while salaries had decreased (Olusanya 1973:86).

African opposition to colonial rule became more vocal during the war, though rarely radical. While there were only three registered trade unions in Nigeria in 1938 (teachers, civil servants, and railway employees), seventy-nine additional unions had emerged by the end of the war. The upper ranks of the colonial civil service had been monopolized by whites before the war, and when many of them were recruited into the armed services, these positions were again opened to literate Africans. A bitter reaction was provoked when returning British servicemen, many of them ill-trained for civil service administrative jobs, were brought into Nigeria after the war, displacing Nigerians from hard-won posts. The shared experience of economic exclusion along racial lines strengthened the ideological unity of the intermediate urban wage-earning sector which had patronized jùjú and other syncretic popular musics during the 1930s.

Returning Nigerian servicemen played an important role in the development of syncretic performance traditions. By 1941, some 16,000 Nigerians had been conscripted into the West African forces (Olusanya 1973:46), many of them serving in East Africa and Burma, where several brigades of Nigerians fought alongside British and Indian troops in 1943 and 1944. Interaction with working-class European soldiers and Indian troops eroded the aura of white superiority promulgated by the British colonists. Many "Boma Boys," as the returning soldiers were called, settled in Lagos and other cities, having "acquired new wants, new tastes, and new desires which could not be satisfied in the villages" (Olusanya 1973:97). Like the sailors and railway workers who influenced popular styles in the early twentieth century, the Boma Boys were an important source of new musical materials and techniques.

British and American servicemen stationed in Lagos also interacted with local musicians, particularly in the bars and brothels which sprang up in increasing numbers during the war. While this development was regarded by the colonial administration as an unfortunate concommitant of the seaport ethos (Great Britain Colonial Office 1946), it represented an important change in the nocturnal informal economy of Lagos. Urban "hotels" serving the multiple functions of brothels, restaurants, and musical venues continued to be an important source of employment for musicians after the War.

The British administration co-opted jùjú and other popular musics. The radio rediffusion ("wired-wireless") service, a medium for BBC war reports and Allied propaganda, was an important medium for the dissemination of styles and the establishment of "stars." In some cases, Lagosian musicians were directly patronized by the government. In 1942, J. O. "Speedy" Araba, a railroad worker who had performed with the jùjú group of Akanbi Wright before the war, made recordings which were shipped to Burma to raise the morale of the Nigerian troops. Songs praising heroic Nigerian servicemen were recorded, including "The Five Nigerian R. A. F." by Akanbi Wright and his Group (His Master's Voice JL 11, released 1943). The exclusion of Africans from service in the Royal Air Force on the grounds that they were malarial (Olusanya 1973:53) had been a source of nationalist grievances against the British. Wright's mass-reproduced praise song celebrated the admittance of five Nigerian trainees into the RAF, a symbolic victory for the nationalist movement. Songs of derision abusing Hitler were also recorded by prominent jùjú groups. "Hitler To Nda Yeru" ("Hitler Who Is Throwing the World into Confusion"), recorded in 1943 by Akanbi Wright (HMV JL 30), was sung by Yoruba school children during the war: "Hitler is throwing the world into confusion, push him with a shovel into the grave" (Olusanya 1973:51).

Conclusion

I have suggested that early jùjú musicians, performing in parlors and palm-wine bars, constructed a syncretic style and a patronage network that over-arched incipient class division between descendants of a Victorian black elite and the predominantly Yoruba-speaking migrant work force. Early jùjú was a musical correlate of the tenuous political networks linking elite nationalist leaders such as Herbert Macaulay to an Yoruba-speaking wage-earning population that included civil servants, merchants, skilled craftsmen, and laborers (Hughes and Cohen 1978). Initially rooted in the competition among Saro, Aguda, and Yoruba "area boys," and eventually patronized by an diversified intermediate sector of urban African society, held together by political clientage and opposition (however ambivalent) to British colonial rule, jùjú music was part of an emergent popular culture linking various African communities in Lagos.

Although I am loathe to push the point too far, broad parallels may be drawn between the emergence of jazz in turn-of-the-century New Orleans and jùjú in interwar Lagos. In both cases the social boundary between a literate bourgeoisie and a large population of migrant workers from the rural hinterland was reflected in musical style and symbolism. The distinction between "refined" and "crude," or "civilized" and "bush" musical styles was one of many ways in which both Creole elites protected their cultural and economic position vis-à-vis the European colonists. The imposition in the late nineteenth century of laws designed to protect white privilege reclassified urban Creoles and Black migrants within a single socioracial category, and created a kind of cultural pressure cooker, heated by shared exclusion and a concommitantly heightened sense of black identity. In both cases, the process of musical syncretism was grounded in the increased rate of interaction of musicians from the two social categories. Though there are many important differences between the two situations— for example, the shift from French to American colonialism in New Orleans, and the importance of the traditionalist Yoruba community in Lagos—the broad parallels are suggestive. In both cases, the construction of cultural identity, and of musical styles, was strongly affected by the imposition of racist legal restrictions.

I would suggest that the historical significance of Tunde King, Ayinde Bakare, and other jùjú pioneers is not limited to their role as predecessors of contemporary jùjú superstars King Sunny Ade and Chief Commander Ebenezer Obey. These early jùjú practitioners were cultural brokers par excellence, symbolically negotiating perceived cultural differences through the manipulation of performance style. In their creative response to the vicissitudes of colonialism and urbanization they fashioned an expressive code that linked clerks and laborers, immigrants and indigenes, the modern and the traditional, within a rhetorical framework deeply grounded in Yoruba values.

4

The Development of Modern
Jùjú (1948–1982)

During the 1950s jùjú music was transformed from a quartet music for contemplative listening, a variant of palmwine guitar style, into a social dance music performed by groups of eight to ten musicians and organized according to traditional principles of Yoruba drumming and praise singing. Its patronage system expanded from a core of literate wage-earning Christians to encompass almost all sectors of Yoruba urban society. By the late 1970s, when my research began, jùjú had become the dominant Yoruba musical style in terms of both stylistic influence and market size.

Postwar Changes in Jùjú Performance Practice

The first change in jùjú performance practice after World War II was the introduction of the Yoruba hourglass-shaped pressure drum or "talking drum." Bandleader Akanbi Ege, who before the war had performed and recorded under the Saro name Akanbi Wright, pioneered in this regard, hiring a talking drummer in 1948. Other jùjú bandleaders in Lagos and hinterland Yoruba towns soon followed his lead; Ayinde Bakare, for example, brought it into his group, the Meranda Band, later that same year. The symbolic importance of this move is linked to postwar Yoruba cultural nationalism, and the political manipulation (and, in some cases, invention) of ìjinlèẹ (deep) Yorùbá tradition.

The pressure drum was, among the diverse membranophone types used by the Yoruba, the best suited for inclusion in a pan-Yoruba musical lingua franca. To begin with, hourglass-shaped pressure drums—ranging from dùndún, the largest, to gángan, the smallest—may be used to substitute for other drums in a wide range of specialized genres (for example, for bàtá drums in ceremonies for Ṣàngó, the òrìṣà with which the bàtá are specifically associated; see King 1961). In addition, while many drum types are restricted to specific regions of Yorubaland, the dùndún, gángan, and other pressure drums are found almost everywhere, particularly within the large area controlled by the kingdoms of Ọyọ and Ibadan in the eighteenth and nineteenth century.

Jùjú music continued to be patronized by Yoruba-speaking Christians after the War. While leaders of the mainstream African churches argued against the use of indigenous musical instruments symbolically associated with "paganism" and "backsliding," the pressure drum was introduced into many syncretist churches and prayer bands as a means of attracting new converts. In *Aláàdúrà* prayer-healing churches, indigenous concepts concerning the supernatural potency of speech, music, and bodily movement were blended with aspects of Christian theology and practice. Whereas drums such as the bàtá, unambiguously associated with òrìṣà worship, were thought intrinsically antithetical to Christian piety, dùndún and gángan drums were regarded by the clergy in many Yoruba popular religious movements as sufficiently generic in their range of customary uses to be appropriate for accompanying hymns.

Various technical features of the pressure drum made it an ideal choice for musicians seeking to create new audiences among an expanding population of rural migrants. In jùjú groups the gángan filled the role of *iyá'lù*, or "mother drum." In Yoruba drum ensembles the iyá'lù has multiple rights and duties: overseeing and focusing the relationships among supporting parts; improvising well-balanced counter-rhythms; and articulating socially appropriate tonemic patterns (Laoye 1959). Musicians suggest that almost anyone can learn to play the jùjú or sámbà frame drums, while competence in dùndún or gángan performance—particularly mastery of formulaic surrogate speech texts—is usually achieved only by individuals born into or apprenticed to specialist patrilineages. While early jùjú drummers were able to articulate surrogate speech phrases, the tambourine is, as one drummer put it, a much less "talkative" instrument than the pressure drum, on which the pitch contour of spoken Yoruba may be clearly yet subtly imitated.

The transformation of jùjú performance practice in the postwar period was also precipitated by the introduction of electronic amplification. According to informants, the first electric guitar in Lagos was brought by Bobby Benson—the father of Nigerian highlife—who returned in 1947 from an eight year sojourn in Great Britain. The first jùjú musician to use an amplified guitar in life performance and on recordings appears to have been Ayinde Bakare, who had been playing since 1935. Bakare experimented with an electric contact microphone, switching from ukelele-banjo to "box" guitar in 1949 because there was no place to attach the pick-up to the body of the banjo (Keil 1966–67). Portable public address systems were introduced during the war, and were first used by jùjú musicians in the late 1940s.

The amplification of voices and guitar allowed jùjú groups to expand along patterns grounded in traditional Yoruba values and techniques. In particular, it enabled the incorporation of more drummers without upsetting the acoustic balance between singing and instrumental accompaniment. Electronic technology thus appears to have facilitated the application of deep Yoruba musical techniques. In short, Westernization of musical means enabled indigenization of musical expression.

The band of Ayinde Bakare, a widely-imitated innovator of the new jùjú style, serves as an example of the expansion of bands during the postwar period [*cassette example 13*].

1939 4 members: ukelele-banjo, jùjú, ṣèkèrè, supporting vocalist

1946 5 members: ukelele-banjo, jùjú, ṣèkèrè, maracas (from Latin dance music), supporting vocalist

1948 6 members: ukelele-banjo, jùjú, ṣèkèrè, maracas, gángan, supporting vocalist

1949 7 members: amplified guitar, jùjú, ṣèkèrè, maracas, gángan, agídìgbo (bass lamellaphone), supporting vocalist

1954 8 members: amplified guitar, jùjú, ṣèkèrè, maracas, gángan, agídìgbo, akúbà (conga drum from highlife and Latin music), supporting vocalist

By 1959, Bakare's Inner Circle Orchestra included electric guitar, jùjú, ṣèkèrè, akúbà, *ògìdo* (a larger conga-type drum), gángan, and two chorus vocalists, who played "clips" (*claves*) and maracas. The overall ratio of instrument types within the group shifted from one stringed instrument (banjo) and two percussion instruments (jùjú and ṣèkèrè) in 1939, to one stringed instrument (electric guitar) and seven percussion instruments (jùjú, ṣèkèrè, clips, maracas, two conga-type drums, and talking drum) in 1959 (Keil 1969). These changes were accompanied by an increase in the size of the responsorial vocal chorus, including specialized singers and other members of the group.

The emergence of modern jùjú style was paralleled and influenced by competing postwar genres, disseminated on discs and radio. *Agídìgbo* or *mámbò* music, for example, was a street drumming style first performed by boys' associations in Lagos [*cassette example 14*]. Agídìgbo bands generally included several large four- or five-key lamellaphones (agídìgbo), conga-type drums, and other percussion instruments. The initial popularizer of the style was Adeolu Akinsanya, whose Rancho Boys and Rio Lindo Orchestras—names derived from the cowboy films popular among Lagosian boys—had a series of hit recordings beginning in 1948. Akinsanya has stated that àgídìgbo music was a Lagosian version of *konkoma*, a dance-drumming style introduced after World War II by Ewe and Fanti migrants from the Gold Coast (Alaja-Browne 1985:64). Other popular àgídìgbo groups included Rosey Show (Mambo) Orchestra and the Lagos Day Orchestra.[1] Àpàlà, a praise song and social dance music, developed in the late 1930s in the Ijebu area, and was popularized by a musician named Haruna Işọla [*cassette example 1*], born in the town of Ijẹbu-igbo (Ọlabọde 1974). Àpàlà groups generally included small hourglass-shaped pressure drums called àpàlà or àdàmọ̀n, an àgídìgbo bass lamellaphone, several conga-type drums, şèkèrè, and a metal idiophone such as an *agogo* or truck muffler (Thieme 1969). Like postwar jùjú, àgídìgbo and àpàlà drew upon Latin American recordings, preexistent popular genres, and deep Yoruba rhetorical devices. These social dance and praise song genres provided an urban-centered musical lingua franca, a set of stylistic coordinates for the construction of modern Yoruba identity. Each of them relied upon indigenous principles as a unifying framework for innovation.

Alaja-Browne (1985:59) suggests that Adeolu Akinsanya's àgídìgbo style exerted a strong influence on jùjú musicians during the 1950s, an assertion corroborated by my informants.

> The introduction of the agidigbo [bass lamellaphone] . . . into juju music at this period marked a significant development . . . , for not only did it begin a trend that was to lead to the exit of the juju drum in juju bands, but its bass-like sounds provided a background rhythm that, in the opinion of the musicians of this period, was preferable to that of the juju drum. Consequently, most juju bands began to show a preference for a heavy instrumental texture in which the beat of the agidigbo . . . was much pronounced.

The expansion of the jùjú ensemble was linked to changes in performance techniques. Traditional principles were applied in establishing musical roles for each new instrument added to the group. The jùjú, sámbà, and conga-type drums were used to play repetitive patterns which combined to form more complex rhythmic gestalts. Idiophones such as the agídìgbo, şèkèrè, agogo, "clips," and maracas also played interlocking cyclical patterns. The gángan, as I have already suggested, occupied the role of the mother drum, improvising, foregrounding aspects of the composite rhythmic framework, and commenting upon the performance and the wider social event of which it was a part.

The expansion and reorganization of the jùjú ensemble was accompanied by a slowing of tempos. For example, recordings made by Ayinde Bakare and his quartet before the Second World War centered around 146–48 pulses per minute, while recordings made with the larger group in the early 1950s ranged from around 108–14 pulses per minute. This shift represents a convergence with Yoruba secular dance drumming (alùjó, lit. "drumming for dancing"), much of which is markedly slower than early jùjú music. Informants describe it as a move "downward," toward "cooler," more "solemn" feelings. The slowing of tempos in the postwar period, along with the incorporation of the talking drum and the development of a standardized hierarchical ensemble structure, made jùjú more deeply and self-consciously Yoruba in form, feeling, and content.

The expansion of jùjú groups was also linked with changes in ensemble texture. Yoruba, like many West African peoples, prefer high-affect contrasts in timbre, modulated by rattling or buzzing devices which create a continuous stream of sound. The expanded jùjú ensembles were able not only to perform satisfying dance rhythms, but also produced a dense sonic texture, built up from the layering of drums, rattles, and electric guitar. Singing and guitar were both channeled through cheap tube amplifiers and public address speakers, augmenting the buzzing quality of the music. The soundscape produced by the enlarged jùjú groups was an important feature of the ambience of social events in which they performed (see chapter 7).

The creative remodeling of jùjú style by urban Yoruba musicians is a clear example of the ideological dimensions of syncretism. The incorporation of the talking drum was the first step in the construction of a stylistic configuration more modern and more Yoruba than early jùjú. Beginning in the early 1950s, jùjú began to attract the patronage of both long-term city residents and recent rural migrants; traders, clerks, artisans, and laborers; Western-educated and nonliterate Yoruba; and Muslims as well as Christians.

The Political Economy of Jùjú Performance during the Postwar Period

The processes of economic expansion catalyzed by the Second World War continued into the postwar period. The bulk of Nigeria's export earnings were, as before the war, derived from cash crops, particularly palm products, cocoa, and rubber. Marketing boards set up in the late 1940s stabilized prices and, thanks to relatively good conditions on the world market, were able to build up substantial cash reserves, used by local authorities to finance ambitious development projects. Although urban industrial development was sporadic, the general vitality of the economy, along with improvements in transportation systems, encouraged the rapid expansion of Lagos and inland towns.

In addition, the "Nigerianization" of government posts, which began around 1953, created new opportunities in the major towns. A mass exodus of British civil servants, especially after the institution of compensation for officers whose posts were Nigerianized, meant that many jobs were left vacant. "Super-scale" positions were rapidly filled, and ambitious education programs were instituted to produce the skilled manpower necessary to run the regional bureaucracy. The universal free primary education scheme, launched by the Western Region government in 1955, was intended both to serve this need and to reinforce the local patronage networks upon which the success of the ruling Action Group party—originally the political arm of the Egbe Omo Oduduwa cultural association—depended. Possession of a grammar school certificate was generally regarded as qualification for employment in the subclerical grades of the civil service. Structural readjustments in the federal and regional governments created new opportunities for upward mobility among African junior civil servants. By Independence (1960) "the shift in personnel of key posts from overseas to Nigerian officers was virtually complete" (Imoagene 1976:70).

The ambitious educational programs of the 1950s had the unintended side effect of producing a large population of primary school dropouts, frequently children of families too poor to pay for textbooks and school uniforms. Many of them migrated to urban centers, attempting to exploit or create niches in the highly dynamic informal economies of Lagos and hinterland towns. In 1950, immigrant Yoruba accounted for about 37% of the population of Lagos (85,042 out of 230,256). According to one estimate, the population of Lagos was augmented during the period 1952–1967 by 644,000 immigrants, 510,000 of which originated in the Western State, most of them in the 15–30 age category (Green 1974:289). Such individuals often entered into apprenticeships with mechanics, tire vulcanizers, watch repairers, carpenters, tailors, drivers, and so on. Others became manual workers for the regional government or private concerns, this generally being regarded as a temporary alternative to setting up a small-scale individually-owned business.

The growth of Lagos and regional administrative and economic centers such as Ibadan, Ijebu-Ode, and Abeokuta created economic opportunities for jùjú practitioners. The emergence of a prosperous urban entrepreneurial elite, many of whom were wealthier than their counterparts in the civil service, provided a new source of patronage. Jùjú ensembles were frequently hired to perform at ceremonies held by upwardly mobile entrepreneurs, who became their most reliable source of profit. Cash prestations to musicians who sang and drummed the praises of the host and other important celebrants took on added importance as a medium for the public assertion of good character and the negotiation of elite status. Yoruba merchants and businessmen, many of them born in rural areas or small towns, became the most prominent patrons of jùjú music.

The number of jùjú groups operating in the towns of southwestern Nigeria increased dramatically during the 1950s. Musicians from hinterland villages and towns migrated to the regional capitals, seeking lucrative markets. Musical performance, largely a nocturnal vocation, provided workers and unemployed migrants with an alternative means of livelihood that did not interfere directly with daytime wagework. Increased economic competition and traditional values encouraging entrepreneurial initiative frequently led to the fissioning of bands, as sidemen set out to establish themselves as leaders. Lagos and Ibadan were each home to a large pool of musicians, who grouped, regrouped, and moved in and out of musical specialization, periodically working as craftsmen, mechanics, drivers, or subclerical workers.

Another important source of patronage for jùjú musicians was the Yoruba political elite, a group interested in the hegemonic possibilities of popular culture. The Richards and Macpherson constitutions (instituted in 1947 and 1951, respectively) established a tripartite national political framework, including three relatively autonomous provinces, each dominated by an ethnic-linguistic group (Hausa in the north, Igbo in the east, and Yoruba in the west). The politicization of hinterland Yoruba, urban workers, and migrants involved in the informal economy accelerated during the 1950s. Yoruba kingdoms which had remained virtually autonomous since the nineteenth century were linked, via local Native Authorities, to a bicameral regional legislature. As Imoagene (1976:50) has suggested, this institutional matrix made it possible for the first time to "weld budding politicians in the different administrative regions together for a common cause."

The implementation of universal suffrage in the Lagos elections of 1950 and the Western Region elections of 1951 quickly led to the establishment of clientage networks linking aspiring politicians, local authorities, and the newly enfranchised masses. Yoruba politicians sought to mobilize local support through the manipulation of traditional symbols of authority.[2] Musical performance, a privileged medium for public political discourse, was one of the expressive systems harnessed by the Yoruba political elite. Musicians ranging from dùndún drummers to sákárà and jùjú bands were hired by political parties to perform at outdoor rallies and fund-raisers. Some popular styles were disseminated via political rallies; for example

the 12/8 dance rhythm called *wǫ́rǫ́*, which originated in western Yorubaland, became a pan-Yoruba style during the 1950s.

Jùjú musicians composed songs supporting the candidates and
groups that patronized them and songs attacking their patrons' enemies.
Such performances made use of the full range of rhetorical techniques
available to Yoruba praise singers and drummers. Jùjú, sákárà, àpàlà, and
agídìgbo groups recorded hundreds of political songs on gramophone
discs. The collection of the Lagos State Broadcasting Corporation, inherited from the old Nigerian Broadcasting Service, today includes dozens of
discs from the 1950s and 1960s marked NTBB (Not To Be Broadcast).
Many of them contain propoganda in support of particular candidates or
parties.

Ojogę Daniel, an Ilęṣa-born bandleader who performed in Lagos and
Ibadan, was a noted supporter of the Action Group, led by Ǫbafęmi Awolowo, and played at party functions during the 1950s and 1960s. Akanbi
Wright—who later changed his name to Akanbi Ege, dropping the British
patronymic in keeping with nationalist sentiments of the times—was, on
the other hand, a supporter of the Lagos-based Nigerian National Democratic Party, popularly known as the "Demos." The NNDP, descendant of
the alliance forced by Herbert Macaulay during the 1920s, allied itself in
1944 with the National Congress of Nigeria and the Cameroons (NCNC),
Nnamdi Azikiwe's party and the major opponent of the Action Group. In
the early 1950s, Akanbi Ege composed a notorious song entitled "Demo
l'o l'Eko" ("The Demos own Lagos"), a partisan commentary on the conflict between the NNDP/NCNC coalition and the Action Group over the
incorporation of Lagos into the AG-controlled Western Region (Sklar
1963:110–12). Akanbi Ege was subsequently afflicted with a crippling disease, rumored by informants to be the effect of a magical attack by supporters of his political opponents. Links between music, speech, and
supernatural power are often invoked in remembrances of the turbulent political scene of the 1950s.

It should be noted that Yoruba nationalism was also expressed in the
emergence of a popular traveling theater tradition. The roots of Yoruba
popular theater lie in the centuries-old *aláàrìnjó* tradition, performed by
itinerant dancer-mummers (Adedeji 1969), and in the Victorian elite enter-
tainments of late nineteenth-century Lagos. Symbolism, rhetoric, and performance techniques—including music and dance—were derived from the
former tradition; certain aspects of staging and narrative from the latter.
The most widely recognized pioneer of Yoruba popular theater was Hubert
Ogunde (Clark 1979), who organized his first productions under the aegis
of an *Aladura* syncretic church in Lagos. From around 1946, his productions, which incorporated ìjinlę̀ę Yorùbá speech, music, and dance within

a framework derived from European musical theater, provided urban migrants with an entertaining and aesthetically satisfying portrayal of the role of tradition in a changing world. In the early 1960s, Ogunde founded his own recording label to release hit songs from his plays. The Yoruba popular theater tradition has continued to blossom since Nigerian independence (see Jeyifo 1984; Barber 1982).

Commercial Mass Reproduction and Dissemination: 1950s–1960s

The rise of jùjú as the dominant Yoruba popular music was conditioned by shifts in the organization of musical mass reproduction and dissemination. EMI, formerly the Gramophone Company, Ltd., continued through the late 1950s to release Yoruba discs on the His Master's Voice JZ series, distributed through the United Africa Company. Senafone releases were imported until the late 1950s by the Compagnie Francaise d'Afrique Occidental. Two relative newcomers had, however, begun to dominate the Nigerian gramophone disc market. Decca, a British company, began recording in West Africa during the mid-1940s, setting up a center of operations in Accra, capital of the Gold Coast, under the direction of Major E. J. Kinder (Akinbọde 1980:1). By the 1950s, Decca (West Africa) Limited had a varied Yoruba catalog and in 1956, set up a two-track facility in Lagos. In 1959, Decca's Lagos operation maintained a expatriate staff of four, and reported an annual turnover of around £100,000, a relatively miniscule proportion of the firm's world market (Akinbọde 1980:4). Decca's major competitor was the Dutch-based firm Philips, which began recording in Nigeria in the 1950s and set up a studio in Lagos around 1957. By 1961, Philips had established two permanent four-track studios, one in Lagos and the other in the Eastern Nigerian town of Onitsha.

The 1950s also saw the establishment of a number of Nigerian-owned record labels, usually established by gramophone record dealers who were contracted by the European firms to oversee wholesale and local retail distribution of discs. The efflorescence of indigenous labels represented an attempt by African entrepreneurs to consolidate brokerage positions linking the European firms, musicians, local retail dealers, and the rapidly expanding audience for mass-reproduced popular music. The autonomy of these local record label owners should not be overemphasized, for they were, until the 1970s, wholly dependent upon recording studios and pressing facilities controlled by European concerns. Nonetheless, they controlled both the access of local musicians to recording opportunities and the distribution of records within Lagos and from Lagos to hinterland urban centers.

The first Nigerian to establish such an enterprise was E. O. Badejọ, an Ijẹbu Yoruba enterpreneur and record dealer based in Lagos.[3] Badejọ, who had been selling gramophone discs of foreign and local popular music since the early 1940s, started recording musicians in his store in 1947. Nigerian businessmen such as Badejọ, his financial partner Mr. Ọlasimbọ, Josy Ọlajoyegbe Fajimolu (an Ijebu merchant who established his label, Jofabro, in the early 1950s), and Mr. Onyekwelu (Philips's contact in the new Eastern Nigerian town of Onitsha) were eager to find overseas facilities for pressing discs from the masters made in their small independent studios. These local labels established agreements with the field agents of European firms—Badejọ with Philips (where he later became an executive), Jofabro first with Decca, and later EMI—who arranged to have the master recordings shipped to England or the Netherlands[4] for pressing. Nigerian entrepreneurs in the Western, Eastern, and Northern Regions oversaw the wholesale distribution of records within Nigeria and guaranteed the profits of the foreign firms.

Acting as middlemen between the multinationals, the consumers, and the musicians, the shrewdest of these entrepreneurs managed to reap considerable profits. The Association of Nigerian Gramophone Record Dealers (ANGARD) was formed in 1948, with O. A. L. Araba as president and Mr. Ṣobọwalẹ as secretary. Other founding members included J. Siwọnku, and early Nigerian record label owners E. O. Badejo and Onyekwelu (Akin Euba, cited in Akinbọde 1980:1). This association, intended to protect the profits of indigenous record dealers and label owners, was troubled by internal dissension and dissolved in 1958. The Nigerian Recording Association, formed in 1958, appears to have followed essentially the same path (Akinbọde 1980:2). Apart from a few prominent success stories, recording and marketing of popular music appears to have been a precarious arena for local entrepreneurship. During the late 1950s and early 1960s, numerous smaller Nigerian-owned labels sprang up, some of them run by musicians and other professional entertainers—for example, Nọṣiru Tunwọn and Affinju Oloko Records, partially owned by a popular sákárà musician; Adeolu Records, owned by agídìgbo bandleader Adeolu Akinsanya; and Ogunde Records, owned by Hubert Ogunde, the popular dramatist. Most of these small-scale enterprises, operating in an atmosphere of intense economic competition, and at a great disadvantage vis-à-vis European firms, disappeared as quickly as they sprang up.

European companies and local merchants sought to expand their patronage networks by building catalogs that included a variety of musical genres, each popular within a given region of Nigeria. Both the dominant European firms (Decca, Philips, and EMI) and more successful Nigerian-owned labels (Badejọ Sound Studios, Jofabro, Alowonle, Star, Association, Zareco, Ajibọla, Ọshunkẹyẹ Brothers) recorded a wide range of Yoruba musical styles in the 1950s and 1960s. Increased prosperity, the spread of electricity and communications infrastructure to hinterland towns, and the emergence of an elite able to purchase record players all contributed to the rapid growth of the market for mass-reproduced music.

Another important factor in the spread of jùjú style throughout Yorubaland was the development of the Nigerian Broadcasting System. As I have already noted, the first broadcasts of Nigerian musicians had been made in 1939 from a 300-watt shortwave station at Ikoyi in Lagos. The main studio was moved from this small wooden building to the top floor of Glover Memorial Hall at the intersection of Custom Street and the Marina, the main facilities of the broadcasting service until 1952. In 1946, radio rediffusion service was available to those who could afford to rent "wired-wireless" boxes in Lagos, Ibadan, Abẹokuta, Ijẹbu-Ode, Port Harcourt, Enugu, Kano, and Zaria.

The 1948 Turner/Byron Report, a survey of broadcasting needs in Nigeria, reported 8,000 rediffusion subscribers in the country. The broadcasting service offered up to 18.5 hours a day of programming, only one hour of which originated in Nigeria. The colonial *Report on Nigeria* for the year 1947 describes the programming on the rediffusion network as consisting mostly of BBC materials augmented with local news reports, lectures in English and various Nigerian languages, and "gramophone records of African songs and music, and performances by African bands and concert parties" (Great Britian Colonial Office 1947:75).

In 1951, the Nigerian Broadcasting Service was inaugurated. Its facilities included the mobile BBC transmitter which had been used to send reports from the Normandy Beachhead, and a collection of some 12,000 catalogued gramophone discs. By 1952, the Director of the NBS claimed a library collection of some 20,000 discs, "the largest collection of West African music in existence" (Mackay 1964:34). The 1951 broadcasting schedule included some twenty hours a week of Nigerian-produced programming, expanding to 58 hours a week by 1953. A variety of performances by local musicians were taped at the NBS studios in Tugwell House (formerly a boarding house for sailors along the Marina) during the 1950s: "The music sessions featured taped and live performances by Nigerian bands and artists, and Nigerian musicians made regular appearances. There was scant interest in western classical music, and the trend was to 'highlife' and disc jockeys, some with strong personal followings" (Mackay 1964:36).

Jùjú music was a staple of the Nigerian network, which by the 1950s reached all of the major Yoruba towns. In December 1955, the administration estimated that there were over 100,000 wireless sets five years old or less in the country, 5,000 of them legally licensed and taxed. There were in addition some 65,000 radio rediffusion boxes. In the same year 2,000 cheap battery-powered radios were imported from Holland, at £6.12.6 each; they were sold out within three months (Great Britain Colonial Office 1955:169). The variety of programming was increased when the Action Group-controlled Western Region government set up its own commercial broadcasting service in 1959.

Although the automobile was the most important indicator of elite status, ownership of sound reproduction equipment was also an important index of upward mobility and urbanity. The wealthy entertained guests with 78-rpm discs played on a turntable/amplifier/speaker unit, while the young migrant worker sought to set aside enough money to buy a short-wave radio. Radio Brazzaville, the official voice of Free France, had been established in the Congo in 1943. General DeGaulle ordered a 50-KW transmitter from the United States, which allowed the *Voix Libre* to be heard over a wide area during the War (Frey 1954:52). By the late 1950s, Congolese guitar-band music, strongly influenced by the Cuban rumba and mambo, had become the craze in Lagos, its popularity sustained in part by the clear broadcasts from Brazzaville. As one informant put it:

> Almost everybody loved Congo music. And if you bought a radio set then you bought it because you wanted to learn to tune to Congo-Brazzaville. Because at that time, Radio Nigeria had rediffusion boxes which could play for five shillings or so, but for foreign music, you had to buy a radio set. They wired the thing to your house, so that you can listen to WNBC programs, without having any other place to tune it to. There permanently, giving you the programs of that place. So, people were tired of that, especially those who were illiterate, they said, "Well, we cannot be bored with talk, talk, talk, talk". Also, the young men moving to the city; the craze of any young man at that time was to have enough money to buy a radio set. Any young man without a radio set, and a carpet in his room, and a curtain to divide the room, a single room, into two, was not considered to be a man leading a full, satisfying life (Adebayọ Faleti; Ibadan, 29 Jan. 1982).

The appeal of Congolese guitar band style was reinforced by the 1962 visit of Franco and the O. K. Jazz Band, "in connection with the inauguration of an air transport link between Nigeria and the Republic of Congo Leopoldville" (Alaja-Browne 1985:85).

The Development of Local Jùjú Styles

In the introduction to this book I suggested that modern pan-Yoruba identity is grounded in mythological accounts of shared origins, and the spread of Standard Yoruba dialect via primary schools and radio. Precolonial kingdom-based allegiances continue, however, to play a prominent role in Yoruba social life. In many contexts, individuals identify themselves as Ẹgba, Ọyọ, Ibadan, Ifẹ, Ijẹbu, Ijẹṣa, Ondo, Ekiti, etc., rather than "Yoruba." Patron-client relationships linking recent migrants to the expanding elite were rooted in notions of the powerful, beneficial, and financially generous olùrànlọ́wọ́, "one who lends a helping hand," or àfẹhìntì, "one upon whom one rests one's back," and were often constructed on the basis of local ethnic affiliation.

> A Yoruba man feels that he can approach a powerful or wealthy man from his home area with whom he has, hitherto, had little or no direct relationship; conversely, he would perhaps be hesitant in seeking help from a person with whom he already has a rather more firmly established relationship, but who is from a different ethnic area (Lloyd 1974:172).

As Nigeria approached independence, Yoruba politics was characterized by oscillation between pan-Yoruba solidarity within the tri-polar national political arena, and fractures along the lines of regional kingdom-based allegiances. Thus, for example, the indigenous and predominantly Muslim Lagosian community of Isalẹ Eko united against the expanding population of hinterland immigrants during the 1950s, while the Ibadan Yoruba, under the charismatic leadership of Adegoke Adelabu, reacted communally against the perceived dominance of the Action Group party by Ijẹbus (Post and Jenkins 1973).

Ethnic identities are embodied in social customs, patterns of facial cicatrization, dialect, and *blason populaire* based upon modal personality types. Thus, for example, Ijẹbu are often regarded by other Yoruba as shrewd but stingy traders (the most common slang term for counterfeit coins in Lagos and Ibadan is "Ijẹbus"); Ibadan natives as open-minded but "trickish," an image probably related to the town's history as a war camp and bustling trade center; the Ekiti as *ará oko*, "people of the farm," simple, hardworking, and coarse in action and speech; and the Ẹgba as sophisticated, magically powerful, and inordinately ostentatious. Yoruba subgroup affiliations are enacted via performance and patronage of distinctive dance and music traditions. Thus, dùndún-ṣẹ̀kẹ̀rẹ̀ music is generally associated with the Ọyọ and related groups such as the Ibadan; bọ̀lọ̀jọ̀ drumming with the Ẹgbado; and àpàlà music with the Ijẹbu.

During the 1950s, jùjú musicians seeking to establish themselves in Lagos and regional urban centers began to experiment with song texts and musical features from their home areas. Though there had been stylistic variation in jùjú since its emergence in the early 1930s, the 1950s saw the first major efflorescence of local substyles. This development was grounded in the efforts of musicians to create distinctive "sounds" or "systems" that might attract the attention of talent scouts from recording companies and appeal to members of their own communities, both in the home area and among migrants in the cities of Lagos and Ibadan.

Among the most popular of these innovators was C. A. Balogun, an Ekiti musician who began performing around 1943. By the mid-1950s, Balogun's style incorporated elements of the music he had grown up with, including local rhythm patterns, song texts in Ekiti dialect, and a distinctive style of polyphonic choral singing involving parallel major seconds [*cassette example 15*]. Balogun's band, called the Abalabi Dandies—the term *Abalabi* referring to an annual harvest festival popular among Yoruba Christians—was, by the mid-1960s, based in the hinterland administrative center of Ilesa (Keil 1966–67:375, 393). His popularity there may be related to the fact that Ijẹsa and Ekiti music share a number of stylistic traits, most notably the distinctive polyphonic choral style (Euba 1967).

Theophilus Iwalokun ("Theo Baba"), a guitarist from Abereke village in the Okitipupa area, is cited as a pioneer in the use of regional dialects in jùjú music (Alaja-Browne 1985:47). Other distinctive substyles were constructed by Kayọde Ige, an Ijẹsa bandleader, and Suberu Oni, a native of Ondo and leader of the popular "Why Worry?" Orchestra. This trend continued during the 1960s in the work of Dele Ojo, an Ekiti musician who in 1962 began to blend elements of his local traditions with highlife music; Idowu Animaṣaun, an Ẹgba Yoruba who formed his Liṣabi Brothers band in Abẹokuta in 1964; I. B. Oriowo, from the Ijẹsa area, who left Kayọde Ige's band during the late 1950s; and Fasco Da Gama, an Ẹgbado Yoruba performing a style strongly influenced by traditional bọlọjọ rhythms.

Although some bands developed styles influenced by and associated with local traditions, most groups emulated the mainstream postwar style established by Ayinde Bakare. The production of commercial recordings of jùjú entirely in local dialects or styles was rare. Recording companies often released discs with a song in Standard Yoruba on one side and a song in local dialect on the other. The idea behind this approach was to maximize the appeal of a given disc among both the Yoruba population as a whole and the local subgroup of the bandleader. As jùjú bandleader Dele Ojo expressed it:

> I want to be identified with my area, you see? I'm not from Lagos,
> I'm not from Ibadan, I'm from Ekiti, where all this music originates.
> So, why not? A lot of my people who cannot dance to the jùjú, real

jùjú music, and they can dance to their native songs. If I want to be popular with my people and the Yorubas, all I have to do is record in Yoruba and record in my Ekiti dialect, and then the record will sell over there and sell in Yorubaland generally. It's a sort of market strategy (Ibadan, 8 Oct. 1982).

Most jùjú bandleaders emulated the mainstream Ayinde Bakare style, including Ojogẹ Daniel (b. Ilẹṣa) and Rose Adetọla (b. Abẹokuta), both based in Ibadan during the 1950s. Others incorporated features from competing popular musical systems and from the reservoir of techniques comprising early jùjú style. For example, Lagos-based bandleader Rafiu Bankọle developed a style strongly influenced by Congolese and Latin rhythms and characterized by a sonorous, nasalized singing style [*cassette example 16*]. The guitar pattern used most often by Bankọle on his recordings during the 1950s was a bluesy variation on the *talo ri* pattern used by palmwine guitarists, emphasizing a flatted seventh scale degree and tonic dominant-seventh (I^7) chords. According to Ojogẹ Daniel, Bankọle's jùjú was particularly popular in Lagos in the late 1940s and early 1950s, and was very similar to the style of Akanbi Ege (Keil 1966–67:364).

Toy Motion

Toy Motion was another important stylistic branch of jùjú, popular in the mid-late 1950s. "Toy" (also a term for marijuana) drew upon earlier traditions such as prewar jùjú and palmwine guitar music. Two Yoruba musicians, members of the skilled African work force established in Lagos during the interwar period, were particularly important in its development. Julius Oredọla Araba (born in Lagos, 24 May 1922) and Joseph Ọlanrewaju Oyeṣiku (born in Abẹokuta, 17 Nov. 1913) were the sons of Christian mission-educated families; and both became skilled technicians for the colonial railway and members of the oldest effective labor union in Nigeria. They were cosmopolitan, educated men approaching middle age, with rich life experiences derived in part from their mobile occupation.[5] Oyeṣiku served in the Nigerian Forces, traveling to East Africa and Burma, and resided in London for a period in the early 1960s; Araba's career included a lightweight boxing title, from which he derived the nickname "Speedy."

These men did not rely upon musical performance for their subsistence. Their musical ideology combined the carefree attitude of the stereotypical palmwine guitarist ("Life is a temporary appointment," as Araba puts it) and the discipline and refinement of the skilled artisan. Musicians such as Tunde King and Ambrose Campbell, early member of the Jolly Orchestra who left Nigeria for London during the 1940s, and whose songs are described by Araba as "superb," functioned as role models for the Toy Motion players. They regarded the jùjú groups formed by recent Yoruba migrants as technically inept, and composed primarily of illiterates motivated by economic rather than aesthetic considerations.

The jùjú music produced by an expanding population of "overnight musicians" in Lagos and other Yoruba cities was measured against memories of the clarity and grace of the Jolly Orchestra and the articulate "sermons" of Tunde King. Araba and Oyeşiku both appear to have regarded the new jùjú style as symbolic of undesirable social change. In discussing changes in the musical life of Lagos, J. O. Araba pointed to the postwar era as a period when the quality of African working class life began to decline:

> In the old days, we used to call Lagos L-A-G-O-S, for "Look And Go On Slowly." You could walk along the Marina in the evening and see and hear so many wonderful things . . . . Before you can get a girl, friends and neighbors will screen you without you knowing. If you dress shabbily, don't speak well, move with hooligans, they will tell the girl's family. Nowadays the world is polluted, no obedience, everything gone haywire. That is what happens when you allow your children to mix with the un-cut. People have forgotten that money is just a means of exchange. They don't know that money can't buy the thoughts you have in your mind (Lagos, 7 Nov. 1982).

Oyeşiku and Araba's musical response to the perceived decline in aesthetic standards was Toy Motion, popular during the late 1950s and early 60s, particularly among educated Yoruba. Araba's group, The Rhythm Blues, was a quartet, consisting of guitar, agídìgbo (large lamellaphone), "side drum" (European parade drum, also called *ilù kékeré*), and maracas. J. O. Oyeşiku's Rainbow Quintette [see plate 5] included guitar, mandolin (played by K. O. Nikoi, a Ghanaian immigrant who wrote the group's biggest hits), agídìgbo, side drum, and sámbà.[6]

Several differences between Toy Motion and other jùjú styles appear to have been regarded as crucial by its practitioners. Mainstream jùjú guitar style of the 1950s was characterized by single pitch melodic lines which supported or bridged between sung phrases. Toy Motion, on the other hand, drew upon harmonic-melodic patterns derived from palmwine music (e.g., *talo ri* and "C-natural"). In Toy style these patterns were enlivened by rhythms derived from more recent styles such as àgídìgbo/mambo and Trinidadian calypso, which became popular among Westernized Nigerians during the 1950s.

Another point of difference between Toy and the dominant large-ensemble jùjú style was related to the ambivalent status of praise musicians. While the new jùjú bands working in Lagos and other cities sang praise lyrics in return for cash donations from their upwardly mobile patrons, Toy musicians regarded the praising of nouveau riche Yoruba patrons as a form of begging. The proper role of the musician, from their perspective, was not to pander to the wealthy, but to provide philosophical commentary on everyday life, and reveal the misdeeds of flawed characters. One Yoruba highlife musician, interviewed in 1967 by Charles Keil, stated that Araba and Oyeṣiku were "big men with other jobs," who did not have to play at urban hotels and only took a few engagements a year. His admiration for Toy Motion musicians was based upon two criteria: their use of "correct scales," as opposed to most jùjú guitarists, who "only tune the guitar with their voice"; and, second, their refined "compositions," a term associated with Western musical practice (Keil 1966–67:151–53).

The two following texts illustrate the ethical focus of Toy Motion songs:

J. O. Araba and His Rhythm Blues. "*Pòtò Pótò*" ("The Swamp"), recorded in Lagos, 1957. Philips 82011.2. [*Cassette example 17*]

> *Pòtò-pótò dáànòn l' ábàtà, enít' áa sí l' ára k' ó foríjìn wá-o-e*
> *Pòtò-pótò dáànòn l' ábàtà, enít' áa sí l' ára k' ó foríjìn wá-o-e*
> *Òrò yìí wá dàbí òwe èyin àgbàgbà, ẹ jòwó ẹ foríjìn wá-o-e*

> The swamp has crossed the road, anyone who gets splashed
> with mud should forgive us, oh
> The swamp has crossed the road, anyone who gets splashed
> with mud should forgive us, oh
> These words are like the proverb of the elders, please forgive
> us, oh

> *B' o bá l' ówó l' ọwọ́, b' o bá l' ówó l' ọwọ́*
> *Má tèl' áṣéwó ìlú Èkó*
> *Tí wọ́n bá bá ẹ jẹ, tí wọ́n bá bá ẹ mu*
> *T' ówó bá tọ́n wọ́n á ní kí-o "jáde òrẹ́!"*
> *Tí wọ́n bá bá ẹ jẹ, tí wọ́n bá bá ẹ mu*
> *T' ówó bá tọ́n wọ́n á ní kí-o "jáde òrẹ́!"*

> If you have money, if you have money
> Don't follow the prostitutes in Lagos town.
> If they eat with you, if they drink with you,
> If the money runs out, they will say, "Leave, friend!"
> If they eat with you, if they drink with you,
> If the money runs out, they will say, "Leave, friend!"

> *B' o bá l' ówó l' ọwọ́, b' o bá l' ówó l' ọwọ́*
> *Ọlọ́lá ni ẹ ní ìgboro Èkó, sàràkí ni ẹ ní ìgboro Èkó*
> *B' áyé bá bá ẹ jẹ, b' áyé bá bá ẹ mu*

T' ówó bá tón wón á ní kí-o "jáde òrẹ!"
B' áyé bá bá ẹ jẹ, b' áyé bá bá ẹ mu
T' ówó bá tón wón á ní kí-o "jáde òrẹ!"

    If you have money, if you have money
    You are a wealthy man in Lagos town, you are the leader of a
    Muslim association in Lagos town
    If the world eats with you, if the world drinks with you,
    If the money runs out, they will say, "leave, friend!"
    If the world eats with you, if the world drinks with you,
    If the money runs out, they will say, "leave, friend!"

Pòtò-pótò dáànòn l' ábàtà, enít' áa sí l' ára k' ó foríjìn wá-o-e

    The swamp has crossed the road, anyone who gets splashed
    with mud should forgive us, oh!

J. O. Oyeshiku and His Rainbow Quintette. Excerpt from "Òrò Ré O Rẹpẹtẹ̀" ("This is the matter, in abundance"). Recorded in Lagos, 1958. Philips 82059.1. [*Cassette example 18*]

Òrò ré o, òrò ré o, òrò ré o rẹpẹtẹ̀
Òrò ré o, òrò ré o, òrò ré o rẹpẹtẹ̀

    This is the matter [i.e., the topic for discussion], this is the
    matter, this is the matter, in abundance
    This is the matter, this is the matter, this is the matter, in
    abundance

Níbi t' ó gbé ńṣe òfófó kiri, níbi t' ó gbé ńṣe òfófó kiri
Atẹ́gùn wá fẹ́ gèlè lọ, atẹ́gùn wá fẹ́ gèlè lọ
Owó bá já bọ́ sọnùn, yerí wá já bọ́ sọnùn
Aṣọ wáa já bọ́ sọnùn, ọmọ bá já s' ílẹ̀

    As she was gossiping all over the place, as she was gossiping all
    over the place
    The wind came and carried her head-tie away, the wind came
    and carried her head-tie away
    The money fell and got lost, then the earrings fell and got lost
    The the cloth [tied around the woman's body] fell and got lost,
    the baby fell to the ground.

Òrò ré o, òrò ré o, òrò ré o rẹpẹtẹ̀
Òrò ré o, òrò ré o, òrò ré o rẹpẹtẹ̀

    This is the matter, this is the matter, this is the matter, in
    abundance
    This is the matter, this is the matter, this is the matter, in
    abundance

Nínú òfófó ṣíṣe ìyàwó kò sí ìgbádùn rárá
Ibi ló máa ńkóbá ni
Ó má ńso ilé di ahoro

Ojú lo máa ńdá tì ni
Ó máa ńbà ilé jẹ́-o
> In gossiping, wife, there is no enjoyment at all
> It generally brings misfortune
> It generally causes a house to fall into ruins
> It generally causes one to be ashamed
> It generally spoils the house

Ọ̀rọ̀ ré o, ọ̀rọ̀ ré o, ọ̀rọ̀ ré o rẹ̀pẹ̀tẹ̀
Ọ̀rọ̀ ré o, ọ̀rọ̀ ré o, ọ̀rọ̀ ré o rẹ̀pẹ̀tẹ̀
> This is the matter, this is the matter, this is the matter, in abundance
> This is the matter, this is the matter, this is the matter, in abundance

The postwar indigenization of mainstream jùjú music was grounded in the emergence of a hinterland-born Yoruba elite. Toy Motion represented a contrastive symbolic strategy, an expressive style intended predominantly for listening rather than dancing, and rooted in the palmwine guitar/early jùjú paradigm. Members of the skilled African work force that pioneered jùjú style in the early 1930s, J. O. Oyeṣiku and J. O. Araba portrayed the "good old days" of prewar Lagos, before the rise of crime, prostitution, and the hinterland-born Yoruba nouveau riche. Toy Motion was an expression of literate African working-class nostalgia, and a symbolic reassertion of the sophisticated "area boys" ethos of early jùjú.

The First Jùjú Superstar: Isaiah Kehinde Dairo, MBE

In 1965 Charles Keil conducted an essay contest based on the question "Who is your favorite musician, and why?" in *Spear,* a Nigerian magazine with an urban audience crossing class and ethnic lines. On the basis of over one thousand ballots, jùjú bandleader I. K. Dairo was the overwhelming favorite, his only close competitor being the Calabar-born highlife bandleader Jim Rex Lawson.

Isaiah Kẹhinde Dairo was born in Ọfa, Kwara State, in 1930. His father was a carpenter for the Nigerian Railway Corporation. He attended a Church Missionary Society primary school in Ọfa for two years, but was forced to withdraw for lack of money. At the age of seven, Dairo returned to his family's community of origin, Ijẹbu-Ijẹsa. According to Okagbere (1969), he became a barber, and spent his time in the evenings listening to local jùjú bands. In 1942, Dairo joined his first band, led by one Taiwo Igese. The band soon broke up, and he moved to Ẹdẹ, where he worked as a pedestrian cloth trader from 1948 to 1950, and lost his job for performing music on the side: "My master travelled and I didn't know he could come back so soon. I went to entertain some people with a group and at the time I came back my master was back, and I was sacked" (Alaja-Browne 1985:68).

After pursuing various sorts of manual labor, including road work, construction, and cocoa farm clearing, Dairo was able to save some cash and move to Ibadan, where he was hired by an expatriate firm contracted to build the new university campus north of town. Working as a carpenter for wages ranging from one shilling and nine pence to two shillings a day, he performed at night with veteran bandleader Ojoge Daniel. In 1957, Dairo returned to Ijebu-Ijeṣa and formed a ten-piece band called The Morning Star Orchestra. This group gained some local notoriety playing marriage, naming, and funeral ceremonies in the Ijeṣa area. I. K.'s meteoric rise began around 1960, just after Nigeria gained its independence from Great Britain. In October the band travelled to Ibadan to play for an Independence Day celebration, sponsored by an important magistrate. They created a sensation, attracting the attention of wealthy Yoruba patrons who thereafter hired the Morning Star Orchestra for their own celebrations.

The expansion of electronic mass media played an important role in Dairo's rapid ascent. Alaja-Browne (1985:68) suggests that Dairo's popularity initially stemmed from radio appearances on the Western Nigeria Broadcasting Service, based in Ibadan, in 1958. Ibadan was also home to the first television station in black-ruled Africa, established in 1957. In 1961, Dairo's band, renamed the Blue Spots, entered a televised competition involving sixteen jùjú bands, winning the contest by general acclaim. A series of hit records with Decca from 1961 through the mid-1960s, when I. K. and àpàlà star Haruna Iṣola established the Star Records label, established Dairo as the dominant figure in jùjú music. He was the first African musician to be awarded the Member of the British Empire medal (MBE), conferred at a ceremony in Ibadan in June, 1963. In 1965, his band represented Nigeria at the Negro Arts Festival in Dakar.

From 1960 until 1968, when the original Blue Spots band broke up, I. K. Dairo was the preeminent jùjú recording star. Alaja-Browne has written that Dairo's style represented the "first significant break between old and new juju music" (1985:66). I would suggest that his enormous success was rooted in a skillful development of jùjú along lines presaged by the developments of the 1950s. Dairo continued the simultaneous modernization and indigenization of jùjú music, attempting to spread the appeal of jùjú across ethnic lines while reinforcing the attraction of the style for Yoruba listeners.

> First, [Dairo] made his music reflect its own tradition more truly by a bit of research: "Many older people have come to ask me for the meanings of some of the words I use in my songs and the majority of

my Yoruba listeners are baffled at some of the incantations, verses and expressions I use . . . I have to travel around, talking to old men who know a lot about such things: I then go back home to turn them into modern music." And second, he designed his modern music to appeal to non-Yoruba: "What I do is to concentrate more on the rhythm, the time, and, most of all, the beat. . . . To make my music appeal, I have introduced various beats and tempos to suit the different tribes" (Roberts 1972:251).

Dairo, an avid member of the Cherubim and Seraphim prayer-healing movement, reemphasized the link between jùjú music and syncretic Christianity. Many of his songs are based upon hymn melodies or texts. The rich choral sound of the Blue Spots was based in part on the distinctive multipart singing style of the Ijẹsa. Dairo was also the first prominent jùjú musician to play the ten-button accordion, using it to fill the role of the guitar. His accordion style, strongly influenced by Latin American music, alternated supporting chords with obligato flourishes. The Blue Spots had nine members during the height of its success. Its instrumentation was, apart from the accordion, typical for jùjú bands of the time: guitar/accordion, talking drum, double toy, àkúbà, ògìdo, clips, maracas, and *agogo* (see plate 6). While incorporating elements of popular Christian and Latin American styles, Dairo was able to exploit patterns of ethnic identity. He accomplished this by composing lyrics in various Yoruba dialects and in languages such as Edo, Itsekiri, Urhobo, Hausa, and Twi, and by using melodic and rhythmic patterns associated with particular areas of Yorubaland.

Dairo's early hits—for example, "To ba fo 'wo kan 'yan" (1959), "Salome" (Decca NWA.5080, 1962), "Elele Ture" (NWA.5079, 1962), and "Omo Alaro" (NWA.5118, 1963)—were released on 78-rpm discs. Dairo mastered the three-minute recording period and refined the generalized form established by jùjú groups during the 1950s. The structure of Dairo's early recordings was almost invariant. He began by stating the melody on guitar or accordion, and singing a verse or two. Then, in a manner reminiscent of the *montuno* in Afro-Cuban recordings, and possibly influenced by Congolese styles and agídìgbo music, he would generally introduce a middle section dominated by drumming and responsorial singing. During this section the talking drum played a prominent role, articulating proverbs and slang phrases. The vocalists frequently repeated the surrogate speech formulas played by the drummer. After the middle section, Dairo would play a short accordion or guitar solo, and sing the final verses. This flexible structure was very influential during the 1960s and may still be heard in the more extended forms used by contemporary jùjú musicians. In general, the first section is more Western, the middle section more African (and, when the talking drum is dominant, specifically more Yoruba), and the last section returns to the cosmopolitan ethos of the first.

A number of the responses to Keil's 1966 *Spear Magazine* essay contest have been published. I. K. Dairo's fans cited a range of ethical and aesthetic criteria for their preference, including clarity of enunciation, compelling dance rhythms, universality of appeal, and philosophical content:

> He begins moderately, sings moderately, ends moderately. No mixing [confusion] of language. No mumble. Different tones, tunes, and beating in each music.
>
> His music is the most unrivalled, distinct, melodious, rhythmical, and intoxicating. Its slow diffusion into my body makes me dance to the tune while jujus shake head to the beats.
>
> Sensible hedonist . . . Dairo's consistent drumming, sedulousity, impartiality and unservitudeness make him the Shakespeare of Music. An earthly god of music!
>
> The man whose music will move the laziest feet to action and will pour undying relief into sorrowful hearts.
>
> The booming of the band which cracks someone's brain and which forces dumb legs to move even if unwilling.
>
> He appeals to all classes of people: politicians, lovers, and common men. He does not blame in his music. He uses indigenous dialect.
>
> His music contains a lot of the up and down of his world. It teaches us knowledge, moral spirits and other things.
>
> His is music without tears (Chernoff 1979: 173–82).

Although Dairo sought to portray the image of an even-handed philosopher, he was inevitably involved in the political turmoil of the mid-to-late 1960s. He was a supporter of Ọbafemi Awolowo, founder of the Action Group Party and chief representative of the Yoruba in the national political arena.

> In 1962, Awolowo's fortunes suffered a severe reversal. A schism in the ranks of the Action Group exploded into a sensational treason trial in which Awolowo and twenty others were charged with plotting to overthrow the government by a coup d'etat. A splinter faction led by Awolowo's former assistant, S. L. Akintola, formed the . . . Nigerian National Democratic Party, which assumed the mantle of Yoruba leadership in the Western Region (Baker 1974:333, n.25).

It is rumored that Dairo, by virtue of his connection with the Aladura church, is able to prophesy future events. He is widely thought to have

predicted the release of Awolowo from prison in 1966. The song "Chief
Awolowo," released in 1964 or 1965, portends Awo's return "to the farm,"
and characterizes his imprisonment as a heroic quest for wisdom (Okagbare 1969:23). S. L. Akintọla was assassinated in Nigeria's first military
coup in January 1966. In a 1967 interview, Dairo claimed political impar-
tiality, but then stated that he sang Awolowo's praises for free, while charg-
ing his enemies prohibitive sums. When Akintọla's men came to him to
ask him to sing praises, he demanded £2000 in cash. They were insulted
and threatened him: "Why don't you sing about our man?" "Be glad to, for
a price," Dairo replied, knowing that they couldn't accept his offer (Keil
1966–67:238).

In 1963, Dairo recorded the song "K'á Ṣọra" ("Let us be careful"),
in which, it is said, he predicted the horrors of the Nigerian Civil War:

> *Gbáú-gbáú l'á ngbọ́ a ò mọ ibi ìbọn tí ńdún*
> *K'ólorí d'orí ẹ mú ó k'á kiyèsí ara*
> *Ọ̀rọ̀ Naijiria yìí-o k'ó máà bò wá d'ogun*
> *O yẹ́ k'á le kiyèsí ara l'ọ́kùnrin, l'óbìnrin, l'ọ́mọdé, l'ágbà*
> *Gbogbo ọmọ Naijiria pátá pò*
> *Ẹ jẹ́ k'á t'ẹ́wọ́ àdúrà sí Olúwa, k'Ólúwa ó gbà ni*
> *K'á má mà r'ògun ẹ̀jẹ̀*
> *K'á mà mà jẹ k'áyé fi tiwa ṣe a rí k'ọgbọ́n, ẹ jàre*

>> We are hearing "boom! boom!," [but] we don't know where the
>> guns are sounding.
>> Let the owner of his head cover his head, hold it, let us be
>> cautious
>> This matter of Nigeria, let it not come to war
>> Please, let us take care, man, woman, child and elder
>> All children of Nigeria, together
>> Let us offer prayer to God, let God receive it
>> Let us not spill blood in war
>> Let us not consume the world, make us see things sensibly,
>> please

> *Ẹ rí iṣẹlẹ̀ ti o ṣe ní Kongo*
> *Ní ọjọ́ yìí ò kò sí ìsinmi rárá*
> *Taní ò ràntí iṣẹlẹ̀ Kongo, taní ò rántí iṣẹlẹ̀ Kongo*
> *Wẹ́rẹ́-wẹ́rẹ́ nwọ́n dìde síi 'ra wọn*

>> See what came to pass in the Congo
>> This is no time to relax, at all!
>> Who does not remember the Congolese Civil War?
>> Stealthily, they rebelled among themselves

> *Bíi ere bíi ere, ilé nwó,*
> *Bíi ere bíi ere, ilè nmì*

Olómo ò m' òmo mó, aláyá ò m' àya mó
  Little by little, the house is collapsing
  Little by little, the earth is shaking
  The parent willlonger know the child, the husband will no
  longer know the wife
K' ólorí d' orí e mú ó k' á kiyèsí ara
Òrò Naijiria yìí-o k' ó máà bò wá d' ogun
Oyé k' á ronú wa wò dákun
Omo ìyá ni gbogbo wa jé dákun kílo wa fà iru eyìí Èdùmàrè
Tó bá je esé Bàbá lo fà' ru èyìí Bàbá daríjìn ni
E f' iyèdénún o, èyin àgbà, e bá wa tún Naijíríà se
  Let the owner of the head [destiny] hold his head, let us be
  cautious
  This matter of Nigeria, let it not come to war
  Please, let us think and watch, please
  Child of mother, all of us, please, what is exacerbating this
  situation, God?
  If it is lack of gratitude, Father, that has caused this, Father,
  forgive us.
  Please, all you elders, help us to repair Nigeria!

In his book, *Songs of I. K. Dairo,* B. C. Okagbare comments on
"K'a Sóra":

Dear reader, what vision, what prophecy has been more vivid, more
picturesque or more graphic than this! Who is he on the European or
African continent other than I. K. Dairo who had foreseen a similar
national catastrophe and had accordingly warned his people before
time? No doubt this I. K. is more than an ordinary musician (Okagbare 1969:75).

I. K. Dairo's songs center on the two major themes common in jùjú
music since its inception: the experience of urban life, and the strength of
ìjinlèe Yorùbá tradition. These two themes often overlap in particular
songs, for example, "Salome," a brisk, crisp performance that "shook the
juju world when it came out" (Okagbare 1969:123) in 1962.

I. K. Dairo and the Blue Spots. "Salome". Recorded in Lagos, 1962. Decca NWA.5080. [*Cassette example 19*]

Sú sú sú bebi-o
Bebi Salome mi-o
Mo fé lo rí bebi-o Salome mi
Màmá Bekun mi

Salome ó wùn mí-o
T' ó bá jẹ́ t' owó, màá tẹpá mó' ṣé owó mi-o Salome
Salome ó dára l' óbìnrin iwa rẹ l' ó wùn mi-o Salome
Eléyin' jú ẹgẹ́
Eyín fún j' owó Salome, eyín m' ẹ̀nu gún-o
Oyìnbó Salo, Salome
Salome, Salome, Salome, Salome, Salome, Salome, Salome,
Salome

> Shoo, shoo, shoo baby
> My baby Salome
> I want to go see my baby, Salome
> Mother of Bekun
> Salome, she attracts me
> If it's a matter of money, I will work hard to make money,
> Salome
> Salome, she is a fine woman, it's her character that attracts me,
> Salome
> She has eyes ["eye-eggs"] that can trap
> Teeth whiter than cowries, teeth that shape the mouth
> Light-skinned Salo, Salome
> Salome, Salome, Salome, Salome, Salome, Salome, Salome,
> Salome

ACCORDION SOLO
DÙNDÚN TALKING DRUM

> *Emì ò ní sí níbẹ̀, èmi ò ní sí níbẹ̀*
> *Níbi wọ́n gbé ṣorí burúkú, èmi ò ní sí níbẹ̀*
> > I will not be there, I will not be there
> > Where they have bad destiny ["head"], I wlll not be there

VOCAL CHORUS

> *Emi ò ní sí níbẹ̀, èmi ò ní sí níbẹ̀*
> *Níbi wọ́n gbé ṣorí burúkú, èmi ò ní sí níbẹ̀*
> > I will not be there, I will not be there
> > Where they have bad destiny ["head"], I will not be there.

DÙNDÙN

> *Ire gbogbo kò ni ṣ' èyìn mi, ní' lé ayé*
> > All the good luck will not happen when I am not present, in this
> > world/life

VOCAL CHORUS

> *Ire gbogbo kò ni ṣ' èyìn mi, ní' lé ayé*
> > All the good luck will not happen when I am not present, in this
> > life

Yes, kẹ̀, o bẹ̀rẹ̀fẹ́; yes, kẹ̀, o bẹ̀rẹ̀fẹ́
   Yes, you start to love; yes, you start to love
Yes, kẹ̀, o bẹ̀rẹ̀fẹ̀; yes, kẹ̀, o bẹ̀rẹ̀fẹ̀
   Yes, you start to joke; yes, you start to joke

DÙNDÚN
   Tà' dí m'ẹ́yìn
      Stick out your ass and move back

CHORUS
   O bẹ̀rẹ̀fẹ̀
      You start to joke

DÙNDÚN
   Tà dí m'ẹ́yìn

CHORUS
   O bẹ̀rẹ̀fẹ̀

DÙNDÚN
   Tà dí m'ẹ́yìn

CHORUS
   O bẹ̀rẹ̀fẹ̀

SOLO VOICE
   Ṣú ṣú bebi Salo, bebi Salome mi-o, bebi-o, bebi, bebi-o, Salo,
   Salome-o,
   Ahh . . . bebi Salome mama-a
   Ahh . . . bebi Salome mama

Dairo's songs emphasize the value of tradition, hard work, and supporters in an uncertain world. In the song "O Wúrọ̀ L'ọjọ́" ("The morning is the day"), one of his last big hits, he deploys ìjinlẹ̀ẹ Yorùbá metaphors to portray entrepreneurial values and ask patrons for support.

I. K. Dairo and the Blue Spots. *"O Wúrọ̀ L'ọjọ́"*. Recorded in Lagos, 1968. [*Cassette example 20*]

LEAD VOICE AND CHORUS
   O wúrọ̀ l'ọjọ-o-o-e, o wúrọ̀ l'ọjọ-o-e
   Akókò kò dúró d'ẹnìkan-o, ọ̀rẹ́ o tẹpá mọ́'ṣẹ́
   O wúrọ̀ ènìyàn n'ílé ayé-o, bí ìpínlẹ̀ ilé l'órí
   Ẹ̀ bá lè kọ̀ s'órí àpáta-o, kẹ̀ má kọ̀ s'órí iyanrìn
   Ayé ẹ gbọ́ s'étí
      The morning is the day, the morning is the day
      Time doesn't wait for anyone, friends, work hard

The morning of a person in the world is like the foundation of a
house
Lay it on a rock, not on the sand
People, listen with your ears

SOLO VOICE

Ẹ jẹ́ áfàárò múra kámá ṣẹ, elé' yà bó d' alé
L'ọ̀kùnrin, l'óbìnrin, l'ọ̀mọdé, l'ágbà
Alẹ́ là ńtoro l'ọwọ Elédùmarè k'ámá ṣẹ ẹlé' yà
Ígbà mẹ́ta n'ígbà ẹ̀dá n'ílé ayé-o
Ígbà ààrò, ígbà àsán, ígbà alẹ́
K' álẹ́ san wá j' òwúrọ̀ lọ̀, bàbá awa mbẹ̀bẹ̀

> Show some enthusiasm in the morning [of life] so that people
> will not ridicule you in the night
> Man, woman, child and elder
> At night [when we're old] we are begging for God's help, so
> that people will not ridicule us
> There are three times that are the times of a person's life
> Morning-time, afternoon-time, night-time
> Let the night benefit us more than the morning, Father, we are
> begging.

LEAD VOICE AND CHORUS

O wúrọ̀ l'ọjọ-o-o-e, o wúrọ̀ l'ọjọ-o-e
Akókò kò dúró d'ẹnìkan-o, ọ̀rẹ́ o tẹpá mọ́' ṣẹ́
O wúrọ̀ ènìyàn n'ílé ayé-o, bí ìpínlẹ̀ ilé l'órí
Ẹ̀ bá lè kọ̀ s'órí àpáta-o, kẹ má kọ̀ s'órí iyanrìn
Ayé ẹ gbọ́ s'étí

> The morning is the day, the morning is the day
> Time doesn't wait for anyone, friends, work hard
> The morning of a person in the world is like the foundation of a
> house
> Lay it on a rock, not on the sand
> People, listen with your ears

SOLO VOICE

Ẹnití a bá ṣẹ kó foríjìn wá
Ọmọ́dé l'a jẹ́, òjò ni wá aò b'ẹ́nìkan ṣọ̀tá
Ẹni eji rí ni eji ńpa
Ẹ bá wa ṣè tójú ẹgbẹ́ Blue Spot ẹgbẹ́ ọlọ́lá
A ṣèṣè bẹ̀rẹ̀, kíl' ẹ tíì rì?

> Anybody whom we offend should forgive us
> We are children, we are rain, we are no one's enemy
> Anyone who is out when it's raining, the rain will beat

Help us to take care of the Blue Spots, honorable group
We are just beginning, you haven't seen anything yet

CHORUS
Ọ̀rẹ́-o-e-e-e, o wúrọ̀ l' awà ọba j' álẹ́ ósan wá
Friends-o, we are in the morning, let the night be better for us

SOLO VOICE
L'ọ́kùnrin, l'óbìnrin, ẹni tó ba'tí gbọ́ wá
K' inú wọn kó ba' lẹ̀
Dídùn dídùn ni, ba' lẹ́ oloyin
A ṣẹ̀ṣẹ̀ bẹ̀rẹ̀, kíl' ẹ tíì rì ọ̀rẹ́ mi-o?
Ṣẹ́ gbọ́?
Ọmọdé l' ágbà dákun ẹyin àgbààgbà, ẹ foríjìn wa-o
A ṣẹ̀ṣẹ̀ bẹ̀rẹ̀ kíl' ẹ tíì rì?
Ọ̀rẹ́-o-e-e-e, o wúrọ̀ l' awà ọba j' álẹ́ ósan wá
Man, woman, anyone who hears us
Let their mind ["stomach"] calm down ["touch the ground"]
It is always sweet in the bee's house
We are just beginning, you haven't seen anything yet, my friend
Do you hear/understand?
Young and old, please, all you elders, forgive us
We are just beginning, you haven't seen anything yet
Friends-o, we are in the morning, let the night be better for us

LEAD VOICE AND CHORUS
O wúrọ̀ l' ọjọ-o-o-e, o wúrọ̀ l' ọjọ-o-e
Akókò kò dúró d' ẹnikan-o, ọ̀rẹ́ o tẹpá mọ́' ṣẹ́
O wúrọ̀ ènìyàn n' ílé ayé-o, bí ìpínlẹ̀ ilé l' órí
Ẹ̀ bá lè kọ̀ s' órí àpáta-o, kẹ̀ má kọ̀ s' órí iyanrìn
Ayé ẹ gbọ́ s' étí
The morning is the day, the morning is the day
Time doesn't wait for anyone, friends, work hard
The morning of a person in the world is like the foundation of a
house
Lay it on a rock, not on the sand
People, listen with your ears

SOLO VOICE
Ẹni bá l' étí kó gbọ́
Akókò ńlọ, àkókò kò dúró d' ẹnikan
Òwe l' á fi pa
Anyone who has ears, let them hear
Time is going, time doesn't wait for anyone
It is proverbs that we use to express it.

LEAD VOICE AND CHORUS
O wúrò l' ọjọ-o-o-e, o wúrò l' ọjọ-o-e
Akókò kò dúró d' ẹnìkan-o, òrẹ́ o tẹpá mọ́' ṣẹ́
O wúrò ènìyàn n' ílé ayé-o, bí ìpínlẹ̀ ilé l' órí
Ẹ̀ bá lè kọ s' órí àpáta-o, kẹ̀ má kọ s' órí iyanrìn
Ayé ẹ gbọ́ s' étí
    The morning is the day, the morning is the day
    Time doesn't wait for anyone, friends, work hard
    The morning of a person in the world is like the foundation of a
    house
    Lay it on a rock, not on the sand
    People, listen with your ears

    Like most jùjú song texts, this lyric operates on multiple discursive levels: it is a prayer; a didactic tale; and an appeal to patrons. Dairo begins with a general philosophical statement about mortality, the unpredictability of life, and the necessity of hard work, themes that are sustained through the entire song. This rhetoric is then applied to the band itself ("Help us to take care of the Blue Spot group"), newly formed in 1968 after the acrimonious breakup of Dairo's original group. Various traditional framing devices are used to establish the position and character of the singer. Dairo presents himself as a fluid, transparent, neutral medium—rain—and then turns the ultimate responsibility for interpretation and moral judgment over to the listener ("anyone who is out when it's raining, the rain will beat," i.e., "if the shoe fits, wear it"). The phrase that precedes the final recapitulation of the verse—*òwe l' á fi pa* ("it is a proverb we recite")—is a traditional means of framing social criticism to protect the performer, a "don't blame the messenger" strategy.
    I. K. Dairo's success in the year following Independence was rooted in a number of factors: slick, carefully organized arrangements; dance rhythms derived from Yoruba drumming traditions and Latin American music; melodies from local sources and Christian hymns; and song and drum texts metaphorically grounding the entrepreneurial strategies of his patrons, and his own struggle for success, in deep Yoruba values.

Tunde the Western Nightingale

Another bandleader who rose to prominence during the 1960s was Ernest Ọlatunde Thomas (alias Tunde the Western Nightingale, The Bird Who Sings At Night), born 10 December 1922 in southern Ijẹbu territory. Thomas, like I. K. Dairo, was a typical jùjú practitioner in terms of life experience and social background. He attended grammar school in Olo-wogbowo quarter in Lagos, and his father, S. Ọladele Thomas, was a civil servant and a noted guitarist (Alaja-Browne 1985:63). Tunde served in the colonial army and was for some time a wageworker in the employ of the Nigerian Railway (Ojogẹ Daniel, Keil 1966–67). He formed his first group in 1944, a trio consisting of guitar, tambourine, and ṣẹ̀kẹ̀rẹ̀. By 1952, his group had expanded to eight members, and, like Ojogẹ Daniel's ensemble, worked at the West African Club in Ibadan, a social center for members of the Action Group party. Although Nightingale's initial commercial recordings on the Jofabro label were not particularly successful, he had by the mid-1960s attracted the enthusiastic patronage of the Lagosian "jet set," members of elite voluntary associations such as the High Society of Nigeria (*Drum Magazine*, Dec. 1981). His hit recordings of the mid-1960s were aimed at a wide Yoruba audience, and included songs about a famous Ijẹṣa warrior ("Gbogungboro") and a praise song for the *Aláàfin* (sacred king) of Ọyọ ("*Ṣẹkẹrẹ Alafin*").

Tunde Nightingale's style was known as *Ṣó Wàmbẹ̀* ("Is it there?"), a slogan interpreted as a reference to the money with which his fans were expected to "spray" him during performances, or as a double entendre referring to beads draped around the hips of dancing women (the proper response to either sense of the question being *Ó Wàmbẹ̀!*, "It is there!"). The most distinctive aspect of Nightingale's style was a high tessitura, tense, slightly nasalized vocal quality modeled upon Tunde King, whom he had heard in Lagos as a young man. It was this vocal quality which earned him the nickname "The Bird That Sings At Night." Nightingale's sound, which incorporated early jùjú vocal techniques into the expanded and reindigenized postwar style paradigm, appears to have been formulated as a strategic response to the style of I. K. Dairo.

> "I was not surprised when I. K. Dairo captured Nigeria with his own brand of jùjú music. He introduced the accordion and made the rhythm more pronounced. Although his own style was very good, I was not convinced that every jùjú orchestra should copy him. I knew that sooner or later people would return to our own form of more relaxed jùjú music" (Ọlatunde Thomas, quoted in Alaja-Browne 1985:66).

In competing with I. K. Dairo, the dominant post-Independence jùjú bandleader, Nightingale reached back to the music he heard and performed growing up in Lagos. Ṣó Wàmbẹ̀ style combined the high-tessitura early jùjú vocal style of Tunde King with the expanded ensemble structure and indigenized rhythms and texture of postwar jùjú [*cassette example 21*].

Once again, we may view this process of stylistic diversification as the product of symbolic and economic strategy. Alaja-Browne (1985:56) quotes from an article in a Lagos magazine (see Daramọla 1967) which asserts that the jet set that patronized Nightingale

> had decided, even when I. K. Dairo was at the peak of his popularity, against Dairo's brand of jùjú music. What was more, they were firm in their belief that jùjú music was for social parties and not for dance halls, and because Dairo was playing more at dances than at social parties, they decided that Tunde was the horse to back. They went all out to patronize Tunde and popularize his type of jùjú music.

Thus, the perceived opposition between the two contexts for jùjú performance—the proletarian bar and the elite party—continued to influence the strategic choices of musicians. In addition, the lavish celebrations of the Lagos jet set may be seen in retrospect as "the seeds of a later period of conspicuous consumption" (Alaja-Browne 1985:57) which strongly affected the fortunes of jùjú musicians.

Dele Ojo and Jùjú-Highlife

During the 1960s, jùjú musicians continued to compete with practitioners of other styles for patronage and recording opportunities. Jùjú and highlife, both revitalized in the late 1940s, developed along contrastive trajectories.[7] Jùjú was an African music with foreign elements woven in, played by Yoruba musicians for Yoruba audiences. Highlife was ballroom music with African and Afro-Caribbean tinges, performed for a varied, though predominantly Christian and literate African audience. Jùjú and highlife practitioners working in the towns of southwestern Nigeria competed for the patronage of the Yoruba elite, and there was in the process a certain amount of stylistic interchange between the styles.

Charles Keil asked Ibadan-based musicians to specify the major distinguishing traits of jùjú and highlife, and to explain why they had chosen to specialize in one genre rather than the other. Their responses may be enumerated briefly: (1) the typical highlife musician used written music, while the jùjú musician performed "from his head," and didn't require as much rehearsal; (2) highlife musicians worked for salary, while jùjú musicians were usually dependent upon cash prestations from patrons; (3) jùjú musicians performed praise songs, while highlife musicians did not; (4) highlife bands used Western wind instruments such as saxophones, trumpets, and trombones; (5) jùjú musicians often wore "native Yoruba dress," while highlife musicians tended to don European clothing; (6) highlife bands did not usually include talking drum, a ubiquitous feature of jùjú ensembles; (7) starting a highlife band required more capital than starting a jùjú band; (8) jùjú musicians sang in Yoruba, while highlife bands sang in English, pidgin English, and various indigenous languages; and (9) highlife musicians were ethnically hetereogeneous and performed music appealing to a varied audience, while jùjú music was essentially by and for Yoruba people. A jùjú musician interviewed in 1966 (Keil 1966–67:100) put it this way:

> One thing I can see from them is this: this highlife band, they play in English way, English songs, so our people, most of them, they don't understand them when they are playing. And what our people like here is that when you are playing either you name them somewhere, you call them, you tell them where you have been knowing them. . . . Let's say you speak what they understand. Well, they will like you.

By the mid-1960s, highlife had begun to decline in popularity among the Yoruba. This decline appears partially to have been precipitated by competition from both local and imported styles. Though highlife retained its popularity in eastern and midwestern Nigeria, it was squeezed out in Lagos, Ibadan, and other Yoruba-dominated cities by the re-indigenized jùjú style, which gained the patronage of the expanding elite. The Civil War also played a role in the decline of highlife music in southwestern Nigeria. Many of the style's leading exponents in Lagos and Ibadan were Igbo, and most left for Eastern Nigeria in 1966 and 1967.[8] In addition, it is often suggested that soul music from the United States—for example, James Brown, Wilson Pickett, and Aretha Franklin—displaced highlife among young, cosmopolitan Yoruba.

In Charles Keil's 1966 *Spear Magazine* poll, the second-place jùjú musician was Dele Ojo, who finished fourth overall. Born near the small Ekiti town of Ilara-Mokin in 1938, he was the son of traditional farmers. His family were first-generation Christians, and he was exposed both to traditional Ekiti music and syncretic Christian hymnody as a child. Ojo first learned to play the cornet, and then the trumpet, in a local grammar school band directed by Roy Chicago, who went on to become one of the most popular Yoruba highlife bandleaders of the 1950s. Ojo was unable, for financial reasons, to enter secondary school. He took a course in short-hand and typing, eventually finding employment as a clerk. In 1955, he moved to the Ekiti town of Igbara-Odo and worked as a band instructor at the local school until 1958, when he was employed as a teacher at Akurę, a large town in Ondo Province. He practiced the trumpet by playing along with recordings of highlife bands broadcast over the rediffusion system. In

1961, Ojo moved to Lagos, where he joined the band of Dr. Victor Ọlaiya ("the evil genius of highlife"), an apprentice of Bobby Benson and the most popular Yoruba highlife bandleader of the period.

> Ọlaiya was very big by then, in Lagos. I had started practicing Ọlaiya's tune while I was in Akurẹ, because I had the opportunity to take my trumpet home, and Ọlaiya was playing on the radio. I listened to him, you know, try to play the way he plays, copy him, just a copycat to Ọlaiya's band. I was employed the very day I interviewed on a salary of fifteen pounds a month, as the first trumpeter in the second band [Ọlaiya ran two units at the time]. Fifteen pounds! Me, fifteen pounds?! Dreaming, was I dreaming?! Because when I left the teaching profession, I was on six pounds-something, or seven pounds-something. How could I rise that high within one or two months?!
>
> Then things went rough. In 1962, August, Ọlaiya had to dissolve the second band. A lot of people thought I would go to first band then, but. . . . I came to Ibadan in 1962, as an insurance agent. I couldn't go 'round looking for jobs in any band, because not every band in Lagos is stable. You go to this place to play a gig and you take your share, you know, I didn't like that type of job.
>
> I came to Ibadan as an insurance agent, and I couldn't earn any money, the first month I walked and walked around Ibadan, no business. Then I met a friend who was working in a hotel. I told him, "Yeah, I'm a musician. I'll get some instruments together, we'll start a little band". The man said "O.K.!". He contacted one Mr. Banjoko [owner of a electronics shop] and got some microphones and a box guitar from him. We started with that box guitar (Ibadan, 8 Oct. 1982).

Dele Ojo's shift from highlife to jùjú music was in part a strategic response to socioeconomic conditions. For one thing, it was relatively easy to find a patron who would purchase the minimal equipment necessary to start a jùjú band. Ojo had started playing guitar during his grammar school days and had learned highlife style from a guitarist in Ọlaiya's band while in Lagos.

> When I came here, this man got the box guitar, and I tried my hand at it, then I would sing to him. I was playing highlife chords, not this two-string jùjú chord, then [laughs]. I was playing real chords, with standard tuning. Small time I bought a flute, and on my first recordings for Philips I played flute and trumpet.

Dele's practical knowledge of highlife allowed him to incorporate aspects of the style into his jùjú style. His first group included a number of musicians who were later to become prominent bandleaders in Ibadan, including Lamina Oguns, E. S. Ọdẹyẹmi, and Jossy Ọla.

> We got these boys together, and rehearsed and rehearsed and rehearsed, and in October 1962, we finally came out, to play to the public. The man at the hotel took us to a television program, they watched us on television. Everybody was amazed. "What type of band is this?!" I played trumpet, I played flute, I played guitar all along. "Who is this man, who is this man?!" That is why the name got out.
>
> Unfortunately, the friend, whom we started together, was very jealous of my success. He was very jealous of my act, and he started to talk to the owner of the hotel, to get the instruments from me, so that he can lead the band. Then we left that hotel, we went to Our Roses Hotel, a small parlor, as small as this place [a single room, ca. 20 × 20 ft.]. My band would stay in a corner. We started playing and people started coming. This is a place where we can make two or three pounds a night, sometimes one pound ten shillings, sometimes one pound fifteen. But, we really had some money to feed ourselves, that was the initial thing.

Ojo's style was popularized through a series of recordings with Philips and Badejo, many of which featured a jùjú-highlife song with Standard Yoruba dialect text on the A-side [*cassette example 22*], and an "Ekiti Native Blues" song utilizing local Ekiti rhythms, instruments, and lyrics on the B-side. A shrewd businessman, he managed to build a substantial patronage network by simultaneously appealing to the older Western-oriented audience which had supported highlife, and to the rapidly growing population of Ekiti Yoruba migrants in Lagos and Ibadan. He traveled to Great Britain and the United States during the late 1960s and 1970s and returned to Nigeria performing a new style influenced by funk music. Ojo was unable to regain his former popularity, due in part to a series of contract disputes with recording companies, and to the domination of the jùjú market by a new generation of recording superstars.

The Oil Boom and the Rise of the Jùjú Mega-stars

The Nigerian Civil War (1967–1970) strongly affected the relations of production of jùjú, though not its essential musical and textual structure. While nightlife in Yoruba towns was adversely affected by the sudden emigration of Igbos, including a number of the most prominent club owners, the war also provided new employment opportunities for jùjú bands that could gain the patronage of officers in the vastly expanded Nigerian Army. Many bandleaders recorded songs lauding powerful officers and military heroes; for example, I. K. Dairo, Ebenezer Obey, and Sunny Ade all released songs praising Col. Benjamin Adekunle ("The Black Scorpion"), who drove the advancing Biafran forces from the town of Ore, in 1968. As I have already noted, the exodus of Eastern Nigerian highlife musicians from Lagos and Ibadan also created new opportunities for jùjú musicians.

Beginning in the early 1970s, the Nigerian economy was transformed by increased demand for crude oil on the international market. Although the agricultural economy had begun to stagnate in the 1960s, taxes on such exports were still the main source of government revenue before the Civil War. Oil production climbed from 140,000 barrels a day in 1968, to 1,080,000 barrels a day in 1970, and 2 million in 1973. The 1970s were characterized by a "succession of oil peaks when the economy was awash with money, punctuated by sharp troughs" (Stevens 1984:3).

The Oil Boom affected the production of jùjú music in several important ways. It led to the formation of a high elite, consisting of an governmental administrative bourgeoisie; a private sector bourgeoisie who accumulate wealth through trade, finance, state contracts, and construction; and highly educated professional and technocratic elites "who mediate between the state and international firms . . . while at the same time, maintaining their own private firms and investments" (Watts and Lubeck 1983:112). Money and power were increasingly concentrated in the hands of a small sector of Nigerian society, exacerbating the gap between wealthy and poor.

This process of socioeconomic differentiation was mirrored during the 1970s by the emergence of the first millionaire jùjú superstars. As the rich got richer, so the stars they patronized rose higher. Bandleaders began in the early 1970s to adopt such unofficial titles as King, Admiral, Senator, Captain, Uncle, and Chief Commander (the last a clever compromise between traditional and military authority). Well-placed band captains were able to accumulate theretofore unheard of amounts of cash for investment in musical and nonmusical enterprises (e.g., recording labels, hotels, construction firms, milk companies). In addition, those with contacts among the high elite gained access to smuggled electronic equipment which, if bought within Nigeria, would have been exorbitantly expensive. The size of the most popular bands increased from around ten performers in the mid-1960s to fifteen or more in the mid-1970s.

The production of commercial recordings in Nigeria was strongly affected during the 1970s and early 1980s by economic fluctuations and by Decree No. 3 (1977), popularly known as the indigenization decree. Section 5, schedule 2 of the Decree stipulates that 60 percent of the share equity of companies involved in the manufacture of plastic products (including record manufacturing plants) must be owned by Nigerian nationals, while up to 40 percent of the remaining paid-up capital may be in

1. Jùjú band: the Honourable Joshua Olufemi (1982).

2. Jùjú band: Captain Jide Ojo and his Yankee System (1982).

3. Celebrants preparing to spray jùjú band captain at àríyá (1982).

4. Talking drummers (Uncle Toye Ajagun and his Olumọ Soundmakers, 1979).

1. Yoruba and Akan musicians performing palmwine guitar music. Note mandolin. (Ibadan, 1982).

2. Yoruba and Akan musicians performing palmwine guitar music (Ibadan, 1982)

3. (Facing page, top) Professional talking drummers (Ibadan, 1982)

4. (Facing page, bottom) "Ju-Orchestra" by M. O. Onimole. *Nigeria Magazine* 32 (1949): 88. Banjo, tambourine, and ṣẹ̀kẹ̀rẹ̀.

5. (Top) J. O. Oyeshiku and K. O. Nikoi of the Rainbow Quintette (Ibadan, ca. 1958). Guitar and banjo-mandolin.

6. I. K. Dairo and his Blue Spots (ca. 1962). Back row, (right to left): clips, maracas, agogo, dùndún. Front row: double toy, ògìdo, accordion, sámbà, àkúbà.

7. Modern Yoruba entre-
preneurship: Jisbo Pub-
licity, School of Signs,
College of Designs
(Ibadan, 1982).

8. Bootleg cassette mer-
chant (Oje Market, Iba-
dan, 1982).

9. Hotel Independence: entrance (Oke Bola, Ibadan, 1982).

10. Hotel Independence: interior.

11. The Ambassador Hotel (Oke Ado, Ibadan, 1982).

Right, Hajji Timmy Tiamiyu Rasaki Aladokun both of King Sunny Ade's African Beats.

12. Newspaper photo of talking drummers at elite celebration, published in Lagos society column.

13. Jùjú band captain and chorus (Honourable Joshua Olufemi, 1982).

14. Jùjú band back line: ṣèkèrè, ògìdo, àkúbà, double toy.

15. Ògìdo and àkúbà (Uncle Toye Ajagun and the Olumo Sound-makers, 1979).

16. Lead and tenor guitars (Captain Jide Ojo and his Yankee System, 1982).

17. Core celebrants dancing and spraying one another at wedding ceremony (1982).

18. Celebrants at wedding ceremony (1982).

19. Sweet stomachs, un-
folded bodies: celebrants
at a house-warming
(1982).

20. Celebrant unveiling amplifier at jùjú band's equipment-launching ceremony (1982).

SOMETIME ago the Egba people marked their centenary in being. Many distinguished Egba sons and daughters gathered in Abeokuta from home and abroad to mark the occasion with festivities.

The Alake of Egbaland, Oba Oyebade Lipede, made several influential people chiefs during the celebrations.

For the foremost 'juju' maestro, Ebenezer Obey Fabiyi, it was time to say "thank you, Royal Highness" for honour done him so far.

OBEY GREETS ALAKE

21. Sacred king of Abeokuta spraying jùjú superstar (1981).

22. Poster for jùjú band's instrument-launching ceremony (1982).

23. Successful jùjú band captain's bus (motto: "God is my power") (1982).

foreign hands. There are three large pressing plants in Nigeria. The first is Record Manufacturers of Nigeria, Limited (RMNL), which in the early 1980s was owned jointly by Decca West Africa (35 percent), Nigerian EMI (25 percent), and various Nigerian concerns, including Take Your Choice Records, founded in 1961 by Yoruba entepreneur Chief Abioro. The second record pressing plant is owned by Polygram, formerly Philips.

The third and newest facility is Phonodisk (Nigeria), Ltd., the brainchild of àpàlà star Alhaji Haruna Iṣọla. The factory, located near Iṣọla's hometown of Ijẹbu-Igbo, has facilities for electro-plating, printing, and pressing. Incorporated in 1976 as Nigerian Musical Industries, Ltd., Phonodisk produced its first discs in 1979, attracting customers dissatisfied with the longer-established companies. King Sunny Ade, for example, has recorded songs on his own label and used Phonodisk's pressing facilities. Several smaller companies, most of them specializing in one aspect or another of the production process, appeared in 1981 and 1982. The Lagos-based company Tabansi Records, for example, has advertised facilities for producing 12-inch LPs, label printing, inner and outer sleeves, jacket design and fabrication, and shrink wrapping.

Despite the apparent growth in Nigerian control over the means of mass-reproducing music, the vigor of the record industry continues to be strongly affected by shifts in Nigeria's balance of trade and in import-export laws, which restrict the flow of raw materials and machinery. Indigenization has not shifted the balance of power between local and foreign concerns; rather, it has served to "rationalize the relationship between the Nigerian bourgeoisie and its patron, international capital" (Ake 1978:49). It is very difficult for entrepreneurs without ties to foreign corporations to break into the record manufacturing business.

The proliferation of record labels, which may record and promote but not physically manufacture records and tapes, has continued since the 1950s. The major labels include Decca, NEMI, Polygram, and the larger Nigerian concerns such as Phonodisk, Take Your Choice, and African Songs. Musicians have on occasion started their own labels—Sunny Alade Records is a notable example—and there have been scores of small labels founded by local entrepreneurs seeking to establish a niche in the music market. As in the 1950s, most of these smaller labels spring up during periods of prosperity and founder during periods of economic retrenchment. The retail distribution of records and tapes in Nigeria is exceedingly complex. Records generally move from the company to private wholesalers in the major cities. Retailing takes place both in record stores and traditional open-air markets.

The contemporary Nigerian music market is characterized by very rapid production and turnover of hit records, partly due to musicians' attempts to stay ahead of tape bootleggers; marked conservatism on the part of wholesalers regarding the introduction of new styles and artists; and domination of the market by pirated tapes and illegally imported recordings. The expatriate heads of Decca West Africa (Robert Oeges) and Polygram (Mr. Van Leeuwen) gave the following estimate of recorded music sales:

Estimated Consumption of Recorded Music Units in Nigeria (1981)

Pirated Cassettes: 6,000,000
Records: 6,000,000
   3,000,000 legitimate locally produced
   1,500,000 legitimate product smuggled into Nigeria
   1,500,000 pirated product

Legitimate local product: 3,000,000	25%
Smuggled legitimate product: 1,500,000	12.5%
Pirated product: 7,500,000	62.5%
Total unit consumption: 12,000,000	100%

This estimate of the informal market in pirated cassette dubs of records and live performances is quite conservative. The practice of copying records on cheap cassettes began in the early 1970s, and expanded rapidly in 1973 and 1974, when government salary increases for upper-level civil servants made the cassette player, formerly a luxury, much more widely accessible. According to Akinbọde:

> traders who needed little or no training in the new "boom" gravitated towards it and before they knew it, the epidemic had caught on in the country and bootleggers carried on their trade in virtually all major cities in Nigeria.
>
> A bootlegger in Yaba Market [Lagos] who chose to remain anonymous told me that he normally bought his empty cassettes from a major wholesaler at Nnamdi Azikiwe Street in Lagos. The "carton" as he called it, contained about 150 empty cassettes . . . at the rate of 60k [kobos] per cassette. After he had bought the empty cassettes, road-side radionics, record-retail shops and some other road-side "recording studios" would record about a dozen empty cassettes for ₦4 or ₦5. In the alternative, the trader might prefer the more arduous [task] of doing the recordings himself. Here his stereophonic equipment at home and a few borrowed cassette recorders placed around the stereo would be used. You would then play the record you desired and get young boys to simulatneously depress the recording buttons. This way you could record ten cassettes at a single playing (Akinbọde 1980:48).

The ability of jùjú musicians to support themselves on returns from recordings is compromised by the size of the bootleg market, by the unwillingness of the Nigerian government to enforce copyright laws (especially Decree 61 [1970], which guarantees protection to "intellectual property"), and by perennial disagreements between recording companies and performers vis-à-vis sales figures and royalty payments. Except for the big Lagos-based superstars, most jùjú musicians are heavily dependent upon earnings from live performance.

Shifts in the global market for oil create fluctuations in the informal sector, resulting in a "boom-bust" economy at the local level. As Karin Barber has written:

> Production in neo-colonial Africa takes place in the context of economies vulnerable to the fluctuations of world prices. But though the whole of society is affected when the economy is hit, it is the intermediate layers that are most likely to be knocked askew. . . . The urban intermediate sector of low-paid workers and the self-employed have no security. Dramatic economic reversals can turn them upside down . . . When an economy suffers, the resulting shortages, decline of local trade, drop in local production, and general worsening of the already precarious position of the majority of the population can drastically affect the production of popular culture (Barber 1987:31).

During the 1980s, the gap between wealthy and poor musicians has continued to widen. For a jùjú band at the bottom of the hierarchy, working within the constraints of a volatile urban cash economy, fortunes fluctuate wildly. Only the most successful groups own their own equipment. Most are indebted to a entrepreneurial sponsor, and "conflict between sponsors and musicians leads to the rapid demise of many bands as equipment is reclaimed" (Collins and Richards 1982:129).

Contemporary jùjú music has been shaped by economic factors, by the influence of popular music from the United States and Europe, and by developments in musical technology. Despite these changes, however, jùjú style has by and large developed along lines presaged by the post-War experiments of Ayinde Bakare, I. K. Dairo, and Tunde Nightingale. I will discuss aspects of contemporary jùjú peformance practice in later chapters. It must suffice for now to note that the arrangement of additional performance roles and sound sources—drums, guitars, and chorus vocalists—has been guided by traditional social and aesthetic values. Instruments are hierarchically arranged in interlocking patterns, and the size of a band broadly indicates the power and popularity of the patron whose praises it sings.

Chief Commander Ebenezer Obey and King Sunny Ade

I conclude my historical sketch of jùjú music with a brief look at the two dominant superstars of the 1970s and 1980s. Chief Commander Ebenezer Obey and King Sunny Ade. Ebenezer Oluwaręmilękun Ǫlaṣupǫ Fabiyi was born 3 April 1942 in Idǫgǫ, Ęgbado Division (Ogun State). His father was a carpenter and farmer on a cocoa plantation (Alaja-Browne 1985: 74). He attended a Methodist school in Idǫgǫ, where he formed an agí-dìgbo group modeled on the popular band of Adeolu Akinsanya. In 1957, he attended school in the Mushin area of Lagos and then entered a Methodist secondary school in Abęokuta. After leaving school at sixteen, he secured employment as a clerk with the Oriental Brothers Pools (football wagering) Company in Lagos. Obey, like most jùjú musicians, began by playing part-time at night to supplement his daily wages. In 1958, he joined the band of Fatayi "Rolling Dollar," former agídìgbo player with J. O. Araba's Afro-Skiffle group. Obey started his own seven-piece band, the International Brothers, in 1964. According to Alaja-Browne (1985:86), the original band included one guitar, double toy, sámbà, agogo, two ṣèk-ęrè, and conga. The International Brothers first single was released by Decca (WA) in 1966.

Obey's style initially derived from the jùjú-highlife framework of Fa-tayi's band, with elements of Congolese guitar band style, soul music, and country-and-western woven in. His songs of the late 1960s focus on typical themes, including prayer, praise, and the treachery of enemies, and draw upon a number of stylistic sources. "Ori Bayemi" (Decca NWA.5490, 1968), for example, is based upon the song "Jolly Papa," a hit by highlife bandleader Jim Rex Lawson, while the song "Olowo Laye Mo" [*cassette example 23*] is a Jim Reeves song, "This World is Not My Home," wth a rumba-influenced dance rhythm and Yoruba lyrics:

Ebenezer Obey and his International Brothers Band. Excerpt from "Olowo Laiye Mǫ". Recorded in Lagos, mid-1960s. Rereleased on Decca WAPS 432. [*Cassette example 23*]

LEADER

> *Olówó l' ayé mǫ̀, Olúwa tèmi dǫwǫ́ rę*
> *Gbogbo làálàá ęda, nítorí owó ni*
> *Ję́ ká yé mi dùn, ṣe mí kí nlè ję́'nìyàn*
> *Tètè fǫnà hàn mí, má ję́ kí ńlǫ lóòfo*
>> It is the rich person that the world knows, my God, my destiny is in your hands.
>> All the struggles of humanity are because of money
>> Let my life be sweet, make me someone notable
>> Show me the way in time, don't let me go empty-handed

CHORUS

> *Olúwa kò s' órẹ́ tó dà bíì rẹ*
> *Tètè fọnà hàn mí, má, jẹ́ kí ńlọ lóòfo*
> *Jẹ́ ká yé mi dùn, ṣe mí kí nlè jẹ́'nìyàn*
> *Tètè fọnà hàn mí, má jẹ́ kí ńlọ lóòfo*
>> God, there is no friend like you
>> Show me the way in time, don't let me go empty-handed
>> Let my life be sweet, make me someone notable
>> Show me the way in time, don't let me go empty-handed

CHORUS

> *Ayé kì ṣe' lé mi àtìgbó ni mo jẹ́*
> *Gbogbo súrà mi yíò ti ńkòjá láwọ̀ sánmà*
> *Àwọn anjeli pè mí, láti ẹnu ọ̀nà*
> *Kò sí tún lè sílé nínú ayé mọ́*
>> The world is not my home, I am only a stranger
>> All my treasures that are passing in the sky
>> All the angels call me, from the entrance to the road
>> There can never be another house in this world again.

On other early recordings Obey praises local business concerns in Lagos, including various football pools companies. In the song "Face to Face" (1970), he sings:

> *Face to Face ni mo ta*
>> It is Face to Face [pools company] that I play
> *Face to Fact ni mo ta lósè yio*
>> It is Face to Face I'm staking, I will play
> *Tó bá fẹ́ lówó, tó bá fẹ́ ta pools, Face to Face ni o ta*
>> If you want to have money, if you want to play pools, it is Face to Face you should play.

Many of Obey's early songs reflect the economic uncertainty of the Civil War period, and the cutthroat competition among bands. In the 1970 release "Ẹ Ṣa Ma Miliki" ("Just Continue Rocking"), Obey attacks his denigrators and competitors, attempts to quell a rumor about smuggled musical instruments, and links his career to the fame of James Brown.

Ebenezer Obey and his International Brothers. "Ẹ Ṣa Ma Miliki" ("Just rocking"). Recorded in Lagos, 1970. Rereleased on Decca WAPS.436. [*Cassette example 24*]
Instrumental Introduction. [Repeated I–V^7 chord pattern.] Bass guitar ostinato derived from surrogate speech phrase:

Ẹ ṣá ma jó, e sá ma yò
Just dance, just be joyful!

LEADER
Kó m' a rotéèti wẹ́rẹ́-wẹ́rẹ́
Let it rotate, gradually, gradually
CHORUS
Ẹ ṣá ma mìlíkì-o, Ẹ ṣá ma mìlíkì-o
Just rocking, oh, just rocking, oh.

LEADER
Kó m' a sakuléètì lọ wẹ́rẹ́-wẹ́rẹ́
Let it circulate, gradually, gradually
CHORUS
Ẹ ṣá ma mìlíkì-o
Just rocking, oh.

LEADER
Kò mà s' éwu l' ọ́rọ̀ wa
There is no danger in our words
CHORUS
Ẹ ṣá ma mìlíkì-o
Just rocking, oh.

LEADER
Kò mà s' èwu l' ọ́rọ̀ wa.
There is no danger in our words
CHORUS
Ẹ ṣá ma mìlíkì-o
Just rocking, oh

LEADER
Lẹ́sọ̀-lẹ́sọ̀ kó ma yí lọ
Gently, gently, let it roll on
CHORUS
Ẹ ṣá ma mìlíkì-o
Just rocking, oh

LEADER
Ẹ ṣá ma sàkàdélìkò
Just be psychedelic, oh
CHORUS
Ẹ ṣá ma sàkàdélì-o, ẹ ṣá ma sàkàdélì-o
Just be psychedelic, oh, just be psychedelic, oh

LEADER
> *Ẹ ṣá ma sàkàdélìkò*
>> Just be psychedelic, oh

CHORUS
> *Ẹ ṣá ma sàkàdélì-o*
>> Just be psychedelic, oh

LEADER
> *Jídé, director mi*
>> Jide, my director

CHORUS
> *Ẹ ṣá ma mìlíkì-o*
>> Just rocking, oh

LEADER
> *Adéníyì, director, bàbá ni*
>> Adeniyi, director, is the father

CHORUS
> *Ẹ ṣá ma mìlíkì-o*
>> Just rocking, oh

LEADER
> *Lẹ́sọ̀-lẹ́sọ̀ kó ma yí lọ*
>> Gently, gently, let it roll on

CHORUS
> *Ẹ ṣá ma mìlíkì-o*
>> Just rocking, oh

LEADER
> *Kó ma sakuléètì wẹ́rẹ́-wẹ́rẹ́*
>> Let it circulate, gradually, gradually

CHORUS
> *Ẹ ṣá ma mìlíkì-o*
>> Just rocking, oh

LEADER
> *Ẹ ṣá ma sàkàdélìko*
>> Just be psychedelic, oh

CHORUS
> *Ẹ ṣá ma mìlíkì-o*
>> Just rocking, oh

LEADER
> *Kó ma rotéètì wẹ́rẹ́-wẹ́rẹ́*
>> Let it rotate, gradually, gradually

CHORUS
> *Ẹ ṣá ma mìlíkì-o*
> Just rocking, oh

TALKING DRUM (PATTERN REPEATED UNDER SINGING)
> *Rìkísí pin alágbède kò rí pépà rọ*
> The mutiny has ended, the blacksmith cannot make paper [i.e., your enemies can't hurt you]

LEADER
> *Jídé director nlẹ́ oṣé*
> Jide, director, thank you

CHORUS
> *Ẹ ṣá ma mìlíkì-o*
> Just rocking, oh

LEADER
> *Jide, ọmọ [?] mi*
> Jide, child of [?]

CHORUS
> *Ẹ ṣá mi mìlíkì-o*
> Just rocking, oh

LEADER
> *Awo Dúpẹ́ ọmọ Awósìkà bàbá*
> Close friend of Dupe, child of Awosika, father

CHORUS
> *Ẹ ṣá ma mìlíkì-o*
> Just rocking, oh

LEADER
> *Ẹ ṣá ma mìlíkì-o*
> Just rocking, oh

CHORUS
> *Ẹ ṣá ma mìlíkì-o, ẹ ṣá ma mìlíkì-o*
> Just rocking, oh, just rocking, oh

LEADER
> *Ẹ ṣá ma sàkàdélìkò*
> Just be psychedelic, oh

CHORUS
> *Ẹ ṣá ma mìlíkì-o*
> Just rocking, oh

LEADER
> *Kó ma rotéètì wẹ́rẹ́-wẹ́rẹ́*
> Let it rotate, gradually, gradually

CHORUS
> *Ẹ ṣá ma mìlíkì-o*
> Just be rocking, oh

LEADER
> *Kó ma sakuléètì wẹ́rẹ̀-wẹ́rẹ̀*
> Let it circulate, gradually, gradually

CHORUS
> *Ẹ ṣá ma mìlíkì-o*
> Just be rocking, oh

LEADER
> *Ká ṣọpé f' Olúwa, ẹgbẹ́ Ebenezer Obey*
> *Ká dúpẹ́ f' Olúwa, ẹgbẹ́ Ebenezer Obey*
> *Àwọn ọ̀dàlẹ̀ wọ́n bà wà jẹ́-o*
> *Wọ́n l' á ò tún lùlù mọ́*
> *Aṣẹ̀ṣẹ̀ bẹ̀rẹ̀ aiyé jíjẹ ni*
> *Obey sì ńlù lọ*
>> Let us praise God, Ebenezer Obey's group
>> Let us give thanks to God, Ebenezer Obey's group
>> The untrustworthy ones have spoiled us [our reputation]
>> They say that we aren't playing music any more
>> We have just begun to eat [enjoy] life
>> Obey still beats [plays] on

CHORUS
> *Ayé-o, ayé-o, ayé ṣòro*
> Life, oh, life, oh, life is difficult

LEADER
> *Ayé màlé-o, ayé-o, ayé màlé*
> Life is hard, oh, life, oh, life is hard

CHORUS
> *Ayé-o, ayé-o, ayé ṣòro*
> Life, oh, life, oh, life is difficult

TALKING DRUM
> *Mágbe mì, ọ̀nọ̀n'fun ò gb' egungun ẹja, mágbe mì*
> Don't swallow it, the throat cannot swallow a fish-bone, don't
> swallow it [don't mess with something you can't handle]

CHORUS
> *Ayé-o, ayé-o, ayé ṣòro,*
> *Ayé-o, ayé-o, ayé màle*
>> Life, oh, life, oh, life is difficult
>> Life, oh, life, oh, life is hard

TALKING DRUM

> *Ẹni a wí fún tó ló hun ònígbọ́*
> *Ẹni afọ̀fọ̀ tó lóhun ònígbà*
> *Ẹni apète pè rò pé ká fi ọwọ́ ẹ̀ bọlè*
> *Pí pele lótún pele si*
>> Someone we talk to and he says he won't listen
>> Someone we talk and talk to, and he says he won't accept it
>> The person whose downfall we've talked about
>> He is now making progress again

LEADER

> *Ilé kí la kọ́-o, owó kí latíì ní*
> *Aṣèṣè bẹ̀rẹ̀ ayé jíjẹ ni*
> *Aó lò gbà yí pẹ́-o*
> *Ọmọ ènìyàn ṣá ni James Brown tó fi jet ṣe ẹsẹ̀ rìn, mo sọ*
>> Which house have we built, which money have we got?
>> We are just beginning to eat [enjoy] life
>> We are going to enjoy for a long time, oh
>> At least James Brown is a person who uses a jet instead of walking with his legs, I say

CHORUS

> *Ayé-o, ayé-o, ayé ṣòro,*
> *Ayé-o, ayé-o, ayé màle*
>> Life, oh, life, oh, life is difficult
>> Life, oh, life, oh, life is hard

LEADER

> *Ayé-o, l'ayé-o, aó lò gbà yí pẹ́-o*
>> Life, oh, in life, oh, we are going to enjoy for a long time, oh

CHORUS

> *Ayé-o, l'ayé-o, aó lò gbà yí pẹ́-o*
>> Life, oh, in life, oh, we are going to enjoy for a long time, oh

LEADER

> *Ẹni tó fi kakí lẹ wúùlù l'aiyé fẹ́-o*
> *Aó lò gbà yí pẹ́-o*
>> The person who patches wool with khaki [a poor person], that's who the world loves
>> We are going to enjoy for a long time, oh

By the early 1970s, with the addition of a talking drummer, bass and lead guitars (the latter played by Monday O. John, a native of Abẹokuta), òrìdo, and two chorus vocalists, Obey's band included thirteen performers. His hit recordings for Decca and connections to the elite allowed him to continue expanding the ensemble, and by the early 1980s, he employed eighteen musicians.

Obey's fans often cite his philosophical depth and knowledge of Yoruba proverbs. Some of his best-known songs are parables about the power of God and the fickleness of human beings. "Kṛtṛ kṛtṛ" (Donkey) (Decca WAPS.98, mid-1970s), recounts the story of a father, his child, and a donkey. As they began their journey, the father put the child on the donkey. The first person they met said, "Foolish old man, you are walking while your child is riding!" The father took his child down, and mounted the donkey. The next person they met asked, "What's going on?! You are riding and your son is walking!" The father dismounted, put his child on the beast, and climbed on behind him. They then came across a third person, who exclaimed, "Goodness, you are merciless! Do you want to kill the donkey?!" The man looked skywards plaintively, dismounted, and took the child down. They met a fourth person, who scoffed, "Ha! Foolish old man! Both of you are walking while the donkey is free!" After long reflection, the old man sang:

> *Ẹ dákun, ẹ f' èyìí k' ógbón*
> Please learn from this
> *K' ó s' ógbón tẹ le dá*
> No matter how experienced you are
> *K' ó s' ìwà tẹ le hù*
> No matter how well behaved you are
> *K' ò s' ónà tẹ le gbà*
> No matter how thorough you are
> *T' ẹ le fi t' ayé l' órun-o*
> You will never satisfy the world-o.

Some of Obey's supporters cite his prophetic powers, which, like those of I. K. Dairo, are widely thought to be derived from syncretic Christianity. One informant cited an Obey song about Jimọ Ejigbadero, an entrepreneur in the Agege area of Lagos who was able, during the mid-1970s, to amass land holdings by manipulating local authorities. One poor farmer whose land was in jeopardy objected, and Ejigbadero shot him dead. He was later executed. Before the event, Obey had released a song about Ejigbadero, including the line:

> *Kò lè yé wọn bi Gbadero ṣe ńlò ígbà*
> One cannot know how Gbadero is using time.

This phrase, initially read as a reference to Ejigbadero's enjoyment of the good life, was later reinterpreted by listeners as a statement about secrecy, ethics, and the fate of the wicked.

The introduction of long-playing microgroove discs in the early 1970s allowed Obey and other jùjú musicians to record longer performances, lasting up to thirty minutes. Obey's recent albums are organized around themes. In the early 1980s, he produced a trilogy for ceremonial occasions, including *What God Has Put Together, Celebration,* and *Ẹ̀bùn Pàtàkì L'ọmọ Bíbí (The Newborn Child is a Precious Gift).* Social and political themes also appear in Obey's work. The LP *Austerity,* released in 1982, comments on the Shagari government's Austerity Measures.

Chief Commander Ebenezer Obey and his Inter-Reformers Band. Excerpt from "Austerity". Recorded in Lagos, 1982. Obey [Decca] WAPS 548. [Cassette example 25]

ÀDÀMỌ̀N TALKING DRUM (SOLO)

> *Ayélabówó, ọmọ Adéṣiyan,*
> *Márìndọ̀tí, Bàbá Tẹ̀miladé*
>> [Traditional introductory salute to the drummer's lineage]
>> Ayelabowo [drummer's father], child of Adeṣiyan [father's mother], someone who is always neat, father of Tẹmilade [the drummer].

[OTHER DRUMS ENTER, STEADY PULSE ESTABLISHED]

TALKING DRUM

> *Dùgbẹ̀, dùgbẹ̀ tí ńrọ̀ l'ókè*
> *Aò mọ̀ rí ẹni ti yíò sọ'lẹ̀ sí*
> *Ọlọ́run, má jẹ́ o sọ'lẹ̀ sórí mi*
>> Something dangerous is falling from on high
>> We don't know who it will fall upon
>> God, please don't let it fall on me

LEADER

> *K'á f'ètò si ká jọ ṣé,*
>> Together, let us be methodical

CHORUS

> *K'á f'èrò si ká jọ ṣé*
>> Together, let us be thoughtful

LEADER

> *K'á f'èrò si ká jọ ṣé,*
>> Together, let us be thoughtful

CHORUS
> *K'á f'ètò si ká jọ ṣé*
> Together, let us be methodical

LEADER
> *K'á f'ètò si ká jọ ṣé*
> Together, let us be methodical

CHORUS
> *K'á f'èrò si ká jọ ṣé*
> Together, let us be thoughtful

LEADER AND CHORUS
> *Austerity Measure yìí ga lọ́lá, Austerity Measure yìí kọ yọyọ*
> *Austerity Measure yìí ga lọ́lá, Austerity Measure yìí kọ yọyọ*
> *O kọ̀n' lówó, ó kọ̀n' lọ́lá, ó kọ̀n mèkúnnù*
> *Ọ̀rọ̀ tó wà nílẹ̀ yìí kò s'ẹ́ni tí ò kọ̀n lára*
> This Austerity Measure is very serious, this Austerity Measure is unbearable
> This Austerity Measure is very serious, this Austerity Measure is unbearable
> It reaches the rich, it reaches the wealthy, it reaches the poor
> This matter leaves no one untouched

LEADER AND CHORUS
> *Ọjà t'ólówó nńọ́n, ni mèkúnnù ńnọ́n*
> *Ata t'ólówó ńjẹ, ni mèkúnnù ńjẹ*
> *Ìresì t'ólówó ńjẹ, ni mèkúnnù ńjẹ*
> *Iṣu t'ólówó ńjẹ, ni mèkúnnù ńjẹ*
> The market that the rich person patronizes, the poor person patronizes
> The pepper that the rich person eats, the poor person eats
> The rice that the rich person eats, the poor person eats
> The yam that the rich person eats, the poor person eats

LEADER AND CHORUS
> *Àmọ́n kiní kọn bà'jàò jẹẹ? Apá ẹ ò gùn jù'tan lọ*
> *A ti f'ọrọ̀ àgbẹ̀ sílẹ̀, a ti f'ọrọ̀ àgbẹ̀ ṣeré*
> *Àmọ́n kiní kọn bà'jàò jẹẹ? Apá ẹ ò gùn jù'tan lọ*
> *Àmọ́n kiní kọn bà'jàò jẹẹ? Apá ẹ ò gùn jù'tan lọ*
> But what is wrong with the *ajao* bird? Its arms are longer than its thighs [i.e., it is overreaching itself, living beyond its means].
> We have put the matter of farmers down, we have made light of farmers

But what is wrong with the *ajao* bird? Its arms are longer than
its thighs
But what is wrong with the *ajao* bird? Its arms are longer than
its thighs

LEADER AND CHORUS

Ọ̀rọ̀ àgbẹ̀, ọ̀rọ̀ àgbẹ̀, ká má f' ọ̀rọ̀ àgbẹ̀ ṣeré-o-e
Ọ̀rọ̀ àgbẹ̀, ọ̀rọ̀ àgbè, ká má f' ọ̀rọ̀ àgbẹ̀ ṣeré-o-e
This matter of farming, this matter of farming, let's not make
light of farmers
This matter of farming, this matter of farming, let's not make
light of farmers

LEADER

Otítọ́ l' epo ńsun, ká má f' ọ̀rọ̀ àgbẹ̀ ṣeré se
True, oil is flowing, but let's not make light of farmers
CHORUS
Ọrọ̀ àgbẹ̀, ọ̀rọ̀ àgbẹ̀, ká má f' ọ̀rọ̀ àgbẹ̀ ṣeré-o-e
This matter of farming, this matter of farming, let's not
make light of farmers

LEADER

Tani kò mọ̀ pé ' ṣu dára l' ẹnu, ká má f' ọ̀rọ̀ àgbẹ̀ ṣeré se
Who doesn't know that yam tastes good, let's not joke about
farmers
CHORUS
Ọ̀rọ̀ àgbẹ̀, ọ̀rọ̀ àgbẹ̀, ká má f' ọ̀rọ̀ àgbẹ̀ ṣeré-o-e
This matter of farming, this matter of farming, let's not
make light of farmers

LEADER

Ibùkún Olúwa l' epo jẹ, ká má f' ọ̀rọ̀ àgbẹ̀ ṣeré se
Oil is a blessing from God, but let's not joke about farmers
CHORUS
Ọ̀rọ̀ àgbẹ̀, ọ̀rọ̀ àgbẹ̀, ká má f' ọ̀rọ̀ àgbẹ̀ ṣeré-o-e
This matter of farming, this matter of farming, let's not make
light of farmers

LEADER

Ọ̀rọ̀ ìbùkún lát' ọwọ́ Olúwa
A blessing from God
CHORUS
Iyẹn ni t' epo jẹ
That's what petroleum is

LEADER

Ọ̀rọ̀ ìbùkún lát' ọwọ́ Olúwa

A blessing from God

CHORUS

Iyẹn ni t' epo jẹ

That's what petroleum is

LEADER AND CHORUS

Ibòsí petrol! Epo! Epo! Ibòsí petrol! Epo! Epo! Ibòsí petrol! Epo!
Epo! Ibòsí petrol! Epo! Epo!
Àmọ́n kiní kọn bà' jàò jẹẹ? Apá ẹ ò gùn jù'tan lọ
Àmọ́n kiní kọn bà' jàò jẹẹ? Apá ẹ ò gùn jù'tan lọ

The unwarranted noise about petrol! Oil! Oil! [sung four times]
But what is wrong with the *ajao* bird? Its arms are longer than
its thighs [twice]

LEADER

T' alẹ́, t' alẹ́

Darkness of night, darkness of night

SOLO CHORUS VOCALIST

T' alẹ́, t' alẹ́

Darkness of night, darkness of night

LEADER AND CHORUS

Kìí b' ọta 'lẹ̀ l' ójú

Shouldn't hurt the eyes of the nocturnal insect [i.e., that which
is natural, like oil, shouldn't be harmful]

Èdùmarè fún wa ní' dẹra baba
Ìdẹra, ìdẹra, ìdẹra, Ọba Olúwa fun wa ní' dẹra náà k' alẹ́

God, give us comfort, father
Comfort, comfort, comfort, King God, give us comfort until
night [whole phrase sung three times]

Àṣẹyẹ l' alákòn ṣ' epo, àṣẹyẹ l' alákòn ṣ' epo
Orí mi, máà jẹ ńsàṣẹ dànùn
Àṣẹyẹ l' alákòn ṣ' epo

The crab produces oil successfully, the crab produces oil
successfully
My destiny, save me from wasting away
The crab produces oil successfully [whole phrase sung five
times]

LEADER AND CHORUS

Ṣ' ọmọ rere ní' dẹra, ṣ' ọmọ rere l' ọ́nà tọ́tọ́

Be a good person in comfort, be a good person on the straight
road

Ṣ' ọmọ rere l' ọ̀nà tọ́tọ́, ṣ' ọmọ rere l' ọ̀nà tọ́tọ́, ṣ' ọmọ rere l' ọ̀nà tọ́tọ́,
s' ọmọ rere l' ọ̀nà tọ́tọ́, s' ọmọ rere l' ọ̀nà tọ́tọ́ [etc.]
Be a good person on the straight road [twenty times]

This is a typical jùjú song text in that it emphasizes the common
interests of, rather than conflicts between, the rich and the poor. Chief
Commander Obey, the prosperous band captain, suggests that the Austerity
Measures instituted by the Shagari government affect all levels of society
equally. The egalitarian metaphor of shared traditional foodways is used to
evoke communal values that crosscut class divisions. Dependence on oil
revenues at the expense of agriculture is portrayed as a problem created by
all the people, rather than by a self-interested elite. The recording ends
with a choral refrain, repeated twenty times, which beseeches the listener
to be good, honest, and (tacitly) to obey the rule of government.

Sunny Adeniyi, the other dominant contemporary jùjú superstar, was
born in Ondo in 1946, and received his primary education at the African
School in Oṣogbo, where his father was church organist (Alaja-Browne
1986:79). Like many other jùjú musicians, he left secondary school pre-
maturely for lack of money. Sunny began his professional musical career
in 1963, playing sámbà drum with the band of Moses Ọlaiya (alias Baba
Sala), who later became a popular actor and comedian. Sunny formed his
own group, the Green Spot Band, in Lagos in 1966.[9] This ten-piece outfit
was modeled on Tunde Western Nightingale's band, and Ade developed a
slightly nasalized, high-tessitura vocal style that represents a fifty-year line
of continuity stretching back through Nightingale's *Ṣo Wàmbẹ̀* sound to the
early jùjú style of Tunde King.

In 1966, when Moses Olaiya switched over from popular music to
popular theatre with the formation of the "Alawada" (comedy) group,
Sunny Ade left [him] and teamed up with Tunde Amuwo to form the
"High Society Band" which was then based at the West-End Coliseum
on Apongbon Street, Olowogbowo area of Lagos. In 1967, Sunny
Ade terminated his contract with Tunde Amuwo, and in the same year,
he and other members of the "Green Spots Band" entered into financial partnership with Mr. Jide Smith, the musician, clerk cum musical
financier who hired out musical instruments to up-and-coming musicians on a businesslike basis (Alaja-Browne 1986:82).

Ade's agreement with Smith, who provided him with instruments and amplifiers, was typical of the exploitative relationship between struggling jùjú
musicians and their sponsors: Smith evidently received two-thirds of all
money made by the band from "spraying," or cash donations. More atypi-

cally, Sunny was able to pay off his debts, and, in 1969, to terminate his relationship with Smith.

Ade developed a reputation as an adept and innovative guitarist, and had a series of hits on the African Songs label, owned by wealthy businessman Chief Bọlarinwa Abioro. His first hits, in 1967, included a praise song for Chief Abioro (African Songs 21A) and a song of praise for a soccer team, entitled "Challenge Cup". In 1970, he added a bass guitar and began to record with sophisticated electronic instruments purchased for him by Chief Abioro; it is at this point that Ade's reputation for technological innovation was consolidated. African Records 97 was the first 45-rpm release featuring Ade's new high-tech style. The A side is entitled *Alújọ̀nù Onígítà* ("Wizard of the Guitar"), Ade's professional *nom-de-plume*, while the B side features a risqué lyric sung to the melody of a well-known syncretic church humn. "*Ẹ gbọ́ òhùn àwọn anjélì ti ńkórin*" ("Listen to the angels singing"), and interrupted briefly by what one urban Yoruba informant described as "a local drum pattern, very bush."

Sunny Ade and His Green Spots Band. "*Wá Wọyàn*" ("Come and look at the breasts"). Recorded in Lagos, 1970. African Songs, Ltd. 97B. [*Cassette example 26*]

> *Wá wọ'yàn àwọn adélébọ̀ tó hún fọ'ṣọ*
> *Wọ́n fọ'ṣọ tọ̀san tòru*
> *Gígé ni, gbogbo wa la bẹ̀rẹ̀ ge*
> *Gígé ni-o, wọ́n ṣè'dí gogoro*
> *Gígé ni-o, wọ́n tun ṣè dí rẹ̀bẹ̀tẹ̀*
> *Wá wọ'yàn àwọn adélébọ̀ tó hún fọ'ṣọ*
> *Ẹ dúró ná, mo wá pàdé bebi ọlọ́yàn méjì kan*
> *Tí óún bá mi léri ó ní bóo lèdí mọ́ mi ma lẹ̀'dí mọ́ ẹ*

> Come and look at the breasts of the married women that are washing clothes
> They wash in the day and the night.
> It is for screwing, all of us, we bend down and screw
> It is for screwing, their bottom is high [like a multi-storied building]
> It is for screwing, their bottom is also fat
> Come and look at the breasts of the married women that are washing clothes
> Wait a bit, I meet a baby with two breasts
> And she's boasting to me that if I paste my bottom on her, she'll paste her bottom on me [i.e., we'll have intercourse]

This lyric encapsulates Yoruba male stereotypical perceptions of rural women. On the one hand, "city dwellers ridicule the unsophisticated

Figure 4.1. Syncro System patterns
Sunny Ade and his African Beats (1974)

'bush' people; their attitudes, as expressed in conversation and proverbs, closely parallel our concept of 'rube' or 'hick'" (Bascom 1955:451). On the other hand, many urban Yoruba men look forward eagerly to a visit to their natal town or village, where they are celebrated as big men, relieved temporarily of the stresses of the city, and receive the attentions of village women, whom they generally regard as simpler, more easily seduced, and more trustworthy than their urban counterparts. A successful urban wage-worker will often keep at least one wife in his home town, and seek to save enough money to build a house there for his parents.

In 1972, Ade split with Chief Abioro, a bitter dispute involving extended legal proceedings. He changed the name of his band to The African Beats, partly to avoid copyright conflicts with a cigarette company which used the name Green Spot (Alaja-Browne 1986:88). In 1974, Ade inaugurated his own label (Sunny Alade Records), initially using Decca's studio and distribution networks. The album *Synchro System Movement,*[10] released in 1976, artfully blended the vocal style Ade had derived from Tunde Nightingale with slower tempos, a tonally ambiguous, almost modal quality, and a langorous electric bass line (see fig. 4.1) This ensemble texture evinces the influence on Ade of Fẹla Anikulapọ-Kuti's Afro-Beat style, a blend of dance band highlife (see chapter 2) with Soul music. This was in part a reaction to the success of Afro-beat and Soul music, which had begun in the early 1970s to cut into the younger portion of jùjú's audience. In addition, *Synchro System Movement* was one of the first jùjú long-play recordings to include a continuous performance on one side, a move away from the three to four-minute limit of mainstream Western popular music, and toward a traditional Yoruba musical practice.

The song text of *Synchro System*, like most jùjú texts, is comprised of a loosely-linked series of exhortations, proverbs, and catch phrases. Like most Yoruba popular songs, its semantic and emotional effect is cumulative, arising from the sequential juxtaposition of verbal images. Both music and text assert the compatibility of new fashions (*àrà*) and ìjinlẹ̀ẹ Yorùbá rhetorical traditions.

Sunny Ade and his African Beats. "Synchro System Movement". Recorded in Lagos, 1976. African Songs AS 26. [*Cassette example 27*]

LEADER

> *Synchro, Synchro system!*
> *A gbé t'àná dànù-o, a túngbé tuntun dé*
> *Àwa lùlù málu t'àná ṣẹ-o, a túngbé tuntun dé*
> *Synchro System, ijó tuntun, ìlù tuntun, Synchromatic Sound*
> *t'African Beat tún gbédé*
> *B'ó bá fé jó Synchro System, ṣo ńgbọ́*
> *Àní t'ó bá fẹ́ jó Synchro System, ṣo gbọ́ mi?*
> *K'ó rọra ṣebí ẹní dúró lójú kan, ṣo ńgbọ́?*
>
>> Synchro, Synchro System, we have thrown away yesterday's thing, oh, we have finally brought a new one.
>> We who don't beat the drum of yesterday, oh, we have finally brought a new one
>> Synchro System, a new dance, a new drum,
>> Synchromatic sound that the African Beat band has finally brought
>> If you want to dance Synchro System, do you hear?
>> The one who wants to dance Synchro System, do you hear me?
>> Do it gently so that it seems you stay in one place, are you listening?

TALKING DRUM

> *Sunny Adé, iwọ l'Ọlọ́run fún, ẹnikan tọrọtọrọ,*
> *Ọlọ́run ò fún, iwọ l'Ọlọ́run fún*
>
>> Sunny Ade, it is you that has been gifted by God
>> A person that asks and asks, God did not give it to him
>> It is you that has been gifted by God

LEADER

> *B'ó bá ṣebí ẹ ní dúró lójú kan*
> *K'ójú sí bebi ẹ, kí bebi ẹ ó k'ójú sí ẹ*
> *B'óò bá l'áya-o, tàbí b'óò bá l'ọkọ, k'ó k'ójú sí Sunny Aládé*
>
>> If you do it as if you are standing in one place, you should face your baby, and your baby should face you

If you have no wife, or you have no husband, you should face
Sunny Alade

LEADER

B'ó bá k'èhìn sí ẹ, kò bọ́si rárá
If she turns her back to you it is not good

CHORUS

Face to face làwá ńfẹ́
It is face to face that we want

TALKING DRUM

Ṣeré fún mi bebi
Display ["play"] for me, baby!

LEADER

B'ó bá k'ẹ̀gbẹ́ sí ẹ, kò bọ́si rárá-o,
If she turns her side to you it is not good, oh

CHORUS

Face to face làwá ńfẹ́
It is face to face that we want

TALKING DRUM

Ṣeré fún mi bèbi
B'óo bá ṣeré fún mi bèbi, màá ṣeré fún ẹ
Ṣeré fún mi bèbi
Display ["play"] for me baby,
If you display for me, I will display for you
Display for me baby!

LEADER

B'ó bá bẹ̀rẹ̀ mọ́'lẹ̀, kò bọ́si rárá
If she bends down it is not good

CHORUS

Face to face làwá ńfẹ́
It is face to face we want

LEADER

À mọ́ ko lọ rántí wípé, láti ìbà'dí ẹ títí lọ dé'sàlẹ̀ níkan k'ó máa ṣiṣẹ́
*Láti ìbà'dí ẹ títí lọ dé òkè orí, k'ó máa rọ́ kẹ́-kẹ́-kẹ́-kẹ́, Super
System*
But remember, you should be working only from your buttocks
down
From your buttocks up to your head should begin to shake and
shake, Super System

TALKING DRUM

> *Nkò ṣòkọn ọmọ tí ò da, eléyìí rẹ̀pẹ̀tẹ̀, nkò ṣòkọn ọmọ tí ò da*
> I don't befriend a girl who is ugly, she is too fat [lit.
> "abundant"], I don't befriend a girl who is ugly

LEADER

> *Synchro System, ẹ máa jó!*
> Synchro System, dance!
> [Police siren]

TALKING DRUM

> *Gbáàtúẹ̀yọ̀ oti ṣe débi ìyàwó*
> Low-life woman, how do you come to be a wife?

LEADER

> *Synchro System*
> Synchro System

CHORUS

> *Ẹ máa jó*
> Dance!

LEADER AND CHORUS

> *Ayé le-o, ọ̀rẹ́ mi, ayé màle*
> *Ayé le-o, ọ̀rẹ́ mi, ayé le-o*
> *Ayé le-o, ọ̀rẹ́ mi, ayé màle*
> *Ẹbẹ mo mà b'ayé, k'áyé mámà bá wa jà*
> *Aṣọ iyì kán má fàya, mọ́ wa lára*
> *Ayé le-o, ọ̀rẹ́ mi, ayé màle*
> The world is hard, oh, my friend, the world is hard [three times]
> I beg the world not to fight with me
> Let my cloth of popularity not be torn by them
> The world is hard, oh, my friend, the world is hard

LEADER

> *Ká rọra fẹ̀ ṣò j'ayé lótó*
> *Ẹni Ọlọ́run bá ṣó o kó ṣọ́ra*
> *Ayé ti gbẹgẹ́*
> *'torípé abánigbélé óńṣeni*
> *Abámi daṣẹ́pọ̀ óndani-o*
> *Ìyàwó t'a fẹ́ sílé óndani*
> *Ọkọ t'ó fẹ́ ni sílé óndani-o*
> *Ẹbí ẹni-o óndani*
> *Àńbọ̀sìbọ́sí aládugbò, ṣo gbọ́?*
> We must take life very easy

The person God takes care of should be very careful
Life that is fragile [that chips, like pottery]
Because your neighbors are doing it to you
Your co-worker is disappointing you
The wife we love in the house is disappointing us
The husband you love in the house is disappointing you
One's blood relations are disappointing
Let alone your neighbors, do you understand me?

O ńlódífá f' okété lójǫ́ kini wípé

Okété-o, báyìí n' ìwàrę, òkété-o, báyìí n' ìwàrę-o

O bá' fá munlę, o dafá

The diviner cast Ifa for the bush rat the other day and said
Bush-rat, this is your character, bush-rat, this is your character, oh!
You swore an oath to the god of divination and then broke it
[you betrayed your friends]

CHORUS

Ayé le-o, ǫ̀ṛę́ mi, ayé màle

Ayé le-o, ǫ̀ṛę́ mi, ayé le-o

Ayé le-o, ǫ̀ṛę́ mi, ayé màle

Ębę mo mà b' ayé, k' áýé mámà bá wa jà

Aṣǫ iyì kán má fàya, mǫ́ wa lára

Ayé le-o, ǫ̀ṛę́ mi, ayé màle

The world is hard, oh, my friend, the world is hard [three times]
I beg the world not to fight with me
Let my cloth of popularity not be torn by them
The world is hard, oh, my friend, the world is hard

LEADER

Ìká wǫ́n ká' lá, kán mámà ká kòkó

Ìká wǫ́n ká' lá, kán mámà ká kòkó

'torí gbígbìn la gb' ǫgędę-o

Lílǫ́ la lǫ́ r' èké

They shouldn't pluck cocoa the way they pluck okra
They shouldn't pluck cocoa the way they pluck okra
Because we plant plantain and we plant sugarcane [i.e., there are many different styles in the world; our own is distinctive].

CHORUS

Ayé, ayé

Ębę mo mà b' ayé, k' áýé mámà bá wa jà

Aṣǫ iyì kán má fàya, mǫ́ wa lára

Ayé le-o, ǫ̀ṛę́ mi, ayé màle

World, world
I beg the world not to fight with me
Let my cloth of popularity not be torn by them
The world is hard, oh, my friend, the world is hard
Aò bá wọn wá, aò màní báwo ńlọ
Kò tètè dé-o, kò ní tètè lọ-o
'torí ní gbẹ̀hìn-gbẹ̀hìn-gbẹ̀hìn l' awá' yé
We didn't come with them [older jùjú musicians] and we won't
go with them
He who does not arrive early will not leave early
Because we came to life later, later, later

CHORUS
Ayé, ayé
Ẹbẹ mo mà b' ayé, k' áyé mámà bá wa jà
Aṣọ iyì kán má fàya, mó wa lára
Ayé le-o, ọ̀rẹ́ mi, ayé màle
World, world
I beg the world not to fight with me
Let my cloth of popularity not be torn by them
The world is hard, oh, my friend, the world is hard
Otítọ́ ni o!
It is true, oh!

In launching his new style, Sunny Ade combines several rhetorical strategies. He begins by asserting the novelty of his brand of jùjú music ("we have brought a new drum"), and of the dance movements that accompany it, distinguishing them from the less refined, though more traditional movements associated with urban low-lifes. Ade suggests that, as a newcomer, he will outlast older bandleaders. The choral refrain portrays the world as a hard, combatative place. "Synchro System Movement" treads the line between innovation and tradition with great care; for even if Ade dispenses with his old "drum" (i.e., his earlier Nightingale-based style), his new style uses deep Yoruba proverbs to evoke traditional themes: competition, destiny, and the value of individual effort.

By 1979, Sunny Ade had expanded his group to sixteen or more members, including two tenor guitars, one rhythm guitar, "Hawaiian" guitar, bass guitar, two talking drummers, jazz drums, synthesizer, and a full retinue of supporting drummers and chorus vocalists. As I have already mentioned, the adoption of fictive titles became ubiquitous among jùjú band captains during the Oil Boom of the mid-1970s. Sunny Ade has borne a series of titles during his career, including Master Guitarist, King, Minister of Enjoyment (M.O.E.), and Golden Mercury of Africa (G.M.A.).

The kingship title appears to have been bestowed upon him by fans after his introduction of the Synchro System style. Ade publicly asserts that he is a member of the royal patrilineage of the Ondo Kingdom. Several informants took a cynical view of this claim, one suggesting that everyone in Yorubaland claims to be linked to royalty when it is to their advantage. Another woman mentioned the traditional association of professional musicianship with begging and low status: "Sunny may have twenty Mercedes, twenty houses, and twenty wives, but he is still a musician. He sings their praises so that he can eat; how can he be one of them?!"

In attempting to gain access to wider markets, Sunny Ade introduced new electronic devices and rhythms from contemporary Afro-American popular music. Although many younger fans cite Ade's modernism in explaining why they prefer him to Obey, this stylistic gambit has clearly cost him some support. As Alaja-Browne (1986:79) phrases the matter: "The innovations Sunny Ade brought have resulted in a progressive differentiation of his brand of juju music from that of his contemporaries and as a result it is widely held in different quarters that [his] music has lost its identity as juju music." The album *Juju Music of the 80s,* aimed at the international pop market, was the subject of much discussion in the Lagos popular press during 1982. These arguments revolved around the concepts of tradition and cosmopolitanism. A number of my informants argued that Ade's attempts to modernize jùjú were well-intentioned and interesting, but that the introduction of too many exogenous elements would lead to a qualitative systemic transformation, and a detachment of Ade's style from the mainstream of Yoruba popular performance traditions. One musician, listening to an Ade record in which five guitar players created an interlocking pattern that filled every available sixteenth-note niche, complained that "the talking drum can't talk!! It's hands are tied!!" "It may be good," said another, "but it's not jùjú!"

Although Sunny Ade is widely considered the most innovative of jùjú musicians, he has sought to maintain a consistent sound throughout his career. His guitar signature motif and slightly nasalized vocal quality are instantly recognized indices of his style. In addition, he often recapitulates textual formulas and melodic themes from earlier hit recordings. On the first disc released on his own label [Sunny Ade Records SALPS 1, recorded in 1974], Sunny sang the following lyric:

> *Ẹ ṣú biri-biri, ẹ bò mi-o*
> *B'íwájú lọ lọ́kọ̀ yìí wà mi lọ*
> *B'ẹyìn ṣá lọ lọ́kọ̀ yìí wà mi lọ*
> *Mi ò mọ̀, mi ò mọ̀, ye-o, mi ò mọ̀*
>> It has become pitch-dark, cover me [my fans], oh

Whether this vehicle [my career] carries me forward
Whether this vehicle merely carries me backward
I don't know, I don't know, please, oh, I don't know

In the early 1980s, when Ade's position as one of the two top jùjú superstars was firmly established, he revived this lyric, with a few crucial alterations:

Ẹ ṣú biri-biri, ẹ bò mi-o
Iwájú lọ lókò̩ yìí wà mi lọ
Ẹ̀hìn kò̩ lọ lókò̩ yìí wà mi lọ
Mo ti mò̩, mo ti mò̩, ye-o, mo ti mò̩
It has become pitch-dark, cover me, oh
This vehicle carries me forward
This vehicle does not carry me backward
I know, I know, please, oh, I know [SALPS 37]

In "Synchro System Movement" (1976), "Ja Fun Mi" (1982), and various
other songs spanning a ten-year period, Sunny has repeatedly used the
phrase shown in figure 4.2.

As we have seen, this sort of self-conscious juxtaposing of new and
old material has been characteristic of jùjú style since the early 1930s.

Despite controversy over the limits of innovation in jùjú music, the
rhetorical techniques employed by King Sunny Ade are firmly grounded in
ìjìnlè̩ Yorùbá idioms. The first song on the LP *Juju music,* the opening
salvo in an attempt to market Ade in the United States and Europe, evokes
the traditional concept of the head (*orí*) as the seat of personal destiny in a
precarious world, shaped by supernatural forces, the profit motive, and
Billboard charts.

A-yé le-o   ò̩-ré̩-e̩ mi a-yé mà le   a - yé   le-

o   ò̩ - ré̩-e̩   mi a - yé   le - o   a - yé   le-

o   ò̩ - ré̩-e̩   mi   a - yé   mà le   e̩ be̩   mo   mà

b'a - yé   k'á-yé   má   mà   bá wa   jà   a-ṣo̩

iyì   kán má fa - ya   mó   wa l'á - ra   a - yé le-

o   ọ̀ - rẹ́ - ẹ   mi   a - yé   mà le

The world is hard, oh, my friend
The world is hard [three times]
I beg the world not to fight with me
Let my cloth of popularity not be torn by them
The world is hard, oh, my friend

Figure 4.2. "Ayé le-o, ọ̀rẹ́ mi, ayé mà le"

King Sunny Ade and the African Beats. Excerpts from "Ja Fun Mi" ("Fight For Me"). Recorded in Lome, Togo, 1982. Produced by Martin Meissonnier. Island Records ILPS 9712. [*Cassette example 28*].

Orí mi yé, jà, jà fún mi, ẹ̀dá mi yé-o, jà, jà fún mi
Orí mi yé, jà, jà fún mi, ẹ̀dá mi yé-o, jà, jà fún mi
'torí, orí agbe a jà fún agbe, orí àlùkò a jà fún-o
'torí, orí agbe a jà fún agbe, orí àlùkò a jà fún-o
Ẹlẹ́ẹ̀dá mi má máà gbàgbé mi yé-o, ò bá mà mà jà-o

> My head, please, fight for me, my spirit, please, fight, fight for
> me
> My head, please, fight for me, my spirit, please, fight, fight for
> me
> Because the Blue Touraco [parrot]'s head fights for the Blue
> Touraco, the head of the Aluko bird fights, oh
> Because the Blue Touraco's head fights for the Blue Touraco, the
> head of the Aluko bird fights, oh
> My Creator, don't forget me, it is better that you fight, oh

Wọn d'òyìí k'ápá, apá ò k'ápá
Wọn d'òyìí k'osè, apá ò k'osè
Wọn d'òyìí ká kọ̀nga, kò ṣe ẹ́ bínú kó sí

> They tried to encircle the Mahogany Bean tree [nocturnal home
> of witches and wizards], they couldn't reach around the
> Mahogany Bean tree
> They tried to encircle the Baobab tree [home of iwin, bush
> spirits], they couldn't reach around the Baobab tree.

They tried to encircle the well, they couldn't do it in anger [i.e.,
my enemies can't harm me]

O-o-o ayé, ayé
Èbè mo mà b'ayé, k'áyé mámà bá wa jà
Aṣọ́ iyì, kán má fàya, mọ́ wa l'ára
Ayé le-o, ọ̀rẹ́ mi, ayé màle

Ohhh, world, world
I beg the world not to fight with me
Let my cloth of popularity not be torn by them
The world is hard, oh, my friend, the world is hard

Ayé tile, ayé tótó, ayé àkàmàrà, ayé
Àtòrì l'ayé, tó bá lọ̀ síwájú, a tún lọ̀ sẹ́hin ni
Àtòrì l'ayé jé, tó bá lọ̀ síwájú, a tún lọ̀ sẹ́hìn ni

Hard world, ultimate world, amazing world, world
The world is a whip, if it swings forward, then it swings
backward in return
The world is a whip, if it swings forward, then it swings
backward in return

Orí mi yé, jà, jà fún mi, ẹdá mi yé-o, jà, jà fún mi
Orí mi yé, jà, jà fún mi, ẹdá mi yé-o, jà, jà fún mi
'torí, orí agbe a jà fún agbe, orí àlùkò a jà fún-o
'torí, orí agbe a jà fún agbe, orí àlùkò a jà fún-o
Ẹlẹ́ẹ̀dà mi má máà gbàgbé mi yé-o, ò bá mà mà jà-o

My head, please, fight for me [etc.]

Orí ẹni ni gbé're ko'ni
Orí wó'bi rere gbé mi dé
Ẹsẹ̀ wó'bi rere gbé mi yá
Orí wó'bi rere gbé mi dé
Ẹsẹ̀ wó'bi rere gbé mi yá
'torí, ko wa nkoloto, ko lo nto ko wa
'torí, ko wa nkoloto, ko lo nto ko wa

One's head [destiny] brings good luck to one
Head, let me land in a good place
Legs, lead me to a good place
Head, let me land in a good place
Legs, lead me to a good place
Because, each person must be responsible for his own affairs
[twice]

Orí mi yé, jà, jà fún mi, ẹdá mi yé-o, jà, jà fún mi
Orí mi yé, jà, jà fún mi, ẹdá mi yé-o, jà, jà fún mi
'torí, orí agbe a jà fún agbe, orí àlùkò a jà fún-o
'torí, orí agbe a jà fún agbe, orí àlùkò a jà fún-o

Ẹlẹẹdá mi má máà gbàgbé mi yé-o, ò bá mà mà jà-o
    My head, please, fight for me [etc.]
Bí kókó bá fẹ ni lédẹẹ, à kìí j' orí ìmàdò
Bá a bá j' orí ìmàdò yẹn, àjókùmọn la ò gbọọdọ náà ni
Bá a bá tún na àjókùmọn, ìwọn àr' ẹni là n mọ
Àìmò 'wọn àr' ẹni, àkóbá ló nkóbá ni
'torí, b' ó ti wú k' ọpọló tóbi tó, ilé ẹ ló mi a mọ
'torí, b' ó ti wú k' ọpọló tóbi tó, ilé ẹ ló mi a mọ
    If a knot develops on our head, we don't usually eat the head of
    the warthog
    If we eat that warthog head, then we must not join a group of
    people fighting with cudgels
    But, again, if we join a group of people fighting with cudgels,
    we should know our limitations
    Failure to know one's limitations lands one in trouble
    Because, no matter how large the toad is when it swells up, it
    always builds its house to suit its size [repeat]
Orí mi yé, jà, jà fún mi, ẹdá mi yé-o, jà, jà fún mi
Orí bàbá mi, jà, jà fún mi, orí mama mi, jà, jà fún mi
'torí, orí agbe a jà fún agbe, orí àlùkò a jà fún-o
'torí, orí agbe a jà fún agbe, orí àlùkò a jà fún-o
Ẹlẹẹdá mi má máà gbàgbé mi yé-o, ò bá mà mà jà-o
    My head, please, fight for me, my spirit, please, fight, fight for
    me
    My father's head, fight, fight for me, my mother's head, fight,
    fight for me
    Because the Blue Touraco's head fights for the Blue Touraco, the
    head of the Aluko bird fights, oh
    Because the Blue Touraco's head fights for the Blue Touraco, the
    head of the Aluko bird fights, oh
    My Creator, don't forget me, please, it is better
    that you fight, oh

King Sunny Ade is the best-known jùjú musician outside Nigeria. The African Beats were signed by reggae magnate Chris Blackwell's Island Records in 1982. Ade's first record for Island, recorded in Togo, intended for export, and tailored to suit Western contexts, tastes, and attention spans, scored a modest success in the United States and Europe in 1983, and was followed by several concert tours.[11] It soon became apparent that King Sunny Ade was not going to take over the role of the late Bob Marley in the world exotic popular music market. Subsequent releases sold fewer copies, and Ade was dropped by Island in 1984.

The recorded performances of Sunny Ade, Ebenezer Obey, and other influential jùjú musicians portray *ayé*—the world, in both its material and social aspects—as a dangerous place. Jùjú singers impressionistically sketch an irrevocable and hostile division between supporters and enemies ("us" and "them"). Invidious comparison is the essence of jùjú rhetoric. Behind prosperity and good luck, potentially malevolent forces are eternally at work; every appearance has its underside, every front its back, every *ayíníké* its *ayínípádà*.

The role of jùjú as a form of praise music anchors it firmly in the social dynamics of local communities. As we shall see in the following chapters, this is particularly true in live performances at neo-traditional life cycle celebrations, where specific personalities, institutions, and events form the basis for lyric composition. However, it should be noted that the recordings of the Lagos-based superstars occasionally evince a broader national or international perspective. Thus, Ebenezer Obey discusses and promulgates government policies, while Sunny Ade has appealed to Nigerians overseas to bring their expertise and wealth home:

King Sunny Ade and his African Beats. "K'álẹ́ San Wá J'òwúrọ̀ Lọ" ("May Our Night Be Better Than Our Morning"). Recorded in Lome, Togo, 1982. Island Records 204 770.

> *Ìmọ̀ràn mi s'awa ọmọ Naijíríà tó ńbẹ l' ẹ́hìn odi*
> *Ìmọ̀ràn mi s'awa ọmọ Naijíríà tó ńbẹ ni' lu ọba*
> *Ẹ bá jẹ́ ká so'wọ́ pọ̀ ká fi mọ̀ sọ̀kan*
> *Ká lè gb'ógo Naijíríà wa ga*
> *Nítoríwípé ìlú eni nì' lú eni*
> *Àjò ò lè dùn titi ko da bí ilé*
> *Èmí á padà sí' lé bàbá mi*
> > My advice to all Nigerians that are abroad
> > My advice to all Nigerians that are overseas
> > Let us be cooperative and thoughtful
> > To bring glory to our Nigeria
> > Because, one's country is one's country
> > A foreign place can never be sweeter than home
> > I will go back to my father's land
> *Ajò, àjò ò lè dùn k'ó ní' lé má re'lé*
> > A sojourn can never be so sweet that a sojourner won't return home
> *Adúrà mi s'awa ọmọ Naijíríà tó ńbẹ lẹ́hìn odi*
> *Adúrà mi s'awa ọmọ Naijíríà tó ńbẹ ni' lu ọba*
> *Ire Olókun, ire Ọlọ́ṣà, á bá yin, dé' lé*
> *Ire Olókun, ire Ọlọ́ṣà, á bá wa dé' lé*

Odídẹrẹ́ kîí kú s' oko, a ó bọ̀ l' áyọ̀
Àwa ọmọ Naíjíríà-o, a ó k' érè oko dé' lé

My prayer to all Nigerians that are abroad
My prayer to all Nigerians that are away from home
The good luck of Olokun [god of the ocean], the good luck of
Ọlọṣa [god of the sea] will accompany you back
The Grey Parrot never dies while on the farm [i.e., away from
home], we will return happily
We children of Nigeria, we will arrive home with harvests

Ìsẹ́ kîí 'sẹ́ ẹja k' ẹja máà wẹ l' omi
Àjò, àjò ò lè dùn k' ó nî lé máà re' lé
Ìsẹ́ kîí'sẹ́ ẹyẹ k' ẹyẹ máà fo l' oke
Àjò, àjò ò lè dùn k' ó nî lé máà re' lé

Poverty does not prevent a fish from swimming in the water
Sojourn, sojourn cannot be so sweet that the sojourner won't
return home
Poverty does not prevent a bird from flying in the sky
Sojourn, sojourn cannot be so sweet that the sojourner won't
return home

Nonetheless, the worldview encoded in most contemporary jùjú texts is clearly grounded in and circumscribed by localized patron-client networks. Incomprehensible patterns of global and national political economy are brought down to earth, focused, and metaphorically recast in images of local social arenas and personal experiences. As ancient symbols of value are reinterpreted and ultimately equated with money (Belasco 1980:38–39), and as the ability to feed a family in the city becomes daily more dependent upon the fluctuations of a dimly understood international oil economy, life is aptly seen as a dangerous place, a "whip" of a world.

Conclusion

This sketch of the postwar development of jùjú music suggests that modernity and tradition may be mutually dependent, rather than opposed processes; that Western technology can catalyze the expression of indigenous values; and that images of deep cultural identity may be articulated and negotiated through cosmopolitan syncretic forms. I have tried to convey—in a necessarily schematic fashion—a sense of relationships between shifts in the political economy of Nigeria and the dynamics of modern Yoruba performance practice, and to follow Szwed's (1970:226) suggestion that studies of popular culture take into account interactions among coexisting styles.

The economic and demographic expansion of jùjú music after World War II cannot be analyzed effectively apart from a consideration of the style's role in symbolically articulating modern Yoruba identity. It is clear that a set of interlinked historical processes expanded the range of economic resources potentially available to Yoruba urban popular musicians during the postwar period. Among the most important of these factors were rapid, if uneven, economic growth; increased rural-urban migration; the rise of new political, bureaucratic, and entrepreneurial elites; the heightened salience of ethnic identity at national and regional levels; and the expansion of communications media linking primary and secondary urban centers within southwestern Nigeria. As Nigerian independence approached, the competition of interest groups for control over state resources was intertwined with the consolidation of Yoruba nationalist ideology.

> [Once] there is a local state rather than a mere dream of one, the task of nationalist ideologizing radically changes. . . . It consists of defining, or trying to define, a collective subject to whom the actions of the state can be internally connected, in creating, or trying to create, an experiential "we" from whose will the activities of government seem spontaneously to flow. And as such, it tends to revolve around the question of the content, relative weight, and proper relationship of two rather towering abstractions: "The Indigenous Way of Life" and "The Spirit of the Age" (Geertz 1973:240).

Jùjú music symbolically mediated these ideological themes—Yoruba essentialism and cosmopolitan epochalism—in the decade leading to independence from Britain. In the process of constructing a syncretic style that was at once autochthonous and modern, jùjú musicians breathed life into residual techniques and forms "effectively formed in the past, but . . . still active in the cultural process" (R. Williams 1977:122). The transformation of jùjú style and its rise to preeminence in the Yoruba popular music market may be viewed as aspects of the emergence of a modern pan-Yoruba identity, an experiential "we" situated on a level intermediate between the nation-state and the precolonial polity.

5

The Social Organization and Contexts of Jùjú Performance in Ibadan

Ibadan, a "city-village" (Lloyd 1967:3) of some three million inhabitants located 150 kilometers northeast of Lagos, is the largest indigenous inland urban settlement in Africa south of the Sahara (see map 4). Founded as a military encampment during the intra-Yoruba wars of the nineteenth century,[1] Ibadan was, by the 1890s, the center of an economic and military empire encompassing around one-third of the total area of Yorubaland and more than half its population (Udo 1982:7). After World War I, it served as the commercial focus of the cocoa belt of southwestern Nigeria and an important bulk-breaking and marketing point in the livestock and agricultural trade linking northern and southern Nigeria. In 1939, Ibadan became an administrative center for the British colonial and, later, Nigerian regional and state governments.

The political and cultural traditions of Ibadan distinguish it from other Yoruba kingdoms.[2] It was from the beginning a cosmopolitan center, a "frontier town" composed of Yoruba from many different subgroups. Immigration of various non–Ibadan Yoruba and non-Yoruba peoples, particularly since the early 1930s, has contributed to the cultural and linguistic heterogeneity of Ibadan. It is nonetheless still a Yoruba metropolis: both the 1952 and 1963 censuses suggest an approximate ratio of nineteen Yoruba to every one non-Yoruba within the city limits (Mabogunje 1969). By 1982, Ibadan covered about 130 square kilometers, and lands in surrounding rural areas along major roads had been purchased by speculators (Areola 1982:71).

Abumere (1982) has identified three major sociospatial zones in Ibadan: first, the core region, in which "the population is almost internally homogeneous, being made up of at least 90% Yorubas, and housing density is fantastically high"; second, the zone of market forces, by far the largest area, in which immigrants compete for cash and housing space;

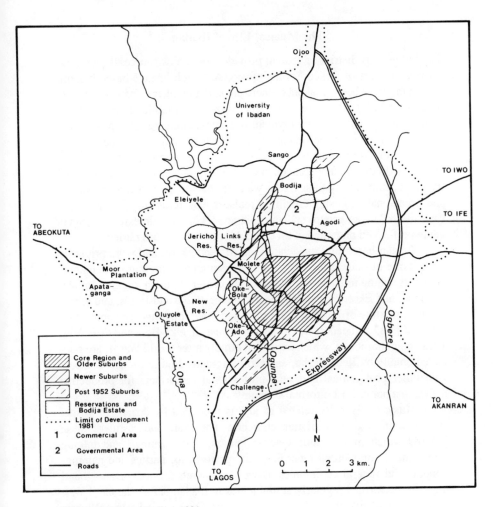

Map 4. The City of Ibadan, 1981
Source: M. O. Filani, ed., *Ibadan Region* (Ibadan: Geography Department, University of Ibadan, 1982)

and third, the institutional zone, reservations and estates established by the government to accommodate senior civil servants, politicians, doctors, lawyers, business executives, and university lecturers (Abumere 1982:232–33). Although demographic variations within each part of the city are inevitably somewhat obscured by this classification, it provides a useful overview of residential patterns.

The Musical Life of Ibadan

The indigenous district of Ibadan provides the major source of patronage for practitioners of ijinlẹ̀ẹ̀ Yorùbá music. Although lineage-based systems of training have been weakened, there are still a number of patrilineal compounds (agbolé) whose residents specialize in particular musical skills. Dùndún drummers find employment in contexts ranging from possession-trance ceremonies for particular òrìṣà to the performance of secular dance music (alùjó, "drumming for dancing") at naming, nuptial, or funerary celebrations. In the commercial centers of the indigenous district, dùndún and gángan drummers ply their trade, walking the streets in search of patrons and occasionally abusing unwilling praisees who refuse to respond with a cash "dash." Other groups specialize in aro-ṣẹ̀kẹ̀rẹ̀, a quintessential Ibadan genre performed on pounded tin cymbals and bottle-gourd rattles.

Ibadan-based jùjú musicians (see Appendix) live and work primarily in the zone of market forces, particularly an area of immigrant neighborhoods stretching to the west of the old city center. To the north are Mọkọla, Inalende, and Ekotedo, established during the 1920s and 1930s, and inhabited by a mixture of Yoruba, Igbo, Edo, and other migrants. The home base for most jùjú bandleaders lies to the southwest, in Oke-Bọla and Oke-Ado. These neighborhoods, which expanded rapidly after World War II, are populated chiefly by Ijẹbu, Ẹgba, and Ekiti migrants. Jùjú musicians compete with other professional and semi-professional performers for productive niches in a boom-bust informal economy.

Music stylistically related to jùjú is produced by dozens of gospel groups sponsored by Christian churches. The more successful of these groups, which may include electric guitars, "jazz drums," and talking drum, make commercial recordings and perform for parties and naming, nuptial, and funeral ceremonies as well as church services. Dance band highlife, performed regularly at nightclubs in Ibadan before the Civil War, is rarely heard live these days. Groups from Ghana and Eastern Nigeria occasionally visit the city, performing in neighborhoods with a high concentration of non-Yoruba immigrants. The only Ibadan-based groups regularly performing the dance band highlife repertoire are the army and police bands, which play at government events and in elite contexts such as the University of Ibadan Staff Club. Members of these formalized ensembles may regroup under a different name as a jùjú band if a lucrative performance opportunity arises.

A number of musical styles are associated with and predominantly patronized by Muslims. Fújì music is the most popular, supported by Muslims at all socioeconomic levels and, increasingly, by adherents of Christian syncretic movements as well. Ibadan-based fújì musicians (see Appendix) are predominantly residents of the indigenous district, the old core of the city. While they perform outside this area, its traditionalist and largely Muslim population provides their major source of patronage. Most fújì musicians identify themselves as ọmọ Ibàdàn (Ibadan indigenes). Fújì groups vary a great deal in size and may include the following instruments: dùndún or àdàmọ̀n talking drums; calabashes (igbá) beaten with ringed fingers; ṣẹ̀kẹ̀rẹ̀ and maracas; agogo iron bells; conga-type drums such as àkúbà and ògìdo; and sákárà and sámbà frame drums. Awurebe music is stylistically related to fújì, and is also performed by Muslim musicians. The originator of the genre, Alhaji Dauda Epo Akara—his last name, "fried bean cake oil," refers to his mother's occupation and evokes a certain earthy quality— is a native of Ibadan. There is also a scattering of groups in the city performing older Muslim styles such as àpàlà, sákárà, and wákà.

The mass-reproduced music economy of Ibadan is centered on an informal cassette industry. Although Nigeria now has three legal record-pressing facilities, long-playing albums cost at least seven naira and the equipment to play them is prohibitively expensive for the majority of city dwellers. "Bootlegged" cassette copies of albums and live performances, on the other hand, are sold in traditional outdoor markets and on the streets for one or two naira each (see plate 8). A smuggled cassette player can be purchased for twenty or thirty naira. Although there has been much public discussion about cracking down on bootleggers—both by recording company executives and the Performing Musicians Association of Nigeria (PMAN), an association of bandleaders formed in 1981—the entrepreneurs who duplicate and sell pirated cassettes defend themselves by asserting that "poor people must have music, too!" These perspectives were expressed in two articles published in the Ibadan tabloid *The Entertainer:*

'WE ARE SUFFERING'

For the first time in recent years, Nigerian musicians are coming together to fight record piracy in the country. Leading the battle is Mr. Sunday Adeniyi, better known as Sunny Ade, the current president of the Performing Musicians Association of Nigeria (PMAN). The musicians are apparently fueled by the increasing wave of bootlegging whereby their music waxed into records are subsequently recorded into cassettes by the record pirates who later sell them at ridiculously reduced prices. In this case, more people buy cassettes than records with the consequence of the musicians losing heavily on their records royalties since these pirates will not give a kobo [penny] to any artiste whose record he recorded for sale.

Meanwhile PMAN now puts its hope for salvation on members of the country's National Assembly. Last month, a delegation of the musicians submitted an eight point memorandum to the National Assembly through Senate President Joseph Wayas. In the memorandum, the association suggested that the existing ineffective copyright act be updated and amendment be made to the royalty act to ensure that government owned radio and television stations pay appropriate royalties to musicians.

The Association did not stop at this level, apart from lobbying some members of the Assembly for a quick answer to their prayers, they also solicited the support of the press to help them fight these bootleggers. Members of the association visited most of the media houses in Lagos to put forward their case and they are also planning to visit media houses outside the federal capital to ask for their support.

Chief Ebenezer Fabiyi Obey leading the Inter-Reformers Band said he would be the happiest man if the government could effectively deal with bootleggers to enable artistes [to] enjoy the fruits of their labour. He claimed that some musicians are almost living from hand to mouth because it is the record pirates who take all the gains from their sweat.

Fuji musician Ayinde Barrister has these to say: "I am always sad whenever I think of these bootleggers. How can a group of people work so hard without enjoying the fruits of their labour. That is what is exactly happening to Nigerian musicians at the moment. The record pirates make all the money leaving little for us and nothing for the government. It is ridiculous that in a country of over 80 million people, a successful musician cannot boast that his record would sell over one million. We musicians have resolved that we shall not rest until we see the end of bootlegging but we cannot take the law into our own hands, that is why we are begging the National Assembly to please save us.

A recording company boss, Mr. Ola Kazim of Ibukun Orisun Iye said on bootlegging: "Those in the recording business are not left out in the loss to bootleggers. They have forced most of us out of business while those of us remaining in the business look for alternative jobs to make ends meet. The federal government is losing heavily too as a result of record piracy because the bootleggers who will not come out to identify themselves because they know it is a criminal business don't pay anything to the government as we do. This is why we are begging the government to please save us."

Bootlegging is a criminal offence which carries a fine of only ₦100 (*The Entertainer*, Feb. 1982, p. 5).

CASSETTE SELLERS REACT

Some record and recorded cassette sellers have reacted to the move by Nigerian musicians to eradicate record piracy in the country. According to one of them, Mr. Billy Obitayo of Ogunpa, Ibadan: it is a "mission impossible" because of the fact that not all Nigerians could afford to buy a record player and amplifier. Mr. Obitayo noted that the increase on record prices was the main cause of the whole thing, pointing out that in the past when an LP record was being sold at ₦2.50 there was nothing like piracy or bootlegging. He stressed that no amount of campaign could help unless the prices of records were beaten down.

"There are some people who, due to financial problem, could only afford to buy a ₦35 tape recorder and ₦1.50 cassette to enable them to listen to their choice of music," he said. He also attributed the fall of record sales to austerity measures in the country. "There is no money in the country now and people cannot afford to spend a lot of money on records," he said.

"What I think the artistes can do to really make their demands work is to reduce the prices of records. You can see now that the prices of records are killing and unless the musicians view it from that angle, the result will be negative. There is no doubt that bootlegging has now become an order of the day in this country and a stop to it might cause a bloodshed," he concluded.

Mr. Lanre Lawal, another cassette seller at Ogunpa says: "We are ready for any action by those musicians. You see, music should not be for only the rich men alone, poor people should also enjoy good music, hence, the establishment of a recording service to the poor people. We offer recording services for people who cannot afford to buy records and this, to my mind, is a kind of promotion for the musicians themselves."

Mr. Lawal stressed that it will be too bad and disastrous if the thousands of cassette sellers in the country are sent out of job. "Those musicians should please bear with the poor people. They should realise that not all fingers are equal."

Another tape recording seller, Mr. Amusa Ojulari of No. 81 New Court Road, Ibadan, has called for the recognition and registration of bootleggers in the country. "The trade should be recognized by the government like other businesses," he said. He suggested that tax should also be collected "on each live play we record" (The Entertainer, Feb. 1982, p. 5).

While most cassette merchants operate on a small scale, retailing out of *bukas* (kiosks) at major markets or at busy intersections in the city, some wealthy entrepreneurs run larger, more sophisticated operations. There is at least one workshop capable of pressing illegal vinyl dubs of domestic and imported discs, and printing counterfeit record jackets.

Ibadan is home to four radio stations, run by the federal and Ọyọ State governments (FRCN and Radio OYO, with AM and FM stations). A wide variety of music is broadcast, including Christian and Muslim religious music, jùjú, fújì, and other Yoruba genres, and imported recordings. The city was also home to black Africa's first television station, and three channels can now be received, including a station in neighboring Ogun State. Television, like radio, provides access to a variety of live perform-ances, some local, others taped in Lagos.

The Economic Organization of Jùjú Ensembles in Ibadan

Jùjú bands may be viewed as socioeconomic operating units, "sets of ac-tors sharing a common adaptive pattern with respect to some portion of the [urban] environment" (Adams 1975:54). The strategies of jùjú groups are organized around a distinction between new and old ensemble types. The old paradigm, referred to as the Ayinde Bakare, Ojogẹ Daniel, or Tunde Nightingale "line," generally includes of eight to ten performance roles: a leader who plays guitar; two or three chorus vocalists, playing clips, mar-acas, and ṣẹ̀kẹ̀rẹ̀; and five or six percussionists, playing conga-type single membrane drums, double toy (bongos), sámbà, and a single àdàmọ̀n talk-ing drum. The contemporary ensemble paradigm, based upon the groups of Lagos superstars Sunny Ade and Ebenezer Obey, includes twelve to twenty roles: the leader; three to five chorus vocalists; two or three tenor guitarists; a lead guitarist; a Hawaiian (pedal steel) guitarist; a bass guitar-ist; five or more percussionists, including two or three àdàmọ̀n drummers, and, in the most affluent groups, "jazz drums" (trap set). I should empha-size that these types are ideal, not rigidly demarcated in practice. Though a clear conceptual distinction is drawn between groups in the Ayinde Ba-kare line and those specializing in more up-to-date "systems," any given band may expand or contract in response to fluctuations in the urban economy.

Jùjú bands are headed by upwardly mobile "band captains" (olóri ẹgbẹ̀ jùjú), intent upon furthering their own interests by manipulating rela-tionships between subordinate musicians ("band boys") and wealthy pa-trons. Though jùjú groups range in size from six to fifteen or more per-formers, their essential structure is invariable. The distribution of performance roles, authority, and remuneration is hierarchical, with the band captain at the apex, the mass of band boys at the base, and a few favored "senior boys" (ẹ̀gbọ́n, "older sibling") who have demonstrated their loyalty to the leader occupying an intermediate position. A common, though primarily nonmusical, role is that of the band manager, usually a trusted friend or kinsman of the band captain who may secure engage-ments, regulate the financial affairs of the band, gather information about important patrons, and oversee the repairing of equipment. While most bands have a manager, his role and authority vis-à-vis other members of the organization varies widely; band managers tend to be more powerful in larger groups. The more prosperous jùjú ensembles also include a retinue of drivers and handlers, who haul and set up electronic equipment and carry out other manual tasks, such as repairing flat tires and fetching refreshments for the band captain and important friends and patrons. This category overlaps with the fluid coterie of hangers-on associated with most groups, on the one hand, and the lower-rank band boys, on the other. Many of the young men who hire on as manual workers for a jùjú band want eventually to move into performance roles, thus beginning the long climb to band captain status.

Ethnicity is an important factor in the formation of jùjú bands. All of the captains and the majority of band boys in Ibadan-based jùjú bands are Yoruba migrants. Of the eighteen active jùjú bandleaders living in Ibadan whose ethnicity was ascertained, nine identified themselves as Ekiti Yoruba. Their natal communities include the largest town in the Ekiti area, Ado-Ekiti, and various smaller communities, including Ilara-Mokin, Ikẹrẹ-Ekiti, Emure-Ekiti, Ikọle-Ekiti, and Aiyetoro-Ekiti. As suggested in chapter 4, Ekiti are traditionally stereotyped by other Yoruba as rustics, blunt in speech and action, but exceptionally hardworking. However, the efflorescence of cocoa cultivation, introduced to the Ekiti area in the 1930s (Berry 1967), and a high rate of Christian conversion (Eades 1980:9) have resulted since the 1950s in rapid economic development, high rates of primary and secondary education, and emigration to modernizing economic and administrative centers such as Ibadan. The Ekiti jùjú bandleaders, many of them primary school educated and all of them Christian, were drawn to Ibadan chiefly by the prospect of cash earnings and status advancement in their home communities.

The next largest group of jùjú band captains is Ẹgba Yoruba, a group with a long history of involvement in Ibadan social and economic affairs. Abẹokuta has long been a center for Islamic proselytization, and two of the three Ẹgba band captains in Ibadan are Muslim. Other Yoruba subgroups are minimally represented (Ondo, Ijẹsa, Ifẹ, Ọyọ), and only one established captain, the youngest, is from the Ibadan area (the satellite town of Idisa). No Ibadan-based jùjú band captains were born within the city limits of Ibadan.

Most band boys are also migrants, their total number fluctuating from around 250 to 300.[3] Yoruba subgroups represented in this population include Ekiti, Ẹgba, Ogbomọṣọ, Oṣogbo, Ijẹsa, Ondo, and Ibadan. Most ọmọ Ibàdàn jùjú musicians are percussionists, particularly talking drummers, who are more likely than other jùjú practitioners to have received some training in a traditional lineage setting.[4] Only a few band boys are of non-Yoruba origin, most of them migrants from neighboring groups such as the Itsekiri and Edo. Such individuals generally have a long history of interaction with Yoruba and are fluent in Standard Yoruba. One band boy,

whose extensive experience as a professional musician involved employment in Lagos, Kano, and Enugu, identified himself as an Idoma.

Many jùjú musicians migrated to Ibadan during the 1950s and early
1960s, a period of economic expansion. Younger musicians arrived during
the oil boom years of the 1970s. They generally share the life goals of other
Yoruba migrants, and organize their socioeconomic strategies around two
concepts: ọlá, or honor, realized via acquisition of honorary titles and a
large and stable set of clients or "followers"; and ọlà, "wealth," represented
by possession of land, a prosperous business, an impressive compound,
wives, children, a private automobile, and access to education for one's
offspring (Lloyd 1974:49). It is almost universally held that these goals are
best pursued through private enterprise. The aspirations of jùjú musicians
are shaped by these values. In the great majority of cases, band captains
are former band boys who served some period of apprenticeship under a
master (ọ̀gá). The career histories of jùjú bandleaders often include membership in a series of groups, often cited as proof of hard-won professionalism and the ability to survive treachery. Bandleaders usually claim to
have achieved some level of skill in all of the performance roles in their
ensemble through such apprenticeship. The prospective band captain must
secure the support of a powerful patron in order to obtain instruments and
contacts for engagements.

> "You see, because we had no musical instruments, my boys
> were not willing to stay. They often left for better established bands as
> I had to hire instruments all about whenever we had engagements.
> Many were not willing to wait for undefinable hopes. It was difficult
> retaining boys who wanted immediate rewards when nothing seemed
> forthcoming.
>
> "But I thank God today for sending us a mentor in the person of
> the managing director of Ade Adebayo Motors. Mr. Ademolu Ade-
> bayo was made the chairman of a party where we entertained with
> hired instruments and because of our performance that day, he became
> interested and volunteered to sponsor the band. It is with joy I'm tell-
> ing you that with his help and the help of God, we were able to launch
> our ₦ 100,000 worth of musical instruments some months ago. Like
> it was magic, he sponsored my trip overseas and the end result is the
> brand new set of Davoli instruments we now boast of in the band"
> (*Lagos Weekend,* 30 Oct. 1981, p. 7).

Popular tabloids are filled with pleas from young musicians for the
support of benefactors. Even established band captains often privately ad-
mit wanting to move out of the music business and into a more secure,
higher status occupation, such as construction or trading.

There is no standardized sequence of skill acquisition within bands, but observation and informant exegesis reveal a common pattern. A new band boy, often a former hanger-on, equipment handler, or a recently arrived younger "kinsman" of the band captain or another band member,[5] begins on an instrument used to produce repetitive patterns, the rhythmic infrastructure of the music. Such instruments include handbeaten single-membrane drums such as *ògìdo*, *agbámolé*, *àkúbà*, or *sámbà*, or idiophones such as *s̩èkèrè̩*, maracas, or clips. As time goes on, the young performer may move to the stick-beaten double toy, learning to play a more highly embellished set of patterns, including flams and single stroke rolls. Another option for a prospective percussion specialist is the àdàmò̩n talking drum. However, the technical difficulty and crucial communicative role of this instrument, and a widespread ideology of talent transmission via lineage "blood," may discourage young players not exposed to it at a young age. The jazz drums are an option in larger groups.

Jùjú bands include from one to six electric guitars, another set of performance roles that a young musician may attempt to master. Initial options include bass or tenor guitar, musical roles involving the production of interlocking melodic-rhythmic ostinatos analogous to those played on the supporting percussion instruments. As with subordinate drumming roles, a tenor guitarist demonstrates his skill by producing steady patterns, a demonstration of musical maturity. Experience with these guitar parts opens the door to foregrounded roles such as lead or Hawaiian guitarist, and prepares the musician to assume the apical status of band captain.

Although some ability on guitar is an important asset for a prospective band leader, praise singing is regarded as absolutely essential. The specialized vocalists who form the chorus harmonize and respond to the praise song sequences performed by the band captain. The chorus singer gradually internalizes a repertoire of melodies, praise texts, and proverbs. Most jùjú musicians state that while it is difficult for a guitarist who cannot sing to become a successful band captain, an experienced chorus singer may quickly acquire the minimal technical competence on guitar necessary to fulfill the role adequately.

Jùjú groups less resemble traditional lineage-based associations of performance specialists than they do the organizations established by practitioners of modern crafts such as sawyer-carpentry, plastering, painting, brick making, automotive repairs, tire vulcanizing, electronics repairs, tailoring, barbering, and public letter and contract writing. One of the most commonly noted features of traditional Yoruba urbanism was the existence of lineage-based craft associations.

> [The lineage head's] authority extends to all matters affecting the craft
> industry as well as the social life of the lineage. At the same meeting,
> the craftsmen will decide about their marriage disputes, farmlands,

prices, the maintenance of high standards of work, or the repair of the
common workshop, . . . and economic activities. . . . The structure
of these organizations was the lineage structure; the lineage meeting
was the craft meeting; the craft head was the compound head, the
oldest man in the lineage (Lloyd 1953:34).

Although craft-specialized compounds existed in all parts of Yorubaland, they were diverse in terms of structure and membership. A distinction has been drawn between the more strongly agnatic northern Yoruba
groups and the cognatic systems of southern Yorubaland (see Lloyd 1966,
1970 for detailed discussion of this issue):

> In Oyo country, large compounds of blacksmiths and male weavers
> are common; ideally, the craft, like the compound itself, is identified
> wih a lineage or a major segment thereof. . . . Woodcarvers, and also
> drummers and praise-singers (two aspects of the same occupation) are
> likewise organized in compounds; the latter appear to be a specialty of
> Oyo country, the tradition of praise-singing being perhaps correlated
> with the strength of lineages. In Ekiti towns, such craft compounds
> are poorer and smaller; weaving is generally a women's craft, carried
> out individually, and drummers and bards do not exist as specialized
> crafts (Krapf-Asakari 1969:87).

The lack of specialization of musical practitioners in southern and
eastern Yorubaland may be a factor in the relatively high involvement of
Ekiti migrants in jùjú music production in Ibadan. Individuals from groups
without a strong ideology of patrilineal training and official validation may
in a sense be better prepared to form flexible organizations adapted to an
unpredictable urban economy.[6]

Contemporary Yoruba urban craft organizations range from a lone
artisan with a few part-time assistants to groups of ten or twenty craftsmen
and apprentices, some of whose members may also operate private shops
in their homes during off-hours. Each of these groups is adapted to a particular niche in the urban economy.

> Although traditional crafts still manage to hold their own in the greatly
> changed environment offered by Ibadan, the old craft association,
> based on the lineage or the compound, has largely been eroded away.
> It is the more modern crafts that have managed to organize themselves
> in a pattern suited to the new conditions (Krapf-Askari 1969:90).

Two studies carried out in Ibadan suggest the important role played
by craft groups in the informal economy. In the early 1960s Callaway
(1967) enumerated a total of 5,135 "small businesses" based upon modern

craftwork, 90 percent of which were started after 1945, 75 percent from 1950 on, and over 50 percent after 1956 (Callaway 1967:159). The rapid expansion of craft enterprises during the late 1950s was triggered by increased government spending, relatively high cocoa prices, and the emergence of the new Yoruba elite, the major consumers of modern goods and services. By the time of Koll's (1969) survey, on the eve of the Oil Boom, around 42,000 individuals out of a total urban population of some 900,000 were employed in the craft sector. This figure included some 14,000 qualified craftsmen and around 28,000 employees and apprentices, as compared with an industrial labor force of some 3,784. Tailors comprised the largest category of craft workers, followed by carpenters, weavers, goldsmiths, pepper-grinders, and barbers, with a smaller number of tinkers, motor mechanics, shoemakers, electricians, watch-repairers, printers, and photographers (Eades 1980:85).

Neither of these surveys discuss the professional musical groups which also began to develop in Ibadan and other southwestern Nigerian towns after World War I. In a demographic sense this is understandable, since the total number of individuals directly employed in the production of popular music in Ibadan is probably under 1,000. The diversity of musical ensembles is rooted in the same processes of socioeconomic adaptation that have shaped the development of nonmusical craft groups. It is clear that the development of syncretic musical styles after World War I, and the establishment of the first jùjú groups in Ibadan during the late 1930s, paralleled the rise of modern crafts such as tailoring and sawyer-carpentry, both associated with the Afro-Brazilian repatriate community (see chapter 2). This correlation is more than fortuitous, for the primary patronage group for both jùjú musicians and the new crafts during the interwar period was a relatively small population of mission-educated African Christians, and wealthy Yoruba entrepreneurs eager to associate themselves with symbols of modernity. In addition, the tremendous expansion of modern craft activity in towns throughout Yorubaland during the 1950s was reflected in a rise in the number of jùjú bands.

While many modern crafts need only one or two workers at a time, the production of jùjú music requires at least six, and usually more, individuals. The specialization of performance roles—guitarist, percussionist, chorus vocalist, lead praise singer—is a point of difference between jùjú bands and most other artisan organizations. The cost of setting up a small business in Ibadan depends upon the initial capital required to purchase the means of production, and the size of the organization needed to produce a given craft or service. While a barber or a sawyer-carpenter can purchase a minimal set of tools for ₦50, and a tailor can start a business for under ₦100, other businesses, such as automotive mechanics, electronics repair, or brick making, require a substantially larger investment. The minimal equipment for a small jùjú group costs at least ₦200, and usually more. The total capital investment involved in outfitting a contemporary fifteen-piece jùjú band, including amplifiers, speakers, mixers, microphones and stands, guitars (often owned by the band captain or a sponsor rather than the players themselves), vehicles for transporting personnel and equipment, and band uniforms, runs into the thousands, and in the case of the most successful groups, tens of thousands of Naira. The life histories of successful jùjú band captains often delineate a gradual progression from a small ensemble with a single amplifier and locally made percussion instruments to the acquisition, celebrated with a lavish "launching" ceremony, of imported musical equipment and one or more band buses (see plates 22 and 23). The success of a jùjú band rests largely upon the ability of the leader to secure financial backing from wealthy patrons.

Another point of comparison between modern craft organizations and jùjú groups is the relationship between master and apprentices. According to Callaway

> the greater the capitalization of a firm, the greater the likelihood that the master-apprentice relationship will approximate to the apprentice-contract conditions of government and of the large firms, particularly in money payments from the master to the apprentice. Examples of this are found among the printing establishments, the modern blacksmiths' and mechanics' workshops, and the improved furniture works (Callaway 1967:161).

I know of no cases in which aspiring jùjú practitioners made formalized payments to the leader of the group in exchange for training. Although the share of profits received by subordinate musicians is generally well below the level needed for independent subsistence or the accumulation of capital needed to start competing groups, the flow of cash is always from the band captain to his band boys. On the other hand, the establishment of a standardized salary schedule is also nonexistent among Ibadan jùjú groups, since the amount of cash paid to each member is dependent upon his place in the hierarchy and the total profits accrued at any particular performance event.[7]

Though jùjú bands are not voluntary associations in the classic sense (Little 1970), they do play a role in the incorporation of urban migrants. Kinsmen or village mates of a band captain or senior band boys may be brought into a group in order to provide them with a little cash. In most cases these individuals are assigned relatively inconspicuous performance roles, such as supporting drum parts. More rarely, jùjú groups may function as a circular credit association, or èsúsú. In this case, a portion of the cash earned during performances is put into a central fund, and payments are made to each member in turn, on a monthly basis.[8] The informant who reported this practice suggested that it was most common in poor, relatively egalitarian jùjú groups, and was "just another way for the captains to cheat their boys."

Fluctuations in the economic environment affect small craft groups differentially; "in some cases, a one-man workshop will close down while the proprietor looks, perhaps fruitlessly, for a temporary job as a labourer, [though] almost all who become hard-pressed manage, however tenaciously, to survive the period of business depression" (Callaway 1967:162). Larger firms with a greater investment in machinery and work space find it more difficult to adjust, though a larger group of apprentices may make it possible to lay off personnel. The structure of performance roles in jùjú bands, and the fact that most band boys in the less successful groups have alternate means of earning cash (e.g., manual labor, driving, carpentry, tailoring, motor or electronics repairs) allow a certain amount of flexibility in the size and composition of ensembles. A group may expand and contract, adding supporting instruments such as akúbà, ògìdo, or sámbà drums, extra idiophones, or tenor and bass guitars for engagements at which a copious cash flow is expected, and reducing the group to the bare minimum of members in less lucrative situations. Under the latter conditions, a chorus singer may double on ṣèkèrè, clips, or agogo, the guitar section of the band is pared down to one, two or three players (the leader and a tenor and/or bass guitar), and a single àdàmòn talking drum is used.[9]

There are, however, practical limits to the variability in size and structure of jùjú ensembles. Without a talking drum, or at least one electric guitar, it is impossible to perform jùjú music that will satisfy patrons. In addition, while there is considerable latitude in the size of the percussion section, there must be at least three membranophones and one or two idiophones to generate the interlocking patterns which form the irreducible core of Yoruba dance rhythms. Finally, there must be vocalists to sing responsorial phrases in alternation with the leader's solo praise singing, and to support and enrich the leader's lines with harmonies.

Musical roles and cash are distributed hierarchically within jùjú ensembles. There is always a gap between the earnings of the captain and other band members. The percentage of net profit distributed to each band boy, after expenses such as petrol and equipment upkeep, is graded by length of tenure, musical skill, and relationship to the captain. Thus, an ògìdo drummer of limited skill with eight years of continual service, an exceptionally adept talking drummer or lead guitarist with only six months service, or a supporting tenor guitarist or chorus singer from the leader's family or community of origin, are all likely to receive more cash per engagement than other band boys.

The distribution of money is a common focus for gossip and recrimination, and the most frequent cause of group break ups. Most band captains are unwilling to provide precise figures, particularly during periods of economic retrenchment when competition among bands is heightened and profits are squeezed upwards to support the status advancement strategies of leaders. Charles Keil was able to collect data concerning the distribution of earnings within several Ibadan-based jùjú bands in 1967. By my calculation, these figures suggest that the captains kept from twenty-two to twenty-nine percent of total earnings, while band boys' shares varied from six to twelve percent, depending upon their place in the group hierarchy. Keil's notes express some skepticism regarding the veracity of these estimates and suggest that band captains purposely underestimated their share for strategic purposes. Though I was unable to convince even those captains with whom I was relatively close to divulge the distribution of cash within their groups—a situation undoubtedly exacerbated by my association with band boys—it was clear that they often take more than fifty percent of band earnings after expenses, while band boys receive from three to ten percent of the total, depending upon their rank, the size of the ensemble, and prevailing economic conditions.

Band captains are often expert impression managers (Goffman 1959), building their own reputation and status while communicating the egalitarian message, "we're all musicians," to subordinate band boys. There is a lot of joking behavior before and after jobs, which temporarily reduces social distance. The captain may make periodic cash advances to certain senior boys, or arrange for a case of beer at each engagement to be shared by all the musicians. He may visit ailing band boys at their homes or, more rarely, provide housing for a few of them in his own compound. One Ibadan band captain owns a Volvo, one of the most expensive cars in Nigeria, and is driven about by a chauffeur. Soon after he acquired the car in 1979, several of his band boys threatened to leave if raises were not forthcoming. The captain assured them that his recording company, Chief Abioro's Take Your Choice Records, had insisted that he accept the car to boost his public image. He, being a common man, certainly did not care for such ostentation. When asked about the contribution of individual band boys to the overall sound of his group, he stated firmly, "I'm a leader, not a boss. A boss commands. I don't command."

A guitarist who performs with various Ibadan-based jùjú bands, and prefers to maintain an independent, if marginal, position in each, expressed another perspective:

> He's not a leader, he's a boss! . . . It is because the boys have no other way to go, [otherwise] he would not have had a single boy. So, also, most musicians in Ibadan . . . they so much like women and

to feel big, whereas they are not, so they don't even care how their boys live. You can imagine some of his boys, they didn't have house, they have no accommodations, some of them sleep in the vehicle, and he doesn't care. If somebody in his position—I mean, by the money he has taken to buy his Volvo, right? He was riding Volvo, two Volkswagen Beetles, and that big civilian bus, and that other *danfo* [van], all at his disposal. I mean, what does he need all those five cars for? He should have spent his money to see that his boys are properly settled in one place.

He is riding a car, and he's telling the boys he's not happy to ride in it. I'm *sure* he's happy to ride that thing. He tells everybody he's not happy. He was telling them that the recording company forced that thing on him. I can't imagine that. I know Chief Abioro, whom he records with. Abioro will be the same yesterday, today, and evermore. He's the same old person. He's a businessman, so he wants to make money for himself. I don't see any reason why he should force a car costing like 18,000 naira or more on your head, when you are not a superstar. . . .

He planned to go to Mecca this year. So he heard the boys murmuring that, "Aha! You bought a car. You're building a house. Then you want to go to Mecca. During the time you're away to Mecca, how do you want us to feed?" He gradually got this information from some of the boys. I think that is why he changed his mind on that. Because he's got the money to go on Hajj (Kọla Oyeṣiku, 12 July 1979).

Social relationships within jùjú bands are suffused with an ideological tension between hierarchical and communal norms that is characteristic of Yoruba society as a whole. This particular captain's strategy had unravelled by 1981, and he was the object of a great deal of gossip when I returned to Ibadan that year. Several senior boys had left him, some moving to Lagos to join another band. He had then been involved in a near fatal accident in one of his Volkswagens and had spent months in the hospital, during which other band members left. The gossip among Ibadan jùjú musicians was framed in terms of Yoruba concepts of retributive justice; it was in fact suggested by several band captains that someone might have put an *oògùn*, "magical power object" in the captain's car. A band boy in another group blamed it on sheer greed and prevarication. When asked about his own captain, he replied rather ambiguously, "Well, I can say that he is trying a little."

Conflicts also erupt between band captains, particularly during periods of economic retrenchment. On one occasion, one bandleader stole an engagement from another. As one musician described it:

A got a play for last Saturday. The celebrant paid him 300 naira to come to that gig. So, while *B* was drinking round the beer parlors, he got hold of it that this woman has given *A* that play for that Saturday. So, *B* tuned the woman so that she went to the bank, to stop them from paying *A* that check, because *B* had convinced her to engage him instead. But unfortunately for her, *A* has already cashed the check. So they have to come to him and tell him they don't want him to play at the gig, and that he should return 200 naira to them. In the end, he gave them 150.

     B must have gone the other way round to win this play for himself . . . you just discover that, most of these cats, they are very, very untrustworthy. What *B* did, if I am the other bandleader, I would take it hard. But *A* can't take it hard because *B*'s well known in the town, so he's got some weapons over him. *C* [a third, more popular captain] can swindle *B*, because I would prefer to take *C* for 250 naira than *B*, musically speaking. So, if *B* has taken 250 from me for a gig, if *C* wants to take it for that 250, I won't mind to get my money out of *B* and give it to *C*. So it happens like that. But when it happens, it's always the big cats that's putting the pounce on the small ones, and there's *nothing* they can do!

Such disputes sometimes erupt publicly during a performance. The same guitarist recounted the story of the launching ceremony for an upwardly mobile Ibadan bandleader's new electronic equipment, held at the exclusive Premier Hotel in Ibadan:

I played with *X* that day. Sunny Ade came from Lagos, he was one of the chief launchers. And *X* fumbled it up. You know, with that kind of occasion, you want to make something and sing about it, so that when you sing people will see the senses of your construction. But *X* felt very inferior . . . so, he just starts singing that [stentorian voice], "I know the person that is older than me in music-o, I know the person that is under me in music." That's what he sang when Sunny was around. I just felt, oh, man, forget about this and sing about something real. I mean, he didn't realize that Sunny's an artist, that an artist is an artist. He can learn something from me; he's got something in his hand, but he can still learn from me. I won't feel all that inferior as to sing that, well, "It's *you* I'm telling this-o, don't think because you are coming from Lagos-o, and they call you King Sunny Alade-o, that you can fuck anybody's ass-o". I mean, it's uncalled for! Let your music talk by itself! Give him something to go home and think about, don't *tell* him to think! *Play,* and let him *hear!!*

     You know, Sunny would have sprayed him that day, because back then there is this rumor that Sunny is fighting with Obey, and *X*, no matter what he is, he's still very close to Obey, because they are both from Abẹokuta. I know that was why Sunny came to lodge himself on Friday, paying his rent at the Premier Hotel. I mean, he would just have given this boy a free field and let him feel free. But, you called him there only to insult him. So Sunny just changed his mind, and starting spraying one-one naira for the band. *One-one naira*!! *X* caused it!! Sunny sprayed *X* one naira, and gave the lead guitar about twenty or thirty, he gave me about five, and the other tenor guitar five. But *X* himself, he only gave a naira!

Although Ibadan is a large city, it is also an economic satellite of Lagos. There are limits on the upward mobility of band captains who choose to stay in Ibadan, and a clear status distinction between the most successful groups in the regional and federal capitals. Most Ibadan jùjú musicians, when asked why they do not move to Lagos, say that life is too difficult and competitive in Lagos; as one band captain put it, "Money dey for Lagos, but in Ibadan we take life cooler." In at least one case, a relatively well-known Lagosian bandleader was able to recruit band boys from an Ibadan-based group:

> Three members of Jide Ojo's band have left the organisation. They are now with Dele Abiodun and his Adawa Super Band. One of the boys is a vocalist while the others play sekere and talking drum.
>
> In his reaction, Jide said he was surprised that Dele could snatch his boys. He declared: "My self and Dele are good friends, why then must he do this to me?"
>
> Jide said that when Dele came to Ibadan he went to him where he was staying to greet him as a friend. "He told me then that he was in town to do some recording for NTA Ibadan. I did not know that he was in town to take away my boys" (*The Entertainer*, March 1982, p. 4).

Although they share a paradigmatic hierarchical structure, the jùjú groups of Ibadan exhibit significant variation. This elasticity may be observed within a single group, as its leader responds to perceived incentives and constraints operative in specific contexts. The dynamics of musical production are strongly influenced by the vicissitudes of the Nigerian oil economy, which "can lurch from excellent to awful in a matter of months" (Stevens 1984:2), setting off ripples that are felt throughout the informal urban economy. Economic factors, ranging from international oil prices to conflicts between captains and band boys, are a crucial aspect of urban Yoruba musical practice.

Performance Contexts: The Hotel

The city of Ibadan is home to scores of beer parlors or "hotels" (see plates 9, 10, and 11). They are scattered throughout the city, although the highest concentration is in immigrant areas such as Mọkọla, Inalende, Ekotedo, Oke-Bọla, Oke-Ado, and Molete.[10] Ibadan hotels generally fulfill the multiple functions of tavern, dance hall, and brothel. They range from small wooden structures with a dance floor surrounded by metal tables and chairs, to larger groups of two or three buildings clustered around an open-air patio with a covered bandstand at one end. Most activity in Ibadan hotels takes place after nine P.M., when they become important nexuses of the city's nocturnal economic structure. A bottle of beer may be purchased for ₦1–1.50, minerals (soft drinks) for 30 kobo, and snacks such as smoked beef or goat meat, chicken, and snails are sold from the bar. Petty traders cluster along the streets adjacent to the hotels, selling more substantial hot food, cigarettes, sweets, and kola nuts.

Another important economic activity associated with the urban hotel is prostitution. The majority of prostitutes in Ibadan are non-Yoruba southern Nigerian immigrants, free from the normative constraints of their home communities. Prostitution is almost universally viewed by its practitioners as a temporary accommodation to city life, a means of accumulating enough cash to move into small-scale trading.

> Prostitutes resident in Ibadan generally have a steady boy friend—a bachelor or a married person whose wife has yet to wean her baby— who pays the rent of her room and gives gifts besides. Since, however, this source of income is not enough to maintain the prostitute, she usually adds to her income by receiving other clients. This is often a source of friction between the prostitute and the boy friend, although any client would acknowledge the prior rights of the boy friend. Quite often such relationships ripen, especially where the woman concerned proves to be steady, reliable and knowledgeable in money matters or in helping forward the career of her chosen boy friend, first into a relationship where the woman gives up her rooms to go and live with the man and later into formal marriage (Okonjo 1967:108).

Prostitution provides migrant women with a means of gradually accumulating independent resources; the brokerage role of the male "pimp" is practically nonexistent. Most prostitutes rent a room, ranging from ₦5 a night at the lower status hotels to ₦10 at more posh establishments. At one popular night spot in the Oke-Bọla area, from twenty to thirty prostitutes work on any given night when business is good. According to a patron, the women generally charge ₦3 for a "round one," ₦2 for a "round two," and are sometimes able to clear ₦10–20 a night after paying rent.

The reasons offered by male hotel patrons for their own attendance on a given night are varied, including domestic squabbles, a desire to see friends, friendship with the owner or manager, and the need for entertainment and diversion, a temporary escape from the daily psychological pressure of the work- or marketplace. One jùjú bandleader who has performed in Ibadan hotels for over a decade emphasized the need for relaxation, the "love of drink," the desire to dance and hear music, and the presence of "free women" as common motivations for individuals to attend. Charles Keil, in his notes on the nightclub scene in Ibadan on the eve of the Civil War, observed that:

> the hard core club-goers are mostly outsiders, "visiting firemen," those who will do things here that they might not want to be seen doing at home . . . the fewer kinsmen, friends of family, etc., one is likely to run into, the more good-timing is done. So, if the away-from-homes go home, attendance suffers very noticeably. Plus the fact that the away-from-homes are away for good money-making purposes (Keil 1966–67:6).

Keil's research led him to suggest a two-pronged pressure on "who goes to clubs": first, the lack of social controls on transients or new arrivals who have come to the city in search of wagework or entrepreneurial opportunities; and second, the fact that migrants exercise more autonomous control over their cash earnings than locals.

The association of urban hotels with prostitution, alcohol consumption, and excessive behavior appears to act as a disincentive for many upwardly mobile Yoruba and older individuals. Aronson (1978) describes the attitudes of an Ijẹbu family residing in the Oke-Ado area, where the majority of jùjú hotels are located, toward the proper use of leisure time:

> Michael and Florence Odusanya have little time or money to spend on "recreation" or "entertainment." While they do spend time together in the afternoon or evening when their jobs allow it, most of their leisure occurs on weekends, especially Sunday, and they spend it on prayer and association meetings, on trips home to visit relatives, or on other forms of social gathering. [Mrs. Odusanya] has never, she says, seen a film, although [she and her family] have been together to one popular play. Music comes from the radio or from groups playing at funerals or other ceremonies; the Odusanyas would not consider going to one of the "night clubs," open-air bars and dance halls, which dot the city (Aronson 1978:72–73).

Hotel patrons are predominantly male wageworkers. There is, however, remarkable variation in terms of occupation and ethnicity. Most hotels have a core of regular customers and a larger group of transients on any given night. During the course of an evening there is an almost constant flow of individuals or small groups of friends. While a few patrons generally stay for hours, most come to sit, drink a few bottles of beer, talk, perhaps visit the prostitutes, and then leave for another night spot or for home.

The typical group of hotel patrons includes clerks, traders, policemen, soldiers, laborers, journalists, artisans and their apprentices, and musicians seeking employment or assessing the competition. Most customers present on any given night are Yoruba, with the various immigrant groups that live in areas such as Oke-Ado and Oke-Bọla predominating. Many of the owners and managers of Ibadan hotels are Yoruba, and informants' accounts emphasize the role of Ijẹbu migrants in these positions. Igbos were heavily involved in the Ibadan hotel scene, both as managers and patrons, in the early 1960s. Their exodus from the western region after the outbreak of violence against Igbo migrants in northern Nigeria led to the closing of a number of popular night spots (e.g., the Paradise Club, Easy Life, Garden City), and played a part in a general disruption of the hotel scene during the war. Mid-western Nigerians also have a history of involvement in Ibadan hotels since at least the early 1960s, when many of the most important establishments were founded. For example, the Independence Hotel in Oke-Bọla, one of the few jùjú clubs mentioned in Keil's 1966–67 fieldnotes that were still featuring live music in 1981–82, has been managed since 1964 by Mr. Ideh, an immigrant from Warri who arrived in Ibadan in 1952. Originally a trader, he gradually saved up enough funds to rent the hotel from its Ijẹbu landlord, to whom he makes annual payments.

The ebb and flow of nightlife in Ibadan is conditioned by economic and political forces, smaller establishments often being forced out of business, and larger hotels cutting back during periods of economic retrenchment. Hotel managers look back fondly on the 1950s, the early 1960s, and the Oil Boom years of the 1970s, when there was "money in town" and business was good. In the summer of 1979, nocturnal entertainment was subdued by the federal elections, since fear of political violence kept many patrons home at night. In 1981 and 1982, slow business was blamed on federal austerity measures, which encouraged individuals to conserve their cash earnings. During annual traditional festivals such as Okè'bàdàn and Egúngún, business drops off. One manager recounted an incident during the early 1970s in which the regional government asked hotels to temporarily avoid the use of music to attract customers. A serious outbreak of cholera had taken place in the city, and a council of herbalists went to the governor to ask him to enforce quiet, in keeping with traditional beliefs linking sound to the transmission of disease.

Since most hotels are open-roofed, business generally drops off markedly during the rainy season (April–November). Frequent interruptions in the supply of electricity are also a problem, although managers of the larger hotels invest in a gasoline generator to power light, refrigerators, and sound equipment. The hotel economy of Ibadan is affected by fluctuations in the oil market, government controls on salaries and imports, the rate of urban migration, conflicts with local authorities, and weather patterns.[11]

While musicians predictably suggest that their performances attract customers, creating profit for the hotel managers, most patrons with whom I spoke did not list music as a major reason for going out to a hotel. Unless the individual was a friend of the bandleader, the primary reasons stated were, as mentioned above, the desire to socialize, to relax, to drink, or to patronize the resident prostitutes. Overall it appears that live music is much preferred to recorded music (used by almost all hotels) because it is regarded as more suitable for dancing, and the musicians can perform praise songs for specific patrons.

Jùjú bands generally do not receive a guaranteed minimum amount of cash. While a few of the most successful bands, usually those that have made popular recordings—for example, I. K. Dairo and his Blue Spots and Dele Ojo and his Star Brothers Band in the 1960s; Captain Jide Ojo and his Yankee System and Uncle Toye Ajagun and his Olumo Sound in the late 1970s—sell tickets at the gate and are guaranteed a minimum by the hotel manager, the great majority of groups depend upon the cash donations of patrons. While a popular band may be "sprayed" more than ₦100 by customers on a good night at one of the larger hotels, profits generally range from a high of ₦75 to a low of ₦5. The captain receives the lion's share, and other members are remunerated according to their place within the band hierarchy.

Keil makes a distinction in his notes between "first- and second-rank" jùjú hotels, a classification upheld by my informants, some of whom divided the clubs and groups that performed at them into three tiers. While rankings of bands and the hotels they regularly perform at are broadly homologous, the constant rotation of groups playing one-night engagements during the week means that second-rank groups sometimes perform at first-rank clubs, and vice versa. In general, the manager of a hotel will book a series of bands for a month at a time. Most bands perform at hotels only on weeknights, reserving the weekends for more lucrative engagements.[12]

Booking schedules are flexible. If a jùjú group has an opportunity to perform in a more lucrative context, they do, leaving the night open for another band. If the power fails, if it rains, or if a quorum of performers fail to show up, an engagement may be cancelled at the last moment. In some cases band captains who are personal friends may share engagements, two or more bands performing on a given night. In general, the hotel jùjú performance scene appeared to have declined somewhat between 1979 and 1982, when several clubs had ceased featuring bands, and those which did had a higher rate of cancellations. According to Ibadan-based jùjú musicians and hotel managers, the decline in live jùjú performance was a direct effect of inflation and government policies. Workers and traders who might have enough for a bottle or two of beer did not have the surplus cash to spray musicians.

In the hotel world of Ibadan, primarily sustained by beer sales and prostitution, the performance of jùjú music is a luxury rather than a necessity. These institutions, patronized primarily by migrants and strangers, and located in a sociospatial zone where the force of community norms is attenuated and hunger, thirst, and sexual desire may be satiated and dysphoria temporarily banished, are a vital part of the diurnal economic structure of Ibadan. Urban Yoruba informants' images of the nightclub world are multifaceted: the hotel is at once a cosmopolitan institution, where one meets friends and acquaintances to discuss the latest news and drink beer, and a liminal zone, in which one must beware of pickpockets, armed robbers, drinks poisoned by rivals, lonely lepers who come out at night when lights are dim, and, as one musician phrased it, "ọ̀tá at'àjẹ́ pápá" ("enemies and witches especially"). The uncertainty, fear, excitement, freedom, and pleasure of urban life are experientially focused in the nocturnal ethos.

Many Ibadan hotel managers view musicians as difficult business partners that create as much hassle (wàhálà) as profit. In a marginal and precarious socioeconomic sphere, where profits are slim, and underlings are frequently suspected of dipping their hands into the till, live music is expendable. Jùjú band captains feel much the same way about the hotel scene, which provides them with a highly uncertain source of profit, and does not generally increase their access to elite Yoruba patrons and recording opportunities. Thus, the more successful jùjú groups based in Ibadan and other Yoruba towns attempt to restrict their appearances to the neotraditional celebrations described in the following section.

Performance Contexts: The Àríyá

Jùjú groups also perform at celebrations called àríyá, a term glossed by Abrahams as "cheerfulness" or "jollification" (1981:64). Another term for these events is ìpàdé, a compound of the terms pa, (to become amalgamated) and dé (to arrive), literally a coming together and fusing of people (Abrahams 1981:540). These two terms map the cultural significance of urban Yoruba celebrations: they generate happiness (inún dídùn, "sweetstomachedness") and pleasure (ìgbádùn, "sweetness reception"), and draw together multiple strands of kinship, patronage, and friendship, actualizing and publicizing a sensual social universe centered on the host(s). Positive affect and social power are twin foci of the modern Yoruba àríyá.

Àríyá are lavish parties celebrating the naming of a baby, weddings, birthdays, funerals, title-taking ceremonies, and the launching of new property or business enterprises. They are sponsored by upwardly-mobile Yoruba wage earners and entrepreneurs, and, on a more opulent scale, by members of the high elite, including wealthy traders, executives, politicians, and university professors. Sandra Barnes, who did research in the Lagos suburb of Mushin, provides a succinct description of the modern àríyá:

> In ceremonial undertakings, *ìdílé* [patrilineal descent group] mates as well as the wider kindred, affines, and even friends, are responsible for making contributions to the events. For those who have been conscientious in their ceremonial giving in the past, the generosity ideally will be returned two-fold when they later stage their own ceremonies.
>
> The ceremony is the symbolic demonstration of the host's resources: material and social. His own wealth and the contributions of his guests are used to make the occasion as satisfying for the participants as possible. In an effort to display generosity, hosts and hostesses buy and distribute gift items; their kinsmen or close friends also can bring and distribute gifts as an added demonstration of their mutual affection and support.
>
> Opulence also is shown in the monetary rewards which are made to musicians. Both hosts and guests are obliged to reward their entertainers, exhibiting their contributions by pressing them to the foreheads of the musicians. The greater the amounts, the higher the esteem accorded the giver; musicians return the favors by extolling the virtues of the donors in their songs of praise.
>
> The ceremony binds together the whole social sphere of the host; it is a reflection of the host's influence and status. Kinsmen, friends, business associates, and political contacts are all gathered together in groups; a host's ìdílé mates may cluster together in one group; his in-laws in another; his voluntary association mates, work colleagues, and friends in still other sets. Social status is additionally measured by the numbers of guests kinsmen and friends bring with them to the ceremonies. It is desireable that they bring guests, since it swells the number of celebrants and attests to the popularity of the hosts (Barnes 1974:111–12).

Naming ceremonies (*ìsọmọnlórúko* or *ikọọmọnjáàdè*) are held about a week after the birth of a child. The ceremony itself, generally in the home of the parents, is centered around a short Muslim or Christian service, and may include ingestion of various substances with traditional symbolic associations, including honey, salt, alligator pepper, palm oil, kola nut, and *orógbó,* or "false kola." If the parents are poor, the sacred service is held without a subsequent celebration. In most cases, however, the father will arrange to slaughter a cow, provide soft drinks, beer, and "hot drink" (schnapps or gin), and hire musicians to entertain guests in his own compound.

Yoruba marriage customs vary from area to area, but there are a number of common features. A series of prestations are made from the prospective groom's lineage to that of the bride. Most young individuals choose their own spouses, though they are generally careful to respect the wishes of their parents. According to Eades:

> The government publishes schedules of the maximum amount in each category of marriage prestation which is recoverable in the case of a divorce. In examples published in the mid-1970s, the total sum amounted to ₦100. In real income terms marriage prestations are probably worth less than they were during the early colonial period, and they may be considerably less than the husband spends either on the wedding celebration or on trading capital to set his wife up in business. The actual celebration may cost very little, but it can become a major occasion for conspicuous consumption, with hundreds of naira being spent on food, drink, the wife's trousseau and payments to musicians (Eades 1980: 57–58).

While weddings are often held in the city in which a couple resides and works (e.g., Lagos, Ibadan), funerals (*isìnkú*) are more likely to be held in the natal community of the deceased. Those individuals who own private cars may spend many hours on the weekends driving to their home towns or villages in order to reaffirm natal connections, or attending the ceremonies given by friends and business associates. The roads between major towns are crowded on Saturdays and Sundays with private vehicles or buses hired by hosts to carry celebrants to and from a ceremony. Funerary customs also vary throughout Yorubaland; in general, the corpse is interred about a week after death. Daily newpapers are filled with funeral announcements, purchased by members of the family or a voluntary association, with a eulogy and photograph of the deceased. Technological developments, available only to the wealthy, have extended the potential wake-keeping period:

> With the increasing number of refrigerated hospital mortuaries, bodies need not be interred immediately but may be kept until the week-

end; in fact I heard of one instance in which the interment of an important man was delayed for three weeks, for the two Saturdays
following the death were already pre-empted by ceremonies which
required the participation of a large number of elite and of clergy
(Lloyd 1974:122).

Informants have more recently claimed to have frozen bodies for periods
of up to six months in order to amass capital for a proper ceremony (personal communication, Andrew Frankel).

The wake following a burial ceremony is generally hosted by the
children and siblings of the deceased, though the expense is borne collectively by the descent group and, to a lesser extent, by close friends and
acquaintances of the deceased, his widow(s), and other affinal relatives.
There may, in the case of particularly wealthy and renowned individuals,
be a series of wakes, hosted by various relatives, and located in various
towns and villages. In addition, there are five- and ten-year commemora-
tive ceremonies, for which musicians are also frequently employed.

Like naming and wedding ceremonies, it is common for wakes to
last all night, with food, drink, music, and various gifts dispensed to guests
as an indication of generosity. The size and opulence of a funerary celebration is related to the age of the deceased—a young person's funeral is not
a cause for celebration—and the wealth of his kin and supporters. The
degree of success of a wake-keeping is often associated with the safe passage of the deceased (*okú*) along the continuum connecting elders (*àgbàl-
ágbà*), ancestors, and *òrìṣà* (deified ancestors) (Morton-Williams 1973).

However, even strongly traditionalist Yoruba are aware of the role of
funeral ceremonies as a medium of communication among the living. Yoruba perceptions of the interpenetration of the supernatural and the social
aspects of death are encapsulated in proverbs (*òwe*). For example, *okú ọlọ́-
mọn kìí sùn gbàgbé,* "the dead parent does not sleep and forget," suggests
that the deceased continue to watch over the welfare of their children. The
proverb *okú ńsunkún okú, akáṣọ lérí ńsunkún araawọn,* "the dead are
mourning the dead; the persons wearing cloth are mourning for each other,"
suggests on the other hand that funeral ceremonies are primarily for the
benefit of the living (Abrahams 1981:467).

These ceremonies, based upon traditional ritual procedures reinterpreted in light of Christian or Muslim beliefs and practices, provide the
upwardly mobile individual with opportunities for status advancement and
reaffirmation of links with patrons, clients, friends and family. At an *àríyá*
the host repays ceremonial debts incurred at previous occasions held by
relatives, friends, and patrons. The celebration provides a ritually framed
setting for the affirmation of consanguineal rights and obligations, and for

the demonstration of magnanimity toward—and implicit evocation of invidious comparison with—less fortunate members of society. One strives
to outdo one's rivals and detractors, while activating crucial socioeconomic
networks.

> At these ceremonies . . . much private business is done between per-
> sons of high status; men who are unavailable in their offices are vul-
> nerable in such situations. But the participants at these celebrations
> are to a large extent ethnically defined, and ethnic cohesion is thus
> enhanced. . . . Weddings, funerals and the like bring men and
> women into renewed contact with their more distant kin, their erst-
> while school and age mates who have remained in the community. By
> a simple greeting the successful emigrant recognises his origins whilst
> the home-dweller affirms his relationship with the eminent (Lloyd
> 1974:122–33).

The ideology of reciprocity which guides behavior at neotraditional
ceremonies is clearly expressed in interviews with Yoruba elites. The individual quoted below, a female chief, former head of a market women's
association, and a well-known proponent of modern education, has maintained a strong attachment to traditional Yoruba values:

> When you were doing yours, I contributed. When he was doing his, I
> contributed. When other people were doing theirs, I contributed. So,
> if I'm doing something, they should come and contribute, too. That's
> all! So that, what you are going to spend, you may get three times
> what you spend. You make money, not only in spraying [cash gifts],
> but also in contributions. I bring food, I bring money, I bring this and
> that. That is the custom. If the father died, and he [the celebrant] is
> ready to spend, he will get a sponsor. All the people he had benefited
> will come round to pay him back. And this is the only time an event
> like this happens.
> I remember when Yinka [her eldest daughter] was married. You
> just can't imagine; everybody felt too happy that all the time I used to
> throw parties for them, give them this and that, and now is the time
> they can repay it. So, the dresses being given to Yinka, it's almost a
> wardrobe.
> This is what we do in the family, if a member of the family is
> getting married. I get a portmanteau and put all the best inside, and
> give it to this girl, the niece or nephew or cousin or whatever the
> relation. Then I count money and contribute it.
> And if a member of the family is dead, one person will be ready
> to prepare the graveyard, another person will buy the coffin, another
> person will buy the shroud. And members of the family will contrib-
> ute money to buy cattle [to feed the celebrants]. So, in fact, if you

don't do it, you are just a loser (personal communication, Chief Janet
Bọlarinwa).

Another informant, a professional architect in Lagos, emphasized
the risks involved in throwing a lavish celebration. From the perspective of
the host(s), an àríyá is an all or nothing affair. "There can be no halfway
celebration!" Ample food must be provided—a good party involves
slaughtering at least two beef cattle, costing several hundred naira each—
as well as hundreds of bottles of beer, soda, shandy, champagne, and hot
drink. Small gifts such as packages of biscuits, imported tins of condensed
milk, sweets, and pencils are also distributed in large quantities. Local
companies specializing in stationary, invitations, and business cards may
be hired to produce personalized paper napkins, plastic cups, plates, and
buckets, each bearing a portrait of the newlyweds or deceased along with
appropriate slogans in Yoruba or English. Metal chairs, tables, and uten-
sils, and a tarpaulin to keep rain and dew off the most important celebrants
must be rented, and a generator procured in case of power failure. Finally,
at least one group must be engaged to perform suitable dancing and praise
music for participants; a first-rate celebration may feature two or more
bands, alternating or performing in different areas, and performers of traditional poetic genres such as *ewì* and *oríkì*. The total cost of an àríyá easily
runs into the tens of thousands of naira.[13]

According to elite informants, the host of a ceremony is compen-
sated through spraying, public cash donations. At the most lavish ceremonies, a wealthy individual closely related to the celebrant by kinship, patronage, or both, may spray thousands of naira to the host, showering him
or her with paper bills. One such informant, after emphatically claiming
that he didn't believe in lavish displays of money at parties, sprayed ₦400
to the host of a housewarming celebration the night before, though the
individual involved was not a close friend or relative ("the husband of a
friend of a friend"). Although it is possible to make money by throwing a
successful ceremony, informants made it clear that the goal is to show generosity, not to turn a profit. Individuals suspected of throwing parties in
order to exploit their guests are scrupulously shunned. Gossip circulates
quickly, and ceremonies are nexus points for positive and negative reeval-
uations of social status and personal character.

The weather provides another potential source of disaster; as one informant expressed it, "rain is the host's nemesis"! At one of his parties,
which, like most, commenced around 9:00 or 10:00 P.M., a light rain began to fall at 4:00 in the morning. Luckily, guests had been coming and
going all night, and much of the food had been consumed. The host encouraged celebrants to cart away surplus cases of beer and soft drinks and

thereby reinforced his reputation as a generous man. However, he said, if it rains earlier in the evening, "both the party and the host are ruined!" It is impossible to effect a last minute change in the date or venue of a party. A large àríyá may be advertised in the host's and deceased's hometown newspapers several weeks in advance as part of a public obituary notice. The unreliability of electronic communications makes it difficult to notify the hundreds of invited guests and workers, including cooks, waiters, musicians, and photographers.

Another potential source of trouble is the scheduling of multiple ceremonies on a given night. If the social networks of two hosts overlap to a significant degree—this being more likely toward the top of the social hierarchy—then invited guests are forced to make a choice between attending one or the other àríyá, or spending some amount of time at both. The last option is unattractive for various reasons, including widespread fear concerning armed robbery en route.[14] The absence of prestigious invited guests is a blow to the host's reputation and can be the stimulus for feuds which last long after the ceremony is over. Conversely, business associates, kinsmen, close friends, and natives of the same home community as the host who are excluded from the invitation list are likely to harbor a grudge for some time. Although my informant stated that he didn't "give a damn what people think," he allowed that there were strong motivations for drawing up an extensive, carefully planned guest list.

I have suggested that live music is crucial to the proper functioning of an àríyá. If a host concentrates his resources on a single well-known band and they fail to appear at the celebration, his status-adjustment strategies are placed in serious jeopardy.

> A Lagos musician, Mr. Dele Abiodun of the Adawa Super System, has been sued for ₦ 100,000 for an alleged breach of contract. The action was taken against the musician by an accountant with DPMS Lagos, Mr. Dele Obimakinde. In suit No. LD/639/82 filed at the Lagos High Court by counsel to the plaintiff, Mr. Kanmi Isola-Osobu, Mr. Abiodun is alleged to have failed to honour a performance engagement for which the defendant had been fully paid.
>
> Mr. Obimakinde allegedly hired the services of Mr. Dele Abiodun and his Top Hitters Band of Adawa Super System as part of an entertainment package for the final funeral ceremonies of the plaintiff's mother in Abeokuta, Ogun State on May 1. The defendant caused Mr. Obimakinde to build a stage area and cement a large area of land to prevent dust around the stage on which the musician was to perform, it was claimed, "but Dele Abiodun and his Top Hitters band did not show up."
>
> Mr. Isola-Osobu said with the presence of eminent personalities

from all walks of life at the ceremony, his client was greatly embarrassed.

Mr. Isola-Osobu said even though he could not quantify the losses and embarrassment, he would just claim special and general damages amounting to ₦ 100,000 (₦ .1 m) from the defendants. No date has been fixed for the hearing (*Lagos Weekend*, 21 May 1982, p. 9).

An additional feature of modern Yoruba ceremonialism must be mentioned: the degree to which these semipublic occasions function as a support system for the poor (*tálákà*) who make up the majority of the population of cities such as Lagos and Ibadan. At any large ceremony a human penumbra surrounds the core of celebrants and musicians. Unemployed or part-time wage workers, small-scale artisans and petty hawkers, and beggars (*alágbe*) are allowed to gather around the edges of the host's compound, and to partake of the food, drink, and gifts circulated among invited participants. This social orbit includes the poorest of the urban unemployed, whose nutritional needs for the coming week may be met by the meat, pounded yam, rice, or cassava porridge they receive. The provision of food, drink, and entertainment for the needy reinforces the host's reputation for benevolence, and expands his network of supporters.

> In Lagos . . . outdoor parties built around transitional events such as birth, marriage, and death have become, to a large extent, institutionalized systems of redistribution adequate to take care of the subsistence needs of many unemployed migrants. Such parties take place very frequently and are, by their nature, open to all comers. It is indeed possible for an indigent but shrewd unemployed migrant not only to have a full square meal a day through these parties but also to turn them into sources of job information and outlets for frustration and despair (Okediji 1978:217).

The neotraditional ceremonial system is conceived as a system of delayed reciprocity, realized inexactly and naturally. The aim of the ideal host is not to make a profit, or to break even, but rather to provide a memorable experience for his guests, and in so doing raise his standing in the community. The successful àríyá is at once a modern rite of passage, a medium for economic redistribution, an aesthetic object, a source of sensual enjoyment, and a frame for transactive behavior.

Yoruba life strategies cluster around one concept: the necessity of cultivating patrons and a large network of supporters to sing one's praises, literally and figuratively. The popular person (*gbajúmọ̀n*, "two hundred eyes know [him/her]") is in a precarious position, for the very supporters who laud her may, having expended her resources by consuming the redistributive largesse she offers them, transfer their loyalty overnight to a solvent patron. The moderately successful trader or politician, or the wage earner gradually accumulating capital with an eye toward launching a private business, must thus strike a careful balance between public generosity and squander.

> Such social investment takes several forms. First, [the Yoruba individual] redistributes part of his income to kinsmen, friends, and neighbors, by giving gifts, especially of money and food. Second, he engages in a special kind of "conspicuous consumption" which involves other *people* more than things. Yorubas comment that someone giving a party is "declaring a surplus." In the continuous and reciprocal obligations of hosting associational meetings or even simple home visiting, in the joint purchase of identical clothing for a holiday or other occasion, in the impressive celebration of a birth, marriage, or death by entertaining dozens or hundreds of guests, and in the monetary gifts and entertainments accompanying the acquisition of a chieftaincy title, he secures the fellowship and good will of his companions while spending high proportions of his income or savings. . . . Most important for rising above other men in power and prestige, he constructs a loose gathering of followers and partisans who have incurred obligations of variable weight to rally around him in times of personal conflict or for the purpose of political competition (Aronson 1978:157–58).

The frequency, size, and ostentation of àríyás is a product of the Nigerian oil economy of the 1970s, which "created a profound cleavage between the 'haves' and the 'have nots'" (Watts and Lubeck 1983:113). However, the organization and ethos of the contemporary àríyá also provide strong evidence of the tenacity and pervasiveness of "deep" Yoruba images of social order. Traditional Yoruba sculpture (see, e.g., Thompson 1971) frequently represents leader-follower relationships. The spatial positioning of figures—the leader elevated above and/or surrounded by his retinue—aesthetically encodes two fundamental tenets of Yoruba political tradition: first, that the king's followers are an essential source of support and protection; and, at a more abstract level, that all power is relational. The economic analogue of this relationship—patron-clientage—has long been a recurrent theme in Yoruba expressive culture. In one of the hundreds of verses (odù'fá) used in Ifa divination—medium of communication between humans and the gods, and source of order in a uncertain universe—the òrìṣà Ifa sings a song to celebrate his wealth:

Kabí owó máa wà o?
Ara ènìòn ni owó mà wà o!
Ara ènìòn l' lowó mà wà o!
> Where are cowries (i.e., money) to be found?
> One's own followers are cowries, oh!
> One's own followers are cowries, oh!
> (Bascom 1969b:363; Belasco 1980:44).

6

The Aesthetics and Social Dynamics of Jùjú Performance at the Yoruba Àríyá

Yoruba neotraditional celebrations, or àríyá, are held either in the city where the host works or in his community of origin, often a small town or village. In the latter case, a jùjú band contracted in Ibadan may take most of a day to reach the site of the event, sometimes traveling hundreds of kilometers on treacherous roads. Though breakdowns, accidents, and armed robbery are matters of constant concern, weekend travel to and from out-of-town engagements is a much-anticipated source of adventure for musicians. The road (ònà), associated in Yoruba thought with danger, movement, trade, innovation, and, in the broadest sense, the world (ayé), offers temporary release from the obligations and constraints of family and wage work. Riding in a bus with the name of the band painted in bright colors on the sides, back and front, each band boy is a gbajúmòn (big shot), greeted by a stream of curious onlookers and admirers.

The arrival of the band at the àríyá site may differ by a number of hours from the time initially agreed upon. Although the host will complain if the group is excessively tardy, it is usually impossible to hire other musicians of acceptable caliber at the last minute. The band captain's excuses—a flat tire, insufficient petrol, poor roads, irresponsibility on the part of a band boy—are almost always accepted after a protracted discussion. Wealthy hosts, such as merchants, corporate executives, or politicians, or those receiving contributions from many kin and friends, may hire several bands. This is done in part to ensure that music will be provided should one of the groups fail to show up. I attended several àríyá at which three bands and various other performers were hired to entertain and sing the praises of host and guests.

In some cases, the hiring of bands from different towns and spatial segregation of guests and dance areas expresses relationships among groups involved in the celebration. At one funeral ceremony, an Ibadan jùjú band entertained one group of guests, an Ibadan fújì band another group, while a jùjú band from Lagos played across the street. In this case, the sociospatial distribution of guests and musical organizations reflected a three-way struggle over inheritance of the deceased's land.[1] At another wake, held in a small town called Imẹsile, some six hours from Ibadan by road, two dance areas were established. An Ibadan jùjú band was hired by the sister's daughter's husband of the deceased, an individual who worked in the city. The other band, Sir Rotor Olusco and his Araga Super Band, came from the northern Yoruba town of Ilọrin, where the deceased had lived at the time of his death. His son, who brought the corpse from the mortuary in Ilọrin to the home community of Imẹsile, hired the second band. Though there was no explicit conflict among groups of participants, the division of the celebration into two zones expressed an Ibadan vs. Ilọrin distinction.

Setting up the amplifiers, an activity carried out by lower-status band boys and, in the larger bands, equipment handlers, takes up to an hour. The band sets up along one edge of a large open space near the house or compound of the host(s). This dance area is surrounded by rows of metal tables, at which celebrants sit. In some cases a table or row of tables is set aside or situated on a raised platform. Celebrants and guests of particular importance are seated at this "high table," visible to all lower-status participants. The spatial arrangement of seats, and the order of service of food, beverages, and gifts to guests portray patterns of social affiliation and status. The layout of jùjú bands is another medium for the portrayal of hierarchy. The praise singers form a line at the front of the band. The captain sits or stands in the middle and is the visual focus of attention (see color plates 1 and 2). To either side of him stand the chorus vocalists, who often entertain observers with horseplay and dancing (see plate 13). Drummers and guitarists form a rear flank behind the band captain and chorus vocalists (see plates 14, 15, and 16).

Although the precise order of events at an àríyá varies, there are some consistent features. Generally the majority of guests, some of whom have traveled hundreds of kilometers to attend the celebration, are already seated and have been served beer, soft drinks, hot drink, and food by the time the band begins performing. There is often a series of speeches by important participants, praising the host(s) and honorees (the deceased at a funeral, the newlyweds at a wedding, the newborn infant at a naming ceremony, etc.). The speakers may include kin, close friends, business partners or patrons, and Muslim or Christian officials. Their speeches may be preceded by a short performance by the band, which initiates the event and focuses the attention of participants on the speakers, who use the band's public address system. Practitioners of ewì, òríkì, rárà, and other heightened speech genres may also perform, praising the host and celebrants, their families, personal accomplishments, and social position. Costumed come-dians (aláàwàdà), who are sometimes hired to perform routines based upon prototypes established by popular Yoruba television performers Moses Ọlaiya ("Baba Sala") and Jacob and Papalolo, tease important par-ticipants, giving them a chance to demonstrate their good humor and equa-nimity.

Jùjú performances begin in earnest around 10:00 or 11:00 P.M. The dance floor is cleared, and a small group of primary celebrants, dressed in imported fabric (aṣọ ebí, "cloth of the consanguines") printed with match-ing patterns vividly symbolizing membership in a kin group or voluntary association, move onto the dance area (see plates 17 and 18). These core participants are expected to dance in the upright, dignified manner tradi-tionally associated with prestige and wealth. At a wedding the first two groups of dancers are representatives of the bride's and the groom's fami-lies. At a funeral members of a voluntary association to which the host belongs, or which helped to arrange and pay for the burial and celebration, may also wear matching sets of cloth. The cloth is generally bought in quantity and paid for by guests, rather than the hosts.

The music continues for six or seven hours, with only one or two pauses. The momentum of the celebration must be maintained, so that guests do not lose interest, grow sleepy, and leave for home. A jùjú per-formance begins with a short instrumental introduction, during which ini-tial adjustments in aural balance are effected. The captain sings solo phrases (dá orin, "initiate song," the verb dá meaning "to create or act alone"; Abrahams 1981:119), segments of which are harmonized by the chorus. He also initiates extended call (elé, from lé, "to drive something away or into something else") and response (ègbè, from gbè, "to support or protect someone") sections, in which he alternates shorter phrases with a fixed phrase sung in harmony by the chorus (ègbè, "supporters" or "pro-tectors"). The song texts performed by leader and chorus are comple-mented by surrogate speech phrases played on the talking drum, or, to a lesser degree, guitar, bass guitar, or congas. Even the ṣèkèrè bottle-gourd rattle can be used to talk by articulating distinctive timbres (Euba 1975:480), although few players in jùjú bands are competent enough to do this.

Single-membraned hand-beaten drums such as ògìdo, gòmbé, àk-úbà, agbámolé, and sámbà play repetitive supporting patterns. These drums are generally not amplified, and are sometimes almost inaudible during a performance. Heard cumulatively, however, they form an essential rhythmic infrastructure. This role is evidenced clearly during power fail-ures, when the amplifiers are incapacitated, and drumming becomes the center of attention. Idiophones such as ṣèkèrè, maracas, agogo, and clips play ostinato patterns which interlock with those played on the hand-beaten drums. The double toy or bongos is played with flexible sticks, producing a penetrating percussive sound which cuts through the dense aural texture of the band. Though single-membrane drums and idiophones may be made to talk through muted strokes, slaps, and other techniques, their primary function is to produce non-text-based dance rhythms (see Euba 1975).

The àdàmọ̀n pressure drum is the most prominent percussion instrument in a jùjú band (see plate 12, color plate 4).[2] As one practitioner put it, "The talking drum can't die out in this music! If a jùjú band shows up without one, they will be asked to leave!" While any instrument capable of producing three distinct pitches—or timbres—may be made to speak, the pressure drum can produce pitch glides imitating the subtle contours of spoken Yoruba, and in the hands of an adept performer, may even imitate distinctions between voiced and voiceless consonants. The talking drum is closely miked, and when possible is run through its own amplifier, separate from the PA system and guitar amplifiers. Volume and bass controls are turned up as far as possible short of feedback, so that the àdàmọ̀n produces a booming cannonlike sound clearly audible over the rest of the band. In the larger groups, with two or three àdàmọ̀n, one drummer takes a dominant role, highlighting aspects of the other drums' patterns and occasionally shifting into speech mode.

The band captain's guitar is usually tuned in an open pattern called "Spanish," in which major or minor triads (either 5–1–5–1–3–5 or 1–5–1–3–5–1, ascending) are played by laying the forefinger of the left hand across one fret, so that, as one jùjú guitarist put it, "it's sweet when you wipe it all across." Few leaders—even superstars such as King Sunny Ade—take extended guitar solos. Their role is rather to punctuate the ensemble texture with percussively struck triads and to signal changes from solo to responsorial singing, or from singing to guitar solos or sections featuring the drums. These signals generally consist of short distinctive motifs. A captain may invent his own signal pattern or copy that of a popular musician. Bandleaders imitating the style of King Sunny Ade, for example, may adopt his signature motif, the pitches 8–7–8 alternated rapidly in a high register. In bands with multiple guitars, a lead guitarist, sometimes using echo, fuzz, or wah-wah effects, takes extended solos. Hawaiian (pedal steel) guitarists embellish the texture of the band with sustained chords and swooping melodic figures, and may be called upon to take solos.

Tenor guitars, like the conga-type drums, play interlocking support patterns. As with the drums, additional guitarists may add a new part or double an existing part. Tenor guitar patterns are frequently harmonized in thirds. Like other instruments in the ensemble, a tenor guitarist may con-

[ò- pó- pó-o mẹ́- ka mọ́n ro - ro   à-lù - já-à - nùn n'í - lé-e wa]

Figure 6.1. Tenor guitar pattern

[Bá   bá mi ṣé -   e - e   bá bá mi ṣé -   e - e]

Figure 6.2. Tenor guitar pattern ("bá mi ṣée")

struct an ostinato pattern out of the tonal contour of a song text. As one guitarist explained:

> What actually influences me in that kind of role is, if somebody sings *straight*, you know, when he doesn't sing so that you don't know where all those beats are supposed to be, then on what he says, you might just have an idea from the song. I remember when we are with Yekini Tomori, he used to praise all these Muslims, *gọnọn* [a lot]. So, when he sings, *òpópó mẹ́ká mọ́n roro, àlùjànún n'ílé wa,* I can pick my tenor. So, when he's singing about all these Muslims, I can play: [The music played is illustrated in figure 6.1.] "The streets of Mecca are very clean, Alujonu [djinns] are in our house." So, yes, you can talk, a lot of the time. (Personal communication, Kọla Oyeṣiku)

A skilled guitarist may adopt a phrase performed by the singers and develop it as a ostinato pattern; for example, a guitarist may take the motif *bá mi ṣée* ("help me to do it"), sung by the band captain on the pitches 5–3–6–5, and built the pattern shown in figure 6.2 from it. It is common practice for a tenor guitarist to move his pick hand steadily in a rapid density referent pattern (Koetting 1970), muting the strings with his left hand for a percussive effect between articulated pitches.

The bass guitar, which one Ibadan band captain refers to as "the father of my background music," is used to perform ostinatos which interlock with dance rhythms played by the àdàmọ̀n pressure drum(s). The bass guitar is treated as a low-pitched drum, the amplifier adjusted so that upper harmonics are attenuated and the fundamental is emphasized, creating a deep rumbling sound. Its function is to anchor the dance rhythm and differentiate between broadly conceived tonic and dominant harmonic centers.

The first group(s) of dancers initiate the sequences of spraying through which patterns of cooperation and competition are enacted on the dance floor. Kin, friends, and associates dance up to the band captain or to one another, withdrawing cash from their pockets or handbags. The money is pressed, bill by bill, to the forehead of the recipient, the process being repeated as many times as the donor wishes or can afford. After half an hour or so the opportunity to sway and spray is open to all, including, as one host put it, "people I've never seen before." These ritualized sequences are a medium for repayment of debts incurred at previous ceremonies; for the symbolic expression and reinforcement of consanguineal, affinal, and clientage relationships; and for the negotiation of social status via the public display of personal wealth, sometimes involving thousands of naira.

Most of the spraying of cash at an àríyá is directed at musicians. This practice has long been a sanctioned response to praise singing and drumming, although the amounts of money involved escalated sharply during the Oil Boom of the 1970s. Cash prestations from participants provide at least fifty percent of a jùjú band's earnings on a given night, though the presence of more than one band,[3] bad weather, or power failure may restrict the flow of money from celebrants to musicians. Spraying, both among guests and to musicians, may take place only when music is being performed. Musical performance establishes norms legitimating public demonstrations of wealth, generosity, and good character. The institution of spraying links musical performance, aesthetic values, and the social strategies of upwardly mobile celebrants. Alaja-Browne (1986:101) has noted the practice of "offering returns," in which

> an aspiring juju musician seeking followership and fame or a successful juju musician seeking to reinforce his status at a social gathering would have already given out money to his patrons with the hope that when the dancing begins, he should be ostentatiously sprayed. This is meant not only to extend his network of patron-musician relationships, but also to attract the generosity of other wealthy patrons who might be around at a given social gathering. After the ceremony, the musician would be given back whatever is left of his money by the patrons after he must have tripled or quadrupled the original amount through spraying.

Spraying is not continuous. After the initial burst at the beginning of an àríyá, there are typically lulls and surges in the flow of cash to the musicians. Controlling the social pulse of spraying so as to maximize profits is among the most important rhythmic skills learned by a jùjú band captain.

At the outer limits of the àríyá, poor residents of the host's neighborhood or village gather, waiting for free food, drink, and a chance to join the dance. Sociospatial boundaries become less clear as the night progresses and the music radiates out into the streets of the city, or the uncul-

tivated bush surrounding the village. Music is a sonic index of the successful àríyá, the first indication a passerby has that something special is
happening. Sound, rather than vision, defines the widest reaches of the
àríyá.

However, it is at the interactional frontier between musicians and
dancers that the link between aurality and social experience is most po-
tently forged. The rich and elderly sway majestically, while the young and
the poor dance more vigorously, exchanging winks, smiles, and mock
glares, sometimes closing their eyes to focus the homology of rhythmic
flow and bodily movement. Body force is focused toward the earth, and
garments may be stretched taut and manipulated to define shifting shapes.
Body parts—a leg, a shoulder, a hip—are autonomously energized, moving in circles while the rest of the body works in a gentle, cool (itútù)
holding pattern.

A competent jùjú band captain controls biographical information
concerning each important guest at a given celebration. In some cases, the
host provides the captain with a written list of key participants. In others,
when the band captain knows few of the celebrants, the band manager will
attempt to collect information from the seated guests, whispering it in the
captain's ear or writing it on a sheet of paper which is then fastened to his
microphone stand for reference during the performance. The captain uses
this information to generate formulaic texts, which form the basis for solo
and call-and-response singing.

The major themes of jùjú song texts are prayer (àdúrà), money
(owó), honor (ọlá), individual destiny (orí), jealousy (ìlara), competition
(idíje), and, most prominently, the praising (yìn) of well-known celebrants
and abusing (bú) of their enemies (ọ̀tá) and rivals (abánidíje). These
themes are often expressed through proverbs (òwe). Urban slang phrases
are used to express excitement, to urge on a dancer, or as a form of teasing
within the band.

An individual sitting at a table or dancing in front of the band hears
the singers call his name (dárúkọ) and the names of his parents, spouse(s)
and offspring. As he and his kin are metaphorically linked to the lofty silk-
cotton tree (àràbà), the elephant (àjànàkú), or a mighty rock on a mountain
(òkè àpáta pìtì), while his enemies are denigrated with references to the
miserly tortoise (ahun) and the treacherous bush rat (òkété), he feels pride
in his accomplishments, confidence in his personal destiny (orí), and
safety in the company of supporters and clients. When the band captain
and chorus begin to sing his praises in call-and-response form, the repeated
phrases rising from the public address system into the evening sky, under-
girded by compelling dance rhythms incorporating deep Yoruba proverbs,
the praisee undergoes an experiential transformation described as a "swelling of the head" (iwúlórí). As one informant put it:

Ó wú mí l' órí, it swelled my head; this means I am feeling the pride of my generations, my accomplishments, my power, and my reputation in the society at large. When singers or drummers do this for you, even a poor man must respond with something, at least a 50 kobo note!

The pressure to join the dance, rock majestically up to the band, and initiate a spraying sequence is intense. The reluctant praisee risks stimulating deleterious gossip (*òfófó*) concerning his character and financial status. As one elite informant put it, "You should never go to an àríyá without cash, especially when you are wearing lace [i.e., expensive cloth]. They will slander you!".

Jùjú Aesthetics

In modern Yoruba ceremonial life pragmatics, sensuality, and aesthetics are inextricably intertwined. Jùjú performance is as much a practical as an artistic process. It is directed toward certain utilitarian ends: the celebration of important events in the individual's life course, the manipulation of public reputation through praise singing and drumming, and the creation of positive affect.

Pleasing form and good feelings are pragmatic; in order to be effective—a quality expressed by the term *ṣe* (to make, do, serve as, act as, function, be certain or definite; Abrahams 1981:607–10)—performances must satisfy aesthetic values. I would argue that a hard-and-fast analytical distinction between the utilitarian and the aesthetic can only obfuscate the full range of values guiding social and musical performance at modern Yoruba rites of passage. Social power, musical sound, poetic rhetoric, and sentiment are woven via performance into whole experiential cloth.

One is not required to respond to a poor performance of jùjú music. If the band is not "up to standard," and cannot generate good feelings—*idùnnún* (happiness, lit., "sweet-stomachedness"), *ìtúraká* (relaxation, "unfolded body"), and *igbádùn* (enjoyment, "sweetness reception")—then few celebrants will spray, usually those most eager to show off their wealth. Inappropriate use of proverbs, lack of knowledge of the participants, and unclear enunciation are all considered major failings.

The voice (*ohùn*) of a band captain may be likened to honey (*ohùn oyin:* evoking sweetness, smoothness), salt (*ohùn iyọ̀:* distinctiveness of flavor), a bird (*ohùn ẹyẹ:* high-pitched, clear), or a metal gong (*ohùn agogo:* distinctive, resonant)—all positive evaluations. A "solemn" voice, appropriate for performing at a funeral, may also be referred to as *ohùn aró* (a mournful voice), while a singer adept at changing the inflection of his voice may inspire the comments *o pa' hùn dá* ("he changed his voice") or *ó*

l' óhùn ("he twisted his voice"). Negative comments focus on lack of resonance or excessive hoarseness, conveyed by the phrases *ó l'óhùn híhá* ("he
has a crowded, confined voice") or *ó kẹ'hùn* ("he has a husky voice," lit.,
a voice which spreads destructively; Abrahams 1981:364). A singer who
drawls may be criticized with the phrase *ó fa'hùn* ("he stretched voice"),
while the verb *kùn,* also applied to rumbling stomachs, bees buzzing, pigs
grunting, and a crowd murmuring, may be used to criticize a singer who
mumbles.

Good jùjú music rushes over the listener in a continuous stream
(*giiri*), or blows flutteringly, like a flag in a strong wind (*fẹ́lẹ́lẹ́*). To cut
through the aural texture of the band, a *ṣèkèrè* or pair of maracas should
ideally sound *kéré-korò* ("small and bitter"), while an agogo iron bell
might sound *sáí-sáí* (penetrating or intense), a term also applied to taste
experiences, or *gbínrín* (piercing, high-pitched). A competent percussion
section emphasizes the interlocking of individual rhythm patterns, con-
trasting sounds which are *kẹ́-kẹ́-kẹ́* (dry sound, a cough, a clock ticking, a
crisp stroke on bongos) with those which are *pọ̀* (dull, without resonance).
A drummer may not only *lù* (beat), but also *gbá* (strike hard) or *pá* (energetically attack) his instrument to create interest. Tenor guitar players *ta*
(shoot a projectile, splash water, kick, puncture, become rapidly, dart,
sting) or *fà* (stretch) their strings, producing percussive, focused attacks.

A effective jùjú performance generates a special world of experienced time. It is possible, and frequently desirable, to *yí* (turn) a song text
or rhythm pattern, that is, to change its relationship to other elements and
thus its place within the flow of performance. Volume and intensity should
be modulated from *kìji-kìji* (intense) or *geere* (bright, rapid) peaks to *kẹ́lẹ́-
kẹ́lẹ́* (stealthy, gentle, quiet) valleys in order to keep the interest of potential
patrons throughout the night. Though different rhythmic and melodic
frameworks may be strung together during the course of a performance,
each individual song should be *mélo-mèlo* (flowing, continuous).

The importance of clarity, order, and control is evident in the evalua-
tive terminology applied to jùjú performances. Unclear, sloppy performances may be referred to as *hẹbe-hèbe, húru-hùru, wára-wàra,* or *bákọn-
bàkọn.* These terms may be applied to walking and dancing as well as
singing and playing an instrument, and each conveys lack of grace and loss
of control, possibly due to intoxication. While the overall texture of a band
may be positively described as *kíkùn* (humming, buzzing), it is also positive to say of the singers that they are *ńkorin ṣáṣá* (singing clearly or
cleanly). A band may sound *gaara* or *gedegbe* ("clear," terms also applied
to transparent or translucent visual percepts). Individual parts should
sound *kete-kete* (distinct) or *gbangba-gbangba* (bright against a consistent
background, as in *òṣùpá yọ gbangba,* "the moon shone brightly"), but no
part should dominate the others.

The most important quality for a performer is responsibility, manifest, particularly in supporting parts such as the single-membraned drums and tenor guitars, in the production of steady patterns. The technique of the virtuoso is admired, but is also a potential source of musical and social imbalance within an ensemble. An individual performer may be described as an *ewèlè* ("bush spirit") if he is particularly adept, but his performance should complement and not dominate the other players. The term *ewèlè* is ambiguous, since such spirits are frequently disruptive. As always, context is crucial to interpreting aesthetic commentary. In Yoruba aesthetics, the boundary between individual prowess and social excess is charged with ambivalence.

Jùjú Song and Drum Texts

One practical problem faced by the jùjú band captain as he fashions lyrics from a memorized corpus of verbal formulas is to ensure that lexemic tone is not altered by melodic contour to a degree that would confuse listeners, particularly the potential wealthy patrons upon whom his success rests. Several factors make the mediation of linguistic tone and melodic contour less of a problem than it might seem at first glance. If the overall contour of a melodic line is preserved, alterations in melodic direction are not noticed as violations of musical norms. Lexemic tone may be also violated within limits, since Yoruba speakers are often able to identify formulaic phrases by their overall contour, speech-rhythm, and semantic context. In addition, many jùjú singers shift between song (*orin*) and speech mode during the course of a performance.[4]

The traditional surrogate speech formulas employed by jùjú instrumentalists are often shortened and simplified to produce patterns appropriate for dance music and to facilitate comprehension by younger listeners. The competent àdàmòn drummer controls a wide range of such materials and is able, on the spur of the moment, to incorporate phrases relevant to the immediate social context into his performance. As an experienced drummer, brought up in a traditional lineage setting, put it:

> If you make a proverb that is not related to the song, it is bad. Some of these jùjú people, they don't know. When you are backing, it should fit the rhythm of the song. If they are singing something solo-chorus-solo-chorus, then you have to back the musicians so that the music will move. It is not all the time that you should make a proverb; the time for proverbs is limited. It is nonsense if you continue to make proverbs like that. If you can't think of another moving backing that you can use behind the chorus, different from the solo, it's better to keep the same (Bisi Adeleke; Ibadan, 2 Dec. 1981).

The àdàmòn drummer must strike a balance between dance and speech modes. A lead drummer may derive a dance rhythm from the tail end of a proverb. At times he may shift into speech mode, articulating tonemic patterns in speech-based rhythm, and then return to a dance rhythm ostinato. Even the most purely dance-oriented patterns may be derived from a linguistic kernel, while phrases that most closely approximate the rhythms of speech must still be related to the underlying metric framework.

Some of the speech formulas used by drummers in jùjú bands are very general and may be used in any context. The following phrase was performed by an àdàmòn drummer at a funeral ceremony, though it might be appropriately employed in almost any context:

> Mo dúpé Olórun kò pa mi l'ékún
> I thank God for not making me cry
> Ori ẹni kò má fí ya jẹ'ni
> One's head [destiny] should not make one suffer
> Àtàrí ẹni kò má f'óṣí ta'ni
> One's occiput should not make one poor
> Mo dúpé Olórun kò pa mi l'ékún
>
> I thank God for not making me cry.

Immediately after this phrase was completed, the àdàmòn began to play a repetitive pattern based on the textual kernel mo-dúpé-mo-dúpé-pé, derived from the proverb just sung. Many of the proverbs performed in jùjú music have an A–B–A or A–A–B–A form. The first line, which serves to identify the proverb, is followed by a contrastive section developing the idea, and a repetition of the opening line. The following phrase, played at the beginning of a performance to announce the prowess of a musical group, follows this pattern:

> A túndé, a túndé
> We're back, we're back
> Àwa l'a mú'gboro dùn
> It is we who make the town happy ["sweet"]
> A túndé, a túndé
> We're back, we're back

The last segment of such a sequence may be used as the generative kernel of a new dance rhythm or "backing" (ẹhin) pattern.

Other proverbs are appropriate only in certain contexts; as one experienced drummer put it, "there is no proverb which you can use in the traditional music that you cannot use in jùjú music; but it depends on the kind of ceremony they are doing at that particular time" (Bisi Adeleke). For example, the phrase

> *Tani ó túu?*
> Who will untie it?
> *Bí ò bá sí tí Jésù l' ókè, ọba mímọ́*
> If not for Jesus on high, holy king
> *Ẹni aráyé so l' ókùn l' ọ̀rùn*
> The person with a rope tied around his neck
> *Tani ó túu?*
> Who will untie it?

is not appropriate for a ceremony held by a Muslim host, while the pattern

> *A ṣeṣe túnṣe*
> We will do it again
> *Bí a bá ṣe yìí tọ́n, áa ṣe míi sì*
> When we have finished this one, we will do another one
> *A ṣeṣe túnṣe*
> We will do it again.

may be performed at a naming ceremony, a wedding, or a birthday, but not a funeral.

The following two drum phrases are particularly appropriate for naming ceremonies:

> (1) *Orí mi máà jẹ́ mpòfo*
> My head, don't let me fail ["become afflicted with emptiness"]
> *Ọmọ l' erè aiyé*
> A child is the profit of life
>
> (2) *Ọlọ́run wò ọmọ náa*
> God, look after this child
> *Ọmọ t' á bí*
> The child that we gave birth to
> *Tí a ńfí ìlù kọ*
> That we are using the drum to teach
> *Ọlọ́run wò ọmọ náa*
> God looks after the child.

Jùjú song and drum texts often use first person plural pronouns to evoke the good fortune of an important patron. This rhetorical strategy draws upon communal values linking the successful individual to his or her supporters, and underlying the redistributive behavior that provides others with chances for upward mobility. The following sequence may be played in praise of a respected elder at any type of ceremony:

> Ìwọ l'a fíṣe, ìwọ l'a fíṣ' àgbà-lágbà
> It is you we made, it is you we made into an elder
> B'ẹ̀nìkan ńṣe kọ̀ndu-kọ́ndu-kọ̀ndu
> If someone else is acting proud, strutting about
> Ìwọ l'a fíṣe, ìwọ l'a fíṣ' àgbà-lágbà
> It is you we made, it is you we made into an elder.

Many verbal formulas used by jùjú singers and drummers boost the reputation of the praisee by attacking his or her enemies. These invidious comparisons generally make use of metaphoric indirection, a technique common to many sub-Saharan African and African-American verbal traditions. The targets of praise lyrics are explicitly named, while the objects of abuse are not. The following sequence may be played by an àdàmọ̀n drummer to praise a celebrant or himself:

> Orí ni
> It is destiny ["head"]
> K'ẹ̀nì mo ni ṣe bo oògùn le
> that which one [a competitor] thinks to be caused by magic.
> Orí ni
> It is destiny

If, for example, the host of an àríyá has recently opened a business after a long period of struggle with competitors, the above phrase asserts that his success is due not to the use of magical charms, but rather to the strength of his orí.

The following phrase was used by a jùjú talking drummer after a sequence of praise singing which emphasized an individual's success in spite of the efforts of bitter rivals:

> Ọ̀pá kò lè pá agogo
> A walking stick can not strike/kill an iron gong

Repeated as an ostinato, this pattern metaphorically portrays the praisee as an iron gong and his defamers as a softer wooden object, asserting that his

enemies can not harm him, try as they might. The ambiguity of the verb
pá, "to strike strongly or to kill," is typical of Yoruba poetic discourse. The
following sequence was used by an àdàmòn drummer during a celebration
hosted by a voluntary association:

> *Ìyẹn náà ninú ḿbí wọn sì*
> It is the thing which is annoying them
> *A lówó-lọ́wọ́ a sì tún l'énìyàn*
> We have money, we also have people [supporters]
> *Ìyẹn náà ninú ḿbí wọn sì*
> It is the thing which is annoying them

Discourse about competition among individuals or groups is under-
lain by the fundamental notion that all phenomena in the material world
are mutable and have an unseen, potentially malevolent aspect. This concept is often expressed with the contrastive terms *àyíníké/àyínípadà*, accompanied by a rotating of the hand to show its two sides. This concept is
metaphorically structured as a distinction between stasis and transformation, the visible and the invisible, or outside and inside. One informant
expressed the concept in the following manner: "You see the bright side of
the moon, but what do you know of its other side?; I smile at you, but how
do you know what's in my mind?"

In some cases, elaborate formulas are shortened and simplified as
they are incorporated into a jùjú performance. The following phrase, for
example, might be used by traditional drummers as a relatively strong and
explicit reference to the enemy:

> *A wí wí wí, elé ò gbọ́*
> We talk, talk, talk, you don't hear
> *A fọ̀ fọ̀ fọ̀ elé ò gbà*
> We speak, speak, speak, you refuse to accept
> *A gbé ìlù sílẹ̀ a tún f'énu wí*
> We drop the drum on the ground [abandon indirection], we
> begin to speak again
> *Àpòtí alákàrà ká bí awu*
> The box of a fried bean-cake seller, that's how it is [greasy,
> dirty]
> *Ohun tí ńṣe ni ńfu yin l'ára*
> The thing you [pl.] have done is making you nervous
> *Ìwà tí ẹ hu ni mbà yin l'ẹ̀rù*
> It is your character that is making you afraid

A mún 'ni ṣí wí, a mun 'ni ṣí sọ
> They cause one to speak blunderingly, they cause one to say
> what one shouldn't say

A mún 'ni tí òkèlè bọ̀ 'mú ni
> They cause one to put a bit of food into one's nose

Bàbá wọn!
> Their father [is like that, too]

As one jùjú drummer put it, "if someone knows you are drumming this about him, he will throw a bottle of beer at your head!" (personal communication, Bisi Adeleke). The version of this sequence used by àdà-mọ̀n drummers in jùjú music would be shorter, leaving out some of the more explicitly abusive passages. Typically, the drummer would extract part of a longer sequence and repeat the first phrase, utilizing the standard-ized A–B–A form:

A wí wí wí, elé ò gbọ́, a fọ̀ fọ̀ fọ̀ elé ò gbà
A gbé ìlù sílẹ̀ a tún f' énu wí, àpòtí alákàrà ká bí awu
A wí wí wí, elé ò gbọ́, a fọ̀ fọ̀ fọ̀ elé ò gbà

Abusive phrases may also be used when one participant starts an argument with another:

Ìwọ ṣá máa jà kiri
> You only go about fighting

Gbogbo ẹgbẹ́ erè ńwọ̀ léèsì,
> You whole group is wearing lace [symbol of wealth]

Ìwọ ṣá máa jà kiri
> [But] you only go about fighting.

If a child is rude to a drummer, but is protected from retribution by his parents, he may be rebuked with the sequence:

Òòlà ikarahun ni ìgbín ajé
> If not for the shell of the snail

Òjo bá rọ̀ a pá ìgbín
> Even the rain would beat the snail

Òòlà ikarahun ni ìgbín ajé
> If not for the shell of the snail.

Conflicts within a jùjú band may also be articulated through surro-gate speech phrases. One drummer told me that the following pattern could be directed at most of the jùjú band captains for whom he had worked:

Yíò bà fùrò rẹ, yíò bà fùrò rẹ
 It will hit you in the anus, it will hit you in the anus
Àwa ń'ṣiṣé l'ọ́ṣẹ̀, ìwọ ńgb'ówó oṣù
 We are working every week, but you are taking the money
 monthly
Yíò bà fùrò rẹ
 It will hit you in the anus

Short slogans may be performed to encourage the dancers and build up excitement. Following are a few of these, used as the generative kernel for dance rhythms:

(1) *Gba bí má gba bẹ̀, gba bẹ̀ mà gba bí*
 Turn this way, don't turn that way! Turn that way, don't turn this way!

(2) *Ẹ bá wa fẹsẹ̀ra, ẹ bà wa fẹsẹ̀ra*
 Help us to dance intensely ["rub legs together"]
Ẹ ra, ẹ ra, ẹ ra
 Rub it, rub it, rub it!
Ẹ bá wa fẹsẹ̀ra
 Help us to dance intensely

(3) *Iró ni jó, ibẹ̀rẹ̀ ni jó*
 Dance standing erect! Dance bending over!

(4) *Bàtàkùn-bàtàkùn*
 Heavily, heavily!
Níbo ní kọ'dí sí? nîì l'ohun?
 Where will I put my buttocks? Here or there?
Bàtàkùn-bàtàkùn
 Heavily, heavily!

A successful performance of jùjú lasts the entire night, with the band taking one or two breaks for food and drink. "As long as the money is coming," says one band captain, "we are enjoying!" As dawn approaches, and the celebration begins to wind down, guests getting into their vehicles for the journey home, the lead talking drummer might play this sequence:

Pàtẹ-pàtẹ ni ó kù
 It is [the type of raffia mat usually used by market women
 displaying] small, small wares that will remain
Bọjà bá tù yíò kù
 when the market closes, that are left

Pàtẹ-pàtẹ ni ó kù
It is small, small wares that remain.

Jùjú performances end entropically, the players jumbling their patterns and creating a chaotic mass of sound. The money sprayed by host and guests is taken out of the beer carton and counted by the band captain, the manager, or a trusted senior band boy, and shares are handed out and debated. Equipment is packed up and loaded onto the band vehicle. When a performance takes place out-of-town, it may be well into the afternoon before the musicians reach home and sleep. Often a band plays successive engagements on weekend nights, traveling from one event to the next and napping during the journey.

Jùjú Performance at an Àríyá

I have thus far offered a description of the Yoruba àríyá that focuses upon the normative, what usually happens. In this section I attempt to provide some sense of the temporal and social patterning of jùjú music by schematically describing a fifteen-minute segment of one performance. This excerpt is included on the cassette that accompanies the book [*cassette example 29*].

It is Saturday, August 4, 1979, the occasion a Muslim funeral celebration in the town of Ogbomọṣọ, some fifty miles north of Ibadan. The host has hired the Olúmọ Soundmakers, led by Ọlatoye Ajagunjẹun, a.k.a. Uncle Toye Ajagun the "Magbe-Magbe Man," one of the most successful band captains based in Ibadan.[5] The son of a lower-level civil servant, Toye was born in 1946 in the Ẹgba Yoruba town of Abẹokuta. His first professional musical experience was as a conga player with the Nigerian Army highlife band. After playing with several jùjú bands in Lagos, he joined the Liṣabi Brothers Band, led by Idowu Animaṣaun, made up mostly of Ẹgba musicians residing in Ibadan. He formed his own group, the Olumọ Soundmakers, named after a sacred hill in Abẹokuta, in 1973. The band was held together by a core of seven young musicians whom Toye had found playing in a band in Ogbomọṣọ, including the lead guitarist, the bassist, and one talking drummer. Uncle Toye's style—the *Máàgbé-Máàgbé ("Don't Carry, Don't Carry") Sound,* a reference to a hold used in wrestling during Muslim festivals—is based loosely on Animaṣaun's àpólà jùjú style, popular in Ibadan during the late 1960s. Toye was picked up by Lagos recording magnate Chief Abioro's *Take Your Choice* label after Sunny Ade left to set up his own label in the mid-1970s. Uncle Toye's fame was partially rooted in his powerful Shure stereophonic PA system, given to him by Chief Abioro. As one competitor put it:

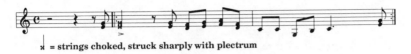

♩ = strings choked, struck sharply with plectrum

Figure 6.3. Introductory theme (Toye Ajagun)

Figure 6.4. Toye Ajagun's signature motif

When Toye goes to a gig, by the superiority of his instruments, his nearness to the crowd can be felt. When you have good instruments, you sing with little effort, and they feel it's shaking the whole floor. Toye was one of the first to get stereophonic sort of equipment, and that was why people felt his sort of music was different from the others.

It is 11:00 P.M., and the Olumo Soundmakers have been playing in front of the host's compound for half an hour. Suddenly, for the second time that evening, the electricity fails, stilling the amplifiers and throwing the celebration into darkness. A great moan arises from the participants: "Oh no!"; *"L'álé yìí ò da-o!"* ["This evening is not good, oh!"]. "NEPA, lepa! [Nigerian Electrical Power Authority, Leper!]". I am seated to one side of the band, and the band manager approaches me and requests that I turn off my tape recorder. After a few moments, the petrol generator is started, and the tape rolls again. Uncle Toye tests his amplifier, arpeggiating a tonic major triad, and signals the band to action (see fig. 6.3). This pattern is gradually picked up by the other guitarists, with the lead and bass guitarists and double toy drummer improvising fills. After nine repetitions of this opening theme, Uncle Toye plays his signature motif on the guitar (see fig. 6.4) and attempts to cool the disgruntled celebrants' feelings by singing:

> *Ẹ má jẹ́ kó bàjẹ́-o-e*
> *Ẹ má jẹ́ kó bàjẹ́-o, kò bàjẹ́ lọ́wọ́ àgbà*
> *Olúwa árọ̀n wá lọ́wọ́-o*
>> Don't let it spoil, oh
>> Don't let it spoil, oh, it does not spoil in the hands of the elders
>> God will help us, oh

This phrase, sung to the melody of a hit record by Ajagun's former captain Idowu Animaṣaun (see fig. 6.5), is intended as a pep talk for the host and

Figure 6.5. Opening vocal line

guests—upon whose mood the night's profits will depend—and for the band itself, which has lost some steam as a result of the repeated interruptions. The celebratory ethos of the àríyá must be rescued. Uncle Toye repeats the line, joined by the five chorus vocalists, who texture and amplify his prayer with three-part harmonies:

> Ẹ má jẹ́ kó bàjẹ́-o-e
> Ẹ má jẹ́ kó bàjẹ́-o, kò bàjẹ́ lọ́wọ́ àgbà, Olúwa árọ̀n wá lọ́wọ́-o
> Don't let it spoil, oh
> Don't let it spoil, oh, it does not spoil in the hands of the elders,
> God will help us, oh

Samuel, the lead talking drummer, inserts a relevant proverb:

> Lọ́wọ́ mi, kò kúkú wùn Elédùmarè, lọ́wọ́ mi
> In my hand, it surely does not please God [to see this occasion spoiled], in my hand

The guitarists continue to make small adjustments, the lead player melodically embellishing the I–V^7 framework established by the tenor guitars, using his echo-plex to soar over the dense ensemble texture. Meanwhile, I fend off a celebrant's request that I behave like a normal human being, that is, that I get up and dance rather than sit next to the band taking notes: "Work first, pleasure later!" He shrugs and heads for the dance area. The opening vocal sequence is repeated, first by Toye, and then by the chorus:

Ẹ má jẹ́ kó bàjẹ́-o-e, ẹ má jẹ́ kó bàjẹ́-o, kò bàjẹ́ lọ́wọ́ àgbà, Olúwa
áròn wá lọ́wọ́-o
Ẹ má jẹ́ kó bàjẹ́-o-e, ẹ má jẹ́ kó bàjẹ́-o, kò bàjẹ́ lọ́wọ́ àgbà, Olúwa
áròn wá lọ́wọ́-o

Samuel, seated at the side of the band, turns toward the bass chorus singer,
and drums:

Yísáù!

Yisau responds affirmatively ("Ẹẹẹẹ"), and Samuel drums him a proverb:

B'éniyàn bínú b'Ọlọ́run kò bá ti bínú àbùṣe-bùṣe
If man is angry and God is not, it is finished [i.e., there is no
problem].

By three minutes into the performance, the supporting patterns have stabilized, and the tenor guitarists have negotiated an ostinato in parallel thirds
(see fig. 6.6). The chorus singers smile and begin moving more fluidly,
teasing one another. One of the tenor vocalists, turning a face of mock
surprise in my direction, calls out:

Òyìnbó!
White man!

Uncle Toye begins a new prayer sequence, his voice echoing powerfully
into the moonlit sky:

Ilàyí Elédùmarè
Elédùmarè, ọba oníbú-ọọrẹ
God in the highest
God, king of a thousand gifts

The tenor guitars continue to play their cool I–V^7 pattern, their right hands
moving in a steady 16th note pattern. After a short pause, Toye enters
again:

Ọba tí gba aláìlárá
Ọba tí pèsè fún àwọn aláìní
Ṣe tèmi níre o, ọba mímọ́n

Figure 6.6. Supporting instrumental patterns
(The Olumo Soundmakers)

> The King [God] has accepted those with no family
> The King has provided for the needy
> Make mine good, holy King

Samuel responds by drumming a fragment from a proverb (see also fig. 6.7):

> *Olọ́wọ́ gbo-gbo-gbo tí ny'ọmọ ẹ l'ọ́fìn, yọ mí*
> Capable person who frees his child from a trap, free me

and Uncle Toye begins another praise sequence:

> *Alájì mi-o,*
> *Mólèyájọ́ bàbá ni*
> My Alhaji, oh
> Moleyajọ is the father

àdàmọ̀n

o- lọ́- wọ́ gbo - gbo - gbo   tí nyọ-mọ   ẹ l'ọ́ - fín   yọ mí

Figure 6.7. Talking drum phrase

A - là - ó   ba - ba ì - bé - jì

[upward slide]

Figure 6.8. Interaction of àdàmọ̀n and guitar

In the back row of the band, Samuel teases the lead guitarist. He flashes his eyes at him and beats:

> *Alàó, bàbá ìbejì*
> Alao, father of twins!

Alao laughs, and responds immediately with an upward slide on his guitar, while one of the chorus singers runs to Samuel and pretends to beat him on the head. Uncle Toye praises Alhaji Moleyajọ and his wife, Iyabode, who sway proudly in front of the band, decked out in white and pale blue lace. Iyabode, ornamented with high heels, necklaces, earrings, and imported silk head-tie, clutches an expensive leather purse.

> *Alájì betilayi, àlájì humura*
> *Mólèyájọ́, mo ba rò de àtàtà*
> *Adúdúyemi, gbajúmọ̀n mi, ẹni re*
> *Ọkọ àlájà-o, ọkọ àlájà Iyábòdé*
> *Mólèyájọ́, gbajúmọ̀n mi àtàtà*
> *Àràbà ṣá ni bàbá*
> *Ẹni a bá l' ábà ni bàbá*
> > Alhaji betilayi Alhaji humura [Muslim salutations]
> > Moleyajo, I follow you out, important person
> > Black and beautiful ["one whose black suits them well"],
> > popular person, good person
> > Husband of the Alhaja, Husband of Alhaja Iyabode
> > Moleyajọ, my popular person, important person
> > The silk-cotton tree is certainly the father [of trees]
> > The person you meet in front of the farm-hut is the father

This proverb implies, first, that Moleyajọ is a father; second, that his own recently deceased father is worthy of great reverence; and, third, that both of them, like giant àràbà trees, tower over other men.

The Olumọ Soundmakers, almost six minutes into their performance, focus their collective attentions on the wealthy host. As Uncle Toye begins another sequence of praise, Moleyajọ glides majestically up to the band. Standing in front of Toye, turned sideways so that all the participants may observe clearly, he pulls a handful of banknotes from the voluminous recesses of his silk gown. Inexorably, bill by bill, he presses the money onto Toye's sweaty forehead. The band captain continues to sing:

> Àlájì betilayi, Mólèyájọ́, gbajúmọ̀n mi àtàtà, ọkọ àlájà Iyábòdé
> Alhaji betilayi, Moleyajọ, my dear important person, husband
> of Alhaja Iyabode

The bass vocalist, Yisau, leans behind the other chorus singers, wiggles his eyebrows at me, and emits a sharp-edged, nasalized imitation of American English into the microphone:

> Òyìnbó!
> White man!

One singer holds the accumulating money against his captain's forehead, while another periodically gathers it in a clump and drops it into a beer carton in the middle of the band. Toye sings a solo call:

> Ìwọ àlájì mi-o
> You, my Alhaji

and, in three-part harmony resounding with electronic reverb, his chorus responds:

> Àlájì mi ọmọ dára o lẹ́wà
> Àṣìkò yíò wu o lè jẹ́, Ọba òkè k'ó fun lá dùn sọ́rọ̀-e
> My Alhaji, good child, you are beautiful
> It might be anytime now that the King will put sweetness in
> your affairs [your reputation, your story].

One of the chorus singers murmurs "Haj!" (Alhaji) into the microphone, and Samuel drums (see also fig. 6.9):

Figure 6.9. Talking drum phrase

> *Ọlọ́run Ọba kìí bínú*
> The Lord God does not get annoyed

Samuel repeats this phrase every four bars, making it into a dance rhythm, a message pulsing subliminally beneath Toye's continued praise singing:

> *Mólèyájọ́, gbajúmọ̀n mi àtàtà, ọkọ àlájà-o, Iyábòdé*
> *Mègídá lojẹ gbajúmọ̀n àyọ̀nfẹ́ lojẹ, adúdúyemí-o tiwa ni*
> Moleyajọ, my popular, important person, husband of Alhaja
> Iyabode
> [Hausa term of respect], you are popular, you are beloved, black
> and beautiful, oh, our own.

Toye pauses, allowing the supporting guitar and drum parts to be heard, and then continues:

> *Ẹ̀sò pẹ̀lẹ́ ọmọ olóyè Mólèyájọ́*
> *To bá mí lọ kírun pè mí dá ní-o*
> *To bá mí lọ kírun pè mí dá ní-o*
> *Afínjú ìmàle tó ńjẹ àlájì nle*
> Gently, son of a chief, Moleyajọ
> If you are going to the mosque call me along
> If you are going to the mosque call me along
> Fastidious Muslim who bears the title Alhaji

As he reaches the end of this ascending melodic phrase, Uncle Toye's voice cracks, and he is forced to play the last word, *nle,* on his guitar. Samuel responds in a split second, drumming the sarcastic observation (see also fig. 6.10):

> *Óò tó bẹ̀ẹ̀!*
> It isn't finished like that!!

The band boys laugh, and Toye turns slightly, fixing the guitarists—though not the talking drummer—with a baleful stare. Moleyajọ has finished past-

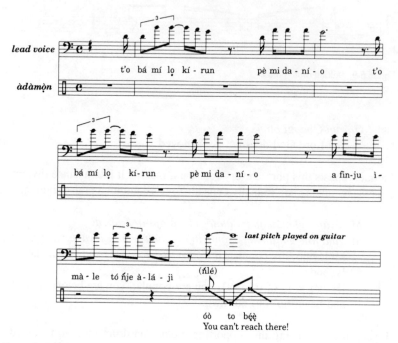

Figure 6.10. Interaction of captain and àdàmọ̀n

ing Naira notes to Toye's forehead, and moved back into the crowd of dancers. The chorus repeats the previous praise sequence:

> *To bá mí lọ kírun pè mí dá ní-o*
> *To bá mí lọ kírun pè mí dá ní-o*
> *To bá mí lọ kírun pè mí dá ní-o*
> *Afínjú ìmàle tó ńjẹ àlájì nle*
> *To bá mí lọ kírun pè mí dá ní-o*
>> If you are going to the mosque call me along
>> If you are going to the mosque call me along
>> If you are going to the mosque call me along
>> Fastidious Muslim who bears the title Alhaji
>> If you are going to the mosque call me along

Samuel tries to drum a proverb, but aborts it abruptly when he collides with the singers. Uncle Toye plays his signature riff to signal the beginning of a guitar solo, supported by an interlocking ostinato pattern in the talking drums and bass guitar. Alao's solo lasts about half a minute before it is cut off with another signal from Toye's guitar. Nine minutes into the performance, he continues his praises, in hopes of inducing the host to come back and continue spraying:

> *'ájì mi-o, Mólèyájǫ́, gbajúmǫ̀n mi àtàtà, bàbá ni bàbá ṣe*
> My Alhaji, Moleyajo, popular, important person, father is father
> [i.e., has seniority]

Samuel drums the pattern:

> *Dúdúwǫnúǫlá, fi wǫn s'ílè̩, máa wòye*
> Honorable black man, leave them [your enemies] be, be careful!

Uncle Toye tries two more lines in honor of Moleyajǫ:

> *Ọkọ Iyábòdé àtàtà ǫlǫ́lá*
> *Mi ò lè gbàgbé gbajúmǫ̀n mi àtàtà*
> Husband of Iyabode, important and respected
> I can't forget my popular and important person

and then redirects his attention to Adebayǫ, a portly man in a gold brocade gown and Alhaji's cap:

> *Àlájì mi-o Adébáyǫ̀ rere, Adébáyǫ̀ mi àtàtà*
> My good Alhaji Adebayǫ, my important Adebayǫ

Samuel attempts to drum another speech pattern, but drops out when he once again collides with the singers. He waits, and then completes the pattern, repeating it as the core of a new dance rhythm:

> *Fún'ra mi, mo ńtijú fún*
> I myself, I am only respecting myself

Toye continues to call Adebayǫ:

> *Adébáyǫ̀ mi áyǫ̀nfę́, Adébáyǫ̀*
> Adebayǫ my dear, Adebayǫ

and his chorus responds:

> *Adébáyǫ̀*

As this leader-chorus exchange is repeated, Samuel attempts to drum another proverb, but cannot finish it before the singers enter. The chorus continues:

> Olówó no bàbá ẹ, ọlọ́lá ni mama ẹ
> Olówó ni bàbá ẹ, ọlọ́lá ni mama ẹ, Adébáyọ̀
>> Your father has money, your mother is respected
>> Your father has money, your mother is respected, Adebayọ

As Samuel drums a salute to a friend in the crowd:

> Adéwalé, ọkún
>> Hi, Adewale!

and Toye continues to shower Adebayọ with praise:

> Adébáyọ̀ mi àtàtà, Adébáyọ̀ mi áyọ̀nfẹ́
> Ọmọ olóyè àtàtà, gbajúmọ̀n mi-o Adébáyọ̀ rere
>> My important Adebayọ, my dear Adebayọ
>> Son of a chief, my popular, good Adebayọ

Samuel tries to interject a speech phrase:

> B' enìyàn sọrọ fun mi . . .

and is again interrupted by the singers. They sing Adebayọ's name twice
more, and the tenacious Samuel is finally able to drum the full slogan:

> B' enìyàn sọrọ fun mi, máa ṣe wèrè fún
>> If someone talks (nonsense) to me, I will give him madness!

The chorus repeats the entire sequence and Toye uses his guitar to signal
for another lead guitar solo, supported by bass guitar and talking drums.
Samuel turns to the lead guitarist, Alao, and beats:

> Alàó ṣe'nu gbàndù!
>> Alao, big-mouth!

Alao sucks his teeth in Samuel's direction. Once again, Toye uses his signature motif to signal a shift back to praise singing:

> Adébáyọ̀ mi àyọ̀nfé, ájì betilayi àlájì humura
> Adúdúyemí mo bá r' òde àtàtà, ẹ fọ́jú olú Ojó tiwa ni

Adebayọ, my dear, Alhaji betilayi, Alhaji humura
Black and beautiful, I follow you to the festivity, take care of
Chief Ojo, our own

Samuel drums:

Ìwọ lo m'ọrọ toò b'Ọlọrun sọ, ṣáà máa kirun
It's you that knows the matter you discuss with God, shall we
pray?

as Toye continues his praises:

Adébáyọ̀ mi-o, adúdúyemí àtàtà
Ọmọ olóyè to ṣ'ọmọ jẹ́jẹ́, Adébáyọ̀
My Adebayọ, black and beautiful, important
Son of a chief, gentle/cool child, Adebayọ

and the chorus answers once again:

Adébáyọ̀

Samuel drums a slogan appropriate for well-mixed gatherings:

Mẹ́ta mẹ́ta mẹ́ta àbùlà
Three, three, three is a fluid mixture [i.e., true comradery
within a group cannot be sundered]

and Toye and the chorus repeat a previous sequence:

Adébáyọ̀, Adébáyọ̀
Olówó ni bàbá ẹ, ọlọ́lá ni mama ẹ
Olówó ni bàbá ẹ, ọlọ́lá ni mama ẹ, Adébáyọ̀
Your father has money, your mother is respected
Your father has money, your mother is respected, Adebayọ

Uncle Toye sings:

Mègídá lojẹ ọmọ olóyè Adébáyọ̀ re
Àyọ̀nfẹ́ 'débàyò mi-o
You are a well-to-do person, you chief's son, Adebayọ
My beloved 'debayọ

and then launches into an extended call-and-response segment based on the phrase "My beloved Adebayọ." The guitars suddenly drop out, and the drummers become more prominent. The junior talking drummer plays an ostinato based on the phrase:

K'ó wọsí wá yanrìn, k'ó wọsí wá yanrìn, k'ó wọsí wá yanrìn
   Bury it (your money) in the sand, bury it in the sand, bury it in
   the sand

as a supporting rhythm, while the lead drummer improvises non-textual cross-rhythms, occasionally shifting into speech mode to play the phrase:

Bẹ́ẹ kí mi, bẹ́ẹ̀ kí mi, àgúngúnlá yín
   If you greet me, if you don't greet me, that is your problem.

As Adebayọ moves forward to spray the band, the leader-chorus, call-and-response sequence continues, with Toye varying his pattern slightly each time:

LEADER
   Àyọ̀nfẹ́ 'débàyọ́ mi-o
   CHORUS
      Àyọ̀nfẹ́ 'débàyọ̀ mi-o
   Àyọ̀nfẹ́ 'débàyọ̀ mi-o
      Àyọ̀nfẹ́ 'débàyọ̀ mi-o
   'débàyọ̀ mi àyọ̀nfẹ́
      Àyọ̀nfẹ́ 'débàyọ̀ mi-o
   Adébàyọ̀ mi àtàtà
      Àyọ̀nfẹ́ 'débàyọ̀ mi-o
   Àyọ̀nfẹ́ 'débàyọ̀ mi-o
      Àyọ̀nfẹ́ 'débàyọ̀ mi-o
   'débàyọ̀ mi-o
      Àyọ̀nfẹ́ 'débàyọ̀ mi-o
   'débàyọ̀ mi-o
      Àyọ̀nfẹ́ 'débàyọ̀ mi-o
   Àyọ̀nfẹ́ 'débàyọ̀ mi-o
      Àyọ̀nfẹ́ 'débàyọ̀ mi-o
   Alájì betilayi
      Àyọ̀nfẹ́ 'débàyọ̀ mi-o
   Àlájì humura
      Àyọ̀nfẹ́ 'débàyọ̀ mi-o
   Ọmọ olóyè to gbáfẹ́ [Stylish son of a chief]
      Àyọ̀nfẹ́ 'débàyọ̀ mi-o

Àyọ̀nfẹ́ 'débàyọ̀ mi-o
Àyọ̀nfẹ́ 'débàyọ̀ mi-o
'débàyọ̀ mi-o
Àyọ̀nfẹ́ 'débàyọ̀ mi-o

Uncle Toye plays his signal motif, the guitars enter, and the band settles back down into the cool accompaniment appropriate for solo praise singing. Toye shifts his attention to Sannia, a paternal relative of the deceased who has driven the 400 kilometers from Lagos to Ogbomọṣọ in his *ọbọ̀kún* [slang for Mercedes Benz; originally an expensive kind of fish].

Sannia mo bá rò de o ọlọ́lá
Sanni arẹwà, ọmọ olóyè tiwa ni
Àláji mi o Sanni, gbajúmọ̀n mi-o Sanni
Sanni yé gbajúmọ̀n mi àtàtà
Sanni yé gbajúmọ̀n mi àyọ̀nfẹ́
Sanni gbajúmọ̀n de gboro Èkó
Sanni gbajúmọ̀n de gboro Èkó
Àyọ̀nfẹ́ l' o jẹ́ gbajúmọ̀n mi àtàtà
 Sannia, I follow you out, respected person
 Beautiful Sanni, son of a chief, our own
 My Alaji, Sanni, my well-known person, Sanni
 Sanni, please, my well-known, important person
 Sanni, please, my well-known, beloved person
 Sanni, well-known person from Lagos town
 Beloved one that is well-known, important

Samuel attempts to insert the proverb:

Ẹ w' ọmọ ẹ̀gbọ́n, ẹ w' ọmọ abúrò
Kẹ́ lẹ́ bí ó, pẹ bí ẹ̀ mọ́-o
 Look at the senior child, look at the junior child
 Everybody should take care of their parents

but is interrupted after the first half of the phrase by Toye's voice. Toye continues to praise Sannia:

Sanni t' ó gbajúmọ̀n mi ẹni ni re
Sanni arẹwà
 Sanni, who is my well-known, good person
 Beautiful Sanni

as the celebrant briefly stops spraying Uncle Toye and dramatically tosses
the sleeves of his lace gown, stamped with Mercedes Benz logos, up over
his shoulders. This movement, popularly called "one-thousand [right arm],
five hundred [left arm]," refers to the price of the cloth. One of the chorus
vocalists shouts:

> Ọmọ Èkó!
>> Child of Lagos!

and Samuel drums the pattern:

> Ẹmá mì lẹ̀gbẹ̀ bí t'Èkó
>> Shake majestically, like a Lagosian!!

followed by a delighted squeal from a female celebrant. Toye sings the solo
phrase:

> Sanni yé gbajúmọ̀n mi àtàtà, oní ilé ọlá
>> Sanni, please, well-known and important, owns the house of
>> honor

and, after some delicate embellishments by the double toy drummer, is
joined by one of the chorus singers in parallel thirds:

> Àràbà ṣá ni bàbá, ẹni abá lábà ni bàbá
>> Only the silk-cotton tree is the father; the one you meet in front
>> of the farm hut is the father.

Samuel, the lead talking drummer, signals a change in the dance rhythm,
and Toye shifts his attention to another wealthy Alhaji, Adeyẹmi

> Awo àlájì-o
> Adéyẹmí mi àtàtà
> Awo àlájì Adéyẹmí
>> Close friend [fellow cult-member] Alaji-o
>> Adeyẹmi, my important person
>> Close friend Alaji Adeyẹmi

A chorus singer interjects a spoken evaluation of the music:

> O pójù!
>> It's too much!

and Toye continues to praise Adeyẹmi:

> *Adéyẹmí mo bá rò de o ọlọlá*
> *Adé ò gbodò tán n' ílé aládé*
>> Adeyẹmi, I follow you out, honorable person
>> The crown must not finish in the house of the king [may your lineage continue]

Samuel begins to drum:

> *Arìnrìn gbẹ̀rẹ̀ níò móyè délé*
> *Aṣíré tete oní móyè jẹ*
>> The person who walks majestically will be made a chief
>> A hustler will not be made a chief

but once again runs into the singers, and is able to play only the first half of the pattern. Toye signals the band to begin another call-and-response section—based on the refrain "Adeyẹmi, child of a king"—as the guitars drop out, the drumming becomes hotter, and Samuel improvises cross rhythms and inserts the proverb:

> *Iyẹmọja yé, Iyẹmọja gbà, Iyẹmọja gb' àlùbọ́sà k' o fi ròfọ́, Iyẹmọja yé*
>> Goddess of rivers, please, goddess of rivers receive, goddess of rivers take onions to mix with vegetables [make life palatable], goddess of rivers, please.

He then finishes off an incomplete proverb from several minutes earlier in the performance:

> *K' ẹ́ lẹ́ bí ó, pẹ bí ẹ̀ mọ́-o*
>> Everyone should take care of their parents.

praises the host's city of residence:

> *Ìbàdàn lo mọ̀, oò mọ̀ Laípo*
>> It is Ibadan you know, you don't know Laipo [the city's inner character]

and salutes Ògún, the tempermental *òrìṣà* of war, hunters, iron, band vehicles, and "engines" (amplifiers):

Ògún korobítí korobítí, Ògún korobìtì korobìtì
Ogun rolls this way, Ogun rolls that way

As the tape ends, the Olumọ Soundmakers continue to roll the àríyá, singing and drumming Adeyẹmi's praises—"Alhaji," "manager," "son of a
king," "my important person," "our very own," "shining black and beautiful"—rhetorically triangulating his position in society, "swelling his head,"
and setting off a torrential shower of Naira.

7

Jùjú Music and Inequality in
Modern Yoruba Society

In this chapter I offer some conclusions concerning the social organization of jùjú music and the role of music in modern Yoruba society. I am aware that specialization may encourage a loss of proportion; that the ethnomusicologist, eager to demonstrate the importance of music in human life, may easily claim too much for it. "Everything that is socially significant and institutionally real . . . is not necessarily represented in musical order, occasions, or resources" (Feld 1984:405). Nonetheless, my field experience and understanding of the literature incline me to the conviction that the relationship between Yoruba musical and social order is not trivial.

I begin by suggesting that music plays an important role in establishing the emotional texture of an àríyá. Musical sound conditions temporal experience and establishes a normative context for ritualized social interaction. Second, I suggest that jùjú performance may usefully be regarded—and is in fact regarded by many urban Yoruba—as a mode of transaction, a means of exchanging valued resources and negotiating status. And finally, it seems to me that the most important link between jùjú performance practice and the distribution of power in Yoruba society is the role of music as a metaphor of social order. Jùjú performance evokes a coherent multisensory image of a communal society, thoroughly cosmopolitan, yet firmly rooted in ìjinlẹ̀ ("deep") Yorùbá values and sentiments. Suspended in and energized by a complex skein of localized patronage networks, jùjú portrays a traditional hierarchy mitigated by the generosity of the wealthy. This persuasive idealized image has helped to reproduce an ideology of cultural cohesion and universal opportunity, and thus, I would argue, to obfuscate ongoing processes of social stratification in post–Oil Boom Nigeria.

Jùjú Music as Context

"Context" is perhaps the most abused term in the ethnomusicological lexicon. In many instances it has been deployed as an prefatory incantation, a means of briefly invoking and effectively circumventing detailed cultural and social analysis. In other cases, a context is any and all factors that may be shown to impinge directly upon the production of musical sound. I would suggest that neither of these perspectives can provide a sufficient understanding of the influence of music and musicality on human social life in general. A conceptual reversal of foregrounded "object" and backgrounded "context" suggests a complementary approach: the study not only of music in context, but of music as a context for human perception and action.

Jùjú music, with voices, guitars, and talking drum amplified at high decibel levels, creates a densely textured soundscape which conditions the behavior of participants in Yoruba neo-traditional life cycle celebrations. Music—or, to be more specific, music properly performed—metacommunicatively frames and legitimates ritualized interactions among participants, and plays an indispensable role in establishing the affective valence of a successful àríyá. Musical sound signals the existence of a celebration over a wide area, and focuses collective attention on the frontier between dancers and musicians, where the most important displays of individual wealth and communal affiliation take place. Without good music and the feelings it engenders—"sweet stomachs," "unfolded bodies," and "swelled heads"—the expected range of symbolic and economic transactions between participants cannot take place.

An àríyá—a loosely structured secular ritual—depends upon the forging of perceptual coherences across multiple sensory modes.

> The participants in a ritual [share] communicative experiences through many different sensory channels simultaneously. . . . Verbal, musical, choreographic, and visual-aesthetic 'dimensions' are all likely to form components of the total message. When we take part in such a ritual we pick up all these messages at the same time and condense them into a single experience (Leach 1976:41).

The sensation of bodily movement, of musical sound, the smell of food and the taste of drink, the pleasures of animated interaction with kin and friends, of word-play and intoxication, collectively define an ethos that sensuously textures and publicly validates the host's social universe.

Perhaps the most important aspect of jùjú performance as a context for social activity is the ability of competent musicians to establish a special flow of lived time. Although the literature on sub–Saharan African music is replete with hypotheses concerning rhythm, only a few scholars have addressed the relationship of musical experience to broader concepts of social or ecological time (Merriam 1982; Stone 1985). Blacking (1973:26–27) suggests that "ordinary daily experience takes place in a world of actual time. The essential quality of music is its power to create another world of virtual time."

Celebrants' experience of time at an all-night àríyá is shaped by music. The establishment of coherence between musical and social time involves a "mutual tuning-in process" (Schutz 1977) on the part of participants. Cooperative involvement in the flow of musical performance, most clearly evinced in dance movements, is focused simultaneously on at least two levels of rhythmic structure: a regular duple pulse, enacted in the side-to-side rocking movements of dancers; and cross-rhythms, reflected in the polymetric opposition of body parts.

The analytical notion of *metronome sense* (R. Waterman 1952)—a subjective framework of regular pulses which forms the basis for interpretation and performance of polymetric music—provides a psychomotor basis for the entrainment (McGrath and Kelly 1986; Hall 1984) of Yoruba musical and social time. The metronome sense hypothesis asserts that temporal experience is strongly conditioned by internalized structures of expectation, and that musical perception is not a passive reception of aural information, but an active search for order shaped by the skill and experience of the perceiver. The metronome sense may be regarded as an anticipatory schemata, a specialized cognitive structure that guides the processing of aural information in musical contexts. "Perception is where cognition and reality meet"; it is "an activity in which both the immediate past and the remote past are brought to bear upon the present" (Neisser 1976:9,14).

Yoruba popular dance music relies upon a kind of temporal "stretching" in which interlocking parts purposefully do not articulate a precise duple or triple division of the pulse. This effect rests upon the same psychological principles as the metronome sense hypothesis, but at a level of temporal discrimination finer than the fastest regular pulse or "density referent." In much Yoruba social dance music, interlocked patterns pull slightly apart in time, maintaining a slight but perceptible tension. My experience performing with jùjú bands suggests that it is these tiny discrepancies (Keil 1986) that propel Yoruba dance music: if strokes consistently fall too far apart from or too precisely on top of a subdivision of the ground pulse, the rhythms lose vitality, celebrants get bored, and the spraying dwindles. The power of supporting musicians stems in part from their skilled control over the temporal elasticities that make rhythms "roll" (yí).

Social organization is interaction ordered through time. At an àríyá, jùjú music establishes an external framework (*zeitgeber;* see McGrath and Kelly 1986:84) for the synchronization of social activity, meshing the interaction rhythms of individuals, and generating a vivid simulacrum of intersubjectivity. The special world of time and sentiment generated in musical performance is regarded as an ideal environment for the public presentation and negotiation of identity. The terms used by jùjú musicians to describe musical intensity and flow—for example, *milíkì* ("rocking"), *fẹ́lẹ́lẹ́* ("fluttering"), *kó má rotéètì, kó má sakuléètì* ("let it rotate, let it circulate"), *synchromatic,* and "kick and start music"—adumbrate a keen appreciation of the power of music to create distinctive domains of experiential time. Numerous informants asserted that a bad performance—one which did not inspire them to dance or spray—could make a celebration seem interminable (*gbọnmọn-gbọnmọn*). In the West, time "flies" when you're having fun; in Yorubaland, powerful music and good times "roll."[1] I would argue that àríyá time, at its most highly ordered, is musical time.

Jùjú Performance as Transaction

> The relationship between musical style and social structure . . . is not just an abstract tautology, with the organization of the symbolic system mirroring the social system for no more direct reason than a general similarity of cognitive pattern. Rather, certain aspects of both the musical system and the social system are related to a set of interactional opportunities and expectations that underlie them (Irvine and Sapir 1976:81).

Another approach to the relationship of musical and social order is suggested by anthropological transaction theory. In the paper "Models of Social Organisation," Fredrik Barth explored the extent to which "patterns of social form can be explained if we assume that they are the cumulative result of a number of separate choices and decisions made by people acting vis-à-vis one another" (1966:2). Barth suggested that individuals engage in a kind of bargaining to establish which of their statuses are to form the basis for interaction. It is through this process that consistency is forged between the standards of evaluation internalized by members of a society. Consensus may be maintained through impression management (Goffman 1959), the skewing of communication about relationships, "*over*-communicating that which confirms the relevant status positions and relationships, and *under*-communicating that which is discrepant" (Barth 1966:3). Although Barth's paper has been criticized for underemphasizing differences in power that constrain the individual's range of strategic choices (e.g., Asad 1972, Paine 1974, A. Cohen 1974), his notion of transaction suggests interesting insights into the role of musical performance at the Yoruba àríyá.

Jùjú performance is a specialized mode of transaction (Wachsmann 1980:148–49) focused on the distribution of economic resources, the negotiation of status, and the management of meaning (Kapferer 1976). Celebrants attempt to accumulate symbolic capital through the public transaction of cash for portrayals of their position in society. By responding to the praise singing and musical skill of jùjú practitioners with an impressive shower of bank notes, a celebrant publicly displays the wealth and personal qualities essential for status advancement. The jùjú band captain, for his part, seeks to accumulate resources such as musical equipment, band vehicles, a private car, a house, and a large family. Many band captains privately aver that they want to leave the low-status and insecure occupation of music making in order to establish themselves as entrepreneurs. The band captain who sings the praises of the elites not only consolidates cash for conversion into symbolic capital, but also has the opportunity to rub shoulders with them, meeting prospective patrons and gathering information about business opportunities.

In Yoruba tradition, sound is an important mode of social and supernatural communication. Powerful speech—the words that placate gods and drive kings to suicide—is made more potent by the patterning of timbre, texture, pitch, and rhythm. Although the commodification of mass-reproduced musical "units" is advanced in contemporary Nigeria, live music remains a privileged mode of symbolic and economic transaction. At the modern àríyá, jùjú performance not only frames and normatively sanctions but is itself a medium of status negotiation and redistribution (cf. Whitten 1970).

I should emphasize, however, that not everyone has equal opportunity to spray musicians and participants during the early, more rigidly structured segments of an àríyá. "Not only are there inequalities within individual exchanges, there are also inequalities of opportunity to make exchanges, and in both cases the power that manifests itself in these inequalities is closely connected with control over communication as a political resource" (Kapferer 1974:80). These constraints underlie one jùjú musician's response to a question about the correlation of musicians' and patrons' status.

> After a day's job, everybody will like to relax different kinds of way. You see, some people would have loved to be at A's band, but they will feel an inferiority complex, one kind of way. I mean, they believe A's status—they are not judging the music, but A personally—is bigger than them. Somebody that will give B one naira will say, "Look! How can I give B just one naira?" So that is why you will have the

younger folks. If B shoots to the limelight now, he will have the bigger ones patronizing him. . . . If a young man should go to A's band, he wouldn't have the chance to dance as he would have loved to dance to B's music. If he has paid B five naira now, he will be happy to dance. But, in A's place, he might want to dance, but when he sees people going there to spray their money, he will feel ashamed. So he will be forced to sit down (C. Waterman 1982:63).

Jùjú Style as a Metaphor of Social Order

Quartets, still lifes, and cockfights are not merely reflections of a pre-existing sensibility analogically represented; they are positive agents in the creation and maintenance of such a sensibility (Geertz 1973a:451).

Music . . . is not just socially structured; the social order is, in part, musically structured since musical activity comprises one important public domain in which a worldview is made patent in a multileveled and powerful form (Turino 1989:29).

Music is fundamentally nondiscursive (Langer 1957:88; Blacking 1969: 38–39), embodying relationships and qualities as aural patterns and textures, rather than denotatively representing them. Metaphor, which establishes synesthesiac correspondences across distinct realms of sensory experience, is an important basis for musical communication. Put simply, it allows us to know one thing in terms of another. Metaphor also plays a fundamental role in the formulation of human identity (Fernandez 1974) and the enactment of cultural values (Turner 1974; Sapir and Crocker 1977; Lakoff and Johnson 1980).

Metaphor operates in jùjú performance at a number of analytically distinct levels, verbal and nonverbal. The rhetorical deployment of metaphors in song and surrogate speech texts—for example, "Adeyẹmi is a silk-cotton tree," "Babatunde is a mighty rock on a mountain," or "Akintọla owns ọbọ̀kún (an expensive kind of fish, a Mercedes Benz)—is perhaps most obvious. But as Lakoff and Johnson note:

Metaphor is not merely a matter of language. It is a matter of conceptual structure. And conceptual structure is not merely a matter of the intellect—it involves all the natural dimensions of our experience, including aspects of our sense experiences: color, shape, texture, sound, etc. (1980:235).

Hierarchy is vividly represented by the superiority of wealthy celebrants vis-à-vis the praise-singer, and of the latter vis-à-vis his "boys." According to one jùjú band captain, a well-organized band cannot have two leaders: "How can two men drive one *mọtọ* [automobile]? Once you are *bàbá* (father), no one go be *bàbá* to you again, oh!". The social distinction between captain and band boys, leader and chorus, individual call and communal response, is visually encoded in clothing and spatial relationships. Unlike the band setups of the 1950s and 1960s, where band boys clustered around their captain in a protective pocket, most contemporary band leaders stand in front of or are flanked by their subordinates. Band captains performing at important social occasions distinguish themselves sartorially from subordinate musicians. In one successful band, the captain sometimes wears a Western tuxedo, while his boys are clothed in matching traditional Yoruba outfits (*agbádá*) (see color plate 2). In another, the leader wears expensive lace against a background of dull brown safari suits (see color plate 1). These images reflect precolonial models of social order, as conventionally represented in wood sculpture (Thompson 1971, 1974).

Hierarchical values are also embodied in the aural structure of jùjú music. The larger bands in Ibadan, based on the Sunny Ade and Ebenezer Obey paradigms (see chapter 5), are comprised of three semiautonomous units. The guitar section includes a lead or solo player (generally not the band captain) supported by interlocking tenor guitars, Hawaiian guitar, and bass guitar. The senior talking drummer improvises on a rhythmic base created by the cumulative interaction of supporting drums. The praise singer is flanked and supported by his chorus. Thus, the fundamental relationship between *elé* (lead part, call, "that which drives ahead of or into something") and *ègbè* (subordinate part, choral response, "supporters" or "protectors") is reproduced in each section of the band. The aural gestalt generated by the intersection of these micro-hierarchies metaphorically predicates an idealized social order: a congeries of localized networks focused on big men.

> In the traditional Yoruba town, the achieved statuses of wealth or power were gained by those who substantially upheld the norms of the society—the trader relying on his popularity with his customers, the chief on the support of the members of his descent group (his constituents). Each stood at the apex of a pyramidal network of social relationships. Interaction between the chiefs and the wealthy did not extend much beyond formal meetings. They formed a category; they were scarcely a status group and certainly not a social class. It is, incidentally, a very similar image of a classless society that contemporary Yoruba politicians . . . are endeavoring to propogate (Lloyd 1973:117.

A countervailing ethic of mutual responsibility and equal opportunity is also enacted in jùjú music. In Yoruba instrumental music each part defines, as it is defined by, the others. The whole is always contingent, dependent upon the principled interaction of the parts.

> A drum in an African ensemble derives its power and becomes meaningful not only as it cuts and focuses the other drums *but also as it is cut and called into focus by them*. Rhythmic dialogues are reciprocal, and in a way that might seem paradoxical to a Westerner, a good drummer restrains himself from emphasizing his rhythm *in order that he may be heard better* . . . . [A] rhythm is interesting in terms of its potential to be affected by other rhythms (Chernoff 1979:59–60).

In Yoruba thought, power (*agbára*) is also a gestalt process generated through relationships. A person becomes powerful only if he or she can maintain a broad network of willing supporters. In precolonial communities "seniority conveyed authority and access to the productive services of others but was also dependent on them" (Berry 1985:8). Jùjú performances at modern celebrations where the wealthy boost their reputations, the struggling entrepreneur seeks elite status, and the poor are afforded free food, drink, and entertainment, externalize these values and lend them visceral impact.

In should be noted that the metaphoric forging of correspondences between musical and social order is not limited to structural analogies. The tendency in Western analytical thought to divorce form from content finds its counterpart in musicological approaches which presume a radical distinction between abstracted musical "structures" (forms, scales, melodic and rhythmic modes) and expressive "qualities" (timbre, texture, rhythmic flow). This is not a meaningful distinction for Yoruba musicians and listeners. The experiential impact of the metaphor "good music is the ideal society writ small" depends upon the generation of sensuous textures. An effective performance of jùjú predicates not only the structure of the ideal society, but also its "feel": intense, vibrant, loud, buzzing, and fluid.

I have argued that jùjú music evokes and affectively grounds Yoruba ideals of social intercourse. The balancing of multiple rhythms and generation of layered backgrounds from interlocked patterns are "a communal examination of percussive individuality" (Thompson 1966:91). Call-and-response singing between band captain and band boys is both cooperative behavior and aesthetic structure, forging coherences across multiple levels of musical and social organization (Blacking 1971:104). *Jùjú* performance does not merely represent society; good jùjú *is* good social order.

"The larger, the more general, abstract and distant in experience the object of our interest, the greater the utility of the metaphor" (Nisbet 1969:240). I suggested in the opening chapter of this book that the notion of a Yoruba people united by a shared autochthonous culture is in certain important regards a modern (that is, a nineteenth and twentieth century) development. Hegemonic values disseminated via print, electronic media, and popular culture portray the Yoruba as a community, a deep, horizontal comradeship united by language, custom, political interests, and ethos. In his book *Imagined Communities,* Benedict Anderson asserts that "all communities larger than primordial villages of face-to-face contact (and perhaps even these) are imagined. Communities are to be distinguished, not by their falsity/genuineness, but by the style in which they are imagined" (Anderson 1983:15). Musical metaphor plays a role in the imaginative modeling of Yoruba society as a hierarchy anchored in communal values, a hand (ọwọ́) comprised of interdependent but inherently unequal fingers. Jùjú style portrays a imagined community of some twenty million people—a sodality that no one individual could know through first-hand experience—and embodies the ideal affective texture of social life and the melding of new and old, exotic and indigenous, within a unifying syncretic framework.

Popular Music and Inequality in Modern Yoruba Society

On the whole, symbolic formations and patterns of action tend to persist longer than power relationships in changing socio-cultural systems (A. Cohen 1974:36).

Musical symbolism may be largely arbitrary but it is not neutral; various interests are served, energies flow in certain directions and not others (Keil 1984:446).

Ethnomusicologists have produced numerous ethnographic accounts of the relationship of music to worldview, values, and social organization.[2] The diverse local perspectives inscribed in these texts provide abundant evidence that music may play an important part in the maintenance of tradition under conditions of social and economic change. But few ethnomusicologists have as yet accepted the challenge articulated by Marcus and Fischer: that is, "how to represent the embedding of richly described local cultural worlds in larger impersonal systems of political economy" (1986:77). This dilemma suggests a repositioning of the insights of acculturation theory within a framework concerned with global networks, the creation of nation-states and peoples, and the invention of tradition.

Until World War II, the Nigerian elite was dominated by a small group of literate men, mostly descendants of the nineteenth century black repatriate elite (chapter 3). The postwar expansion of primary education, a massive intake of Nigerians into the colonial civil service, and the emergence of a new generation of professional politicians led to the formation of a broad-based traditionalist Yoruba elite during the 1950s and 1960s (chapter 4). During the 1970s, the Nigerian economy underwent a rapid shift from agricultural export production to reliance upon petroleum as a sole major source of capital accumulation. By the time of my research, the Nigerian political economy was "an inverted pyramid, teetering precariously on a hydrocarbon pinnacle" (Young 1982:219).

Nigeria is a rentier state, in which revenues derive from taxes or rents on production, rather than from productive activity. "Practically all aspects of exploration, production and marketing are dominated by international capital, typically in the form of the transnational corporation" (Graf 1988:219). Rentier economies are highly vulnerable to fluctuations in global markets and breakdowns in technology. This generalization applies to the Nigerian music industry, which is heavily dependent upon external materials and technological expertise. Change in the international demand for Nigerian crude oil sends ripples throughout the informal economy, directly impacting the social and material conditions of urban musical practice.

Terisa Turner (1985) has suggested that "government by contract" is the essential characteristic of the Nigerian economy. The Nigerian elite is enmeshed in and sustained by a commercial triangle which includes foreign partners (the major beneficiaries), local middlemen, and state officials, who receive a commission on behalf of the state. This system requires "a huge army of middlemen, commission-takers, import-export agents, facilitators and contact men. This group links international suppliers or lenders with the state. In the period to 1980 many projects intended to increase production in Nigeria were started but because they were controlled by the private-public comprador alliance, these products were ill-organized, except to achieve the sponsors' real objective of primitive accumulation" (T. Turner 1985:23).

The Nigerian elite, subdivided by particularistic economic interests and ethnicity, has not coalesced into a broad-based, self-aware "class for itself."

> As a sectionalised, segmented, tribalised and therefore divided class, it possesses no historical *raison d'etre* capable of mobilising the popular classes for social goals. Because it is particularised and self-centred, it is incapable even of creating a broad, universally accessible infrastructure to underpin its continued domination. . . . The Nigerian state class in a sense fashions its 'private' infrastructure, endowing itself with expensive cars and private jets, with individual generators and water tanks, with fenced compounds and private armies—all paid for with surpluses realised at the expense of society as a whole (Graf 1988:233).

The literature on Nigerian perceptions of social inequality suggests a "conspicuous absence of class terminology among even the English-speaking Nigerians and the virtual absence of an ideology proposing a radical restructuring of society in a more egalitarian form" (Lloyd 1974:3–4). Peter Waterman, who interviewed stevedores working for the Nigerian Port Authority in Lagos, wrote that:

> It is striking to observe that the NPA workers literally cannot identify any enemies to themselves. They do not think of any social category in such terms. Said one, "I cannot say we have enemies. There is inability to reason along with modern demands. But we do not have *visible* enemies as such". Given their resentments, the extent to which they accept a view of society as existing of one community is remarkable (P. Waterman 1976:50).

The lack of class identity has also been noted among urban elites: "Even though there is a growing consciousness among members of the Nigerian national bourgeoisie that in the final analysis they have common interests to defend against the masses of their people, this class consciousness is still in an embryonic stage and is far from being fully formed" (Oṣọba 1978:71).

Modes of analysis that presume the historical inevitability of class conflict have had to explain the lack of class consciousness among Nigerian workers and elites.

> [The Nigerian bourgeoisie's] tribalism is the outcome of its lack of control of the productive resources of the economy and hence of the competition among the bourgeoisie for favored access to scarce resources, and the need to manipulate particularistic interests and sentiments among the poor to maintain the bourgeoisie's political domination (G. Williams 1976:34).

Watts and Lubeck, writing after the Oil Boom, asserted that "the differentiating effects of rapid economic growth and the experience of exclusion from the purported benefits of the petroleum boom have not only created a profound cleavage between the 'haves' and the 'have nots' but [also] create an objective set of inequality experiences that possess the potential to launch a popular political movement in the future" (1983:114).

Despite the increase of oil revenues during the 1970s, the economic conditions and life-chances of the inhabitants of rural areas and urban slums declined considerably (International Labor Organization 1982). This situation has been exacerbated during the 1980s by wild fluctuations in the international demand for oil and the imposition of government "austerity measures." However, even among those groups best known for class-based action—i.e., skilled workers in the public sector, who have a history of work stoppage going back to 1897 (Hopkins 1966; Peace 1974), and independent rural smallholders located near urban distribution centers (Beer 1976; G. Williams 1976:121–31; Berry 1985)—collective action remains sporadic. Among the Yoruba urban poor, including the *táláká* (destitute, homeless, and unemployed) and the *mèkúnnùn* (common people such as poor craftsmen or petty traders) class-consciousness is tempered by the near-universal belief that every individual has a powerful kinsman or hometown mate who might be persuaded to act as a sponsor.

In a study of Yoruba perceptions of inequality, P. C. Lloyd (1974) suggested that patron-client and class strategies were guided by two conceptual models of society, the "ego-centered cognitive map" and the "externalized analytic structure":

> In using an analytical structure the individual stands outside his society—though noting his own place within it. He sees the society as an integrated whole and is concerned with the interrelationship between the constituent parts. In the cognitive map the individual is placed at the centre; surrounding him is the personal network of relationships; the map specifies the goals available to him, the routes by which he can attain them. . . . To some extent the distinction between the models . . . parallels a dichotomy between a national (or worldwide) view of society and the view of a local community (Lloyd 1974:8).

An individual's perception of the overall structure of society and his purposive action in particular contexts are not mechanically linked. The class-conscious actor may view the "haves" and "have nots" as dichotomously opposed categories. However, if he is in the latter category he may decide that the costs of actively opposing the "haves" exceed the potential rewards. He will therefore seek to advance his interests by forging patronage networks on the basis of kinship or ethnicity. "An actor is not concerned with abstract problems of whether his choice of resources reflects 'ethnicity' or 'class consciousness': he wants a combination that will work" (Eades 1980:146).

The description of modern Yoruba ceremonial behavior presented in this book suggests that what works best for many urban Yoruba are the particularistic network strategies vividly portrayed in jùjú and other forms of neo-traditional praise music. However, it should be noted that the class-oriented "externalized analytic structure" also has its counterpart in Yoruba popular music. *Afro-beat,* a branch of the dance band highlife genre, influenced by soul music and jazz, is patronized by "a cosmopolitan cross-section of Nigerian youth, sophisticated in terms of 'street sense' " (Collins and Richards 1982:122), including unemployed migrants, wage workers, and college students. Unlike jùjú, the genre is focused on one charismatic individual, Fẹla Anikulapo-Kuti.[3]

First arrested in 1974 on marijuana charges, Fẹla has a long history of confrontations with authorities, including an infamous attack by soldiers on his residence, and his imprisonment from 1984 to 1986 on currency smuggling charges. In 1979, he organized Movement of the People (M.O.P.), a political party disqualified by the Federal Electoral Commission (FEDECO) for lack of organized support. Fẹla is highly articulate about his ideological position:

> Yes, if you're in England, you sing of enjoyment. You sing of love or
> . . . who you're going to be with *next!* But my society is underdeveloped because of an alien system imposed on my people. So there's no music for enjoyment, for love, when there's such a struggle for people's existence. So, as an artist, politically, artistically, my whole idea about my environment must be represented in the music, in the arts. So art is what's happening in a particular time of people's development or underdevelopment. Music must awaken people to do their duty as citizens and act (Grass 1985:142).

The song "No Bread" (1975) focuses on the inequality of Africa and the West, ironically juxtaposing the poverty of the Lagosian night-soil carrier (*àgbépo*) and the natural wealth of Africa:

> For Africa here him to be home
> Land boku (*beaucoups*) from north to south
> Food boku from top to down
> Gold dey underground like water
> Diamond dey underground like sand
> Oil dey flow underground like river
> Everything for overseas
> Na from here him de come
> Na for here man still dey carry shit for head

In other songs, he uses traditional metaphors to portray class conflict:

> Everyday everyday, I dey hungry
> Everyday everyday, no house to stay
> Monkey dey work, baboon dey chop [eat]
> Baboon dey hold dem key of store
> Monkey dey cry, baboon dey laugh
> One day monkey eye come open now

The song "Authority Stealing" (1980) abandons indirection entirely, focusing on the corrupt bureaucracy of the Shagari government:

> Instead of workers, we have officials
> Instead of busses, dem dey ride motorcar
> Instead of motorcycles, na helicopter
> Instead of dem waka, na worker to go waka for dem
> Authority people dem go dey steal
> Public contribute plenty money
> Na him authority people dey steal
> Authority man no dey pick pocket
> Na petty cash him go dey pick
> Armed robber him need gun, Authority man him need pen
> Pen get power, gun no get
> If gun steal eighty thousand naira, pen go steal two billion naira
> We Africans must do something about this nonsense!

Fẹla's work has since the mid–1970s consistently presented a class-stratified image of Nigerian society. However, his core audience is limited. As Collins and Richards (1982:139) phrase it, "merchants and the professional elite, major patrons of jùjú music, have less use for the uncompromisingly dramatic style of urban politics pursued by the proletarian 'youth'." Afro-beat is much less popular overall than social dance and praise musics such as jùjú and fújì. Most urban Yoruba dismiss Fẹla and his ideological mix of black essentialism, male superiority, and class struggle—expressed in the urban lingua franca of pidgin English—because of his deviant public image: he *shaks* (smokes marijuana), takes advantage of young migrant women from the village, defies constituted authority, and engages in explicit abusive language (*yabis*). A typical comment is "there is truth in what he sings, but he is not responsible." These people are aware of social inequality on a grand scale, but they also feel that their destiny lies with the traditionalist patronage networks epitomized by the success stories of the ruling elites.

The popularity of jùjú across all levels of Yoruba society is related not only to continuity in musical values, but also to the preeminence of network strategies. Despite objective inequalities in wealth and access to education, most urban Yoruba, including elites, small-scale traders, craftsmen, and the mass of urban unemployed, continue to believe that status advancement results from individual effort, and that anyone may rise to prominence in society. "The fact that everyone regards upward mobility as potentially attainable not only removes emotional strain between the high and the low but reconciles them to an extent that the latter tend to become insensitive to the incipient class structure" (Imoagene 1976: 297–98).

I have argued that competent musical performance is an indispensable aspect of the successful Yoruba naming, wedding, wake, or business launching celebration (chapters 5 and 6). Jùjú music externalizes, comments upon, metaphorically grounds, and helps to reproduce the hegemonic values that guide behavior at urban secular rituals. Hierarchy is lauded and, as the "long-legged" ọlọlá extends a helping hand to the struggling mẹkúnnùn, related to ìjinlẹ̀ Yorùbá redistributive values. The àríyá demonstrates the elites' embeddedness in traditional social relationships, and asserts their Yorubaness, their openhandedness, and their belief in the ability of all individuals to overcome the hardships of life. The Yoruba elites' sponsorship of such events is "instrumental to the extent that the classless image so projected helps to becloud the nascent class structure" (Imoagene 1976:296). Put simply, jùjú performances advance the following arguments concerning the relationship of individual to culture and community: 1) "We're all Yoruba"; 2) "Our values are intact"; and 3) "Keep working". Viewed as a system of rhetoric arguing for a particular vision of society, jùjú simultaneously legitimates inequality and argues that all actors may become wealthy and powerful, a kind of African Horatio Alger ideology. In the face of widening disparities in wealth, education, and health, music plays a role in the reproduction of hegemonic values.

Appeals to "deep" Yoruba tradition are made with an eye toward present and future interests. I want to emphasize, however, that the relationship between deeply held cultural values and emergent patterns of social inequality need not be conscious to be effective. Yoruba elites, members of an internally divided economic class, are not consistently aware that àríyás sanction individual success while veiling broader patterns of class conflict. The power of jùjú performance to structure experience and forge consensus lies precisely in the fact that the metaphoric correlation of social-structural, ideological, and aural patterns takes place largely on an unexamined, commonsense level, "the expression of a complex idea, not by analysis, nor by direct statement, but by sudden perception of an objective relation" (Read 1952:23). This tendency of root metaphors to become "natural" (Becker and Becker 1981:203) is what Steven Feld is driving at when he asserts that Kaluli metaphors "are not metaphors to Kaluli, but simply what is real" (Feld 1984:406).

Claude Lévi-Strauss has suggested that metaphor "can change the world" (1963:201–2). This is by no means a straightforward proposition. The metaphoric portrayal of traditional values and social perceptions in modern Yoruba musical performance has helped to conceal a profound political and economic transformation: the consolidation of a potentially self-reproducing comprador elite with privileged access to international markets and overseas education. In this case, it appears that metaphor may help to transform the world by sustaining the illusion that it remains, in some deep and essential sense, the same.

The stylistic trajectory of jùjú music has for over fifty years been grounded in processes of urban adaptation, including the creation of economic niches, the development of new patterns of social interaction, and the negotiation of cultural identities and values. Early jùjú style, created in the 1930s by the cosmopolitan "area boys" of Lagos, and shaped by the interplay of class, ethnic, and religious identity, declined as the social and ideological patterns from which it drew significance were superceded. Modern jùjú music, complete with the electric guitar and talking drum, emerged with the postwar Yoruba elite, accompanied them on their rise to power, and is now helping them to defend and celebrate their gains.

In the end, however, I am reluctant to conclude that jùjú music is necessarily or unambiguously supportive of social inequity. Every expressive tradition discloses the gaps and contradictions that make transformation possible. In jùjú music, as in the bulk of Yoruba song and poetry, "the existence of multiple variant texts is a fundamental and inescapable feature of the mode of transmission. There is simply no possibility of establishing a single authoritative version on which all critics would agree" (Barber 1984:508). The contingent nature of jùjú performance patterns, the interpretive open-endedness of jùjú song texts, and the tenacity of values concerning the interdependence of leader and followers preserve, as they conceal, alternative "readings."

Talking drummers, the artisans closest to the wellsprings of Yoruba identity, are still feared for their ability to unmask the corrupt through surrogate speech and metaphor. Despite the progressive hardening of class boundaries, Yoruba musicians may retain the power to chasten and dethrone irresponsible leaders, and to foster among their people the sense of national and regional purpose upon which Nigeria's future in an inequitable world economic order so crucially depends.

Appendix

Roster of Ibadan-Based Jùjú and Fújì Bands

Ibadan-Based Jùjú Bands, 1981–1982

1. Micho Ade ("Sunny Ibadan") and His Jùjú Group.
2. Ade-Wesco and His Western Jùjú-Highlife Band.
3. Sule Agboola and His Jùjú Band.
4. Uncle Toye Ajagun ("Magbe-Magbe Man") and His Olumo Soundmakers.
5. Abayomi Domingo and His Oduduwa Brothers Band.
6. Chief Bode Esan and His Jùjú Group.
7. The Great Chief Mayowa Ilesanmi and His Noble Band.
8. K. K. Kolade and His Melody Makers.
9. Prince Ola Kollington and His Afro Super-Star Organization.
10. Sir Suppy Joe and His Afro Sound International.
11. Mighty E. S. Odeyemi and His Valiant Band.
12. Lamina Oguns and His African Tempos Band.
13. Captain Jide Ojo and His Yankee System Organization.
14. Captain J. K. Ojo and His Active Sports Band.
15. Jossy Ola and His Jùjú Group.
16. Jimmy Olorebi and His Salam Salam Jùjú Band.
17. Honourable Joshua Olufemi and His Morning Star Band.
18. Abiodun Omoleye and His Rainbow Stars International.
19. Humble Oyebanjo Omotele and His Happy Brothers Organization.
20. Bayo Orija and His Unity Brothers Band.
21. Daniel Ajayi Owaduge and His Group.
22. King Bayo Owo-Ola ("Maccelo King") and His Royal Brothers Band.
23. Michael Robinson and His Everready Orchestra.
24. Yekini Tomori and His Okebadan Social Brothers Band.
25. Senator Sola West and His Afrogay Stars International.

Ibadan-based Fújì Bands, 1981–1982

1. Alhaji Taju Ayinla Abiodun and His Fújì Group.
2. Sulaimon Adigun ("Golden Fújì Lecturer") and His Group.

3. Akanbi-Ade Commissioner and His African Fújì Republic.
4. Alhaji Fancy Aiye Alamu and His Ikebe Fújì Band.
5. Alhaji Ayinde Sule Apollo and His Superior Fújì Organization.
6. Sikiru Ayinde and His Ibadan Fújì Group.
7. Admiral Tunde Ayinla and His Fújì Group.
8. Captain Nureni Akande Bonanza ("Fújì King of Ibadan") and His Group.
9. Alhaja Alamu Majester and Her New Brain Fújì Sound.
10. Wahabi Alagbe Nacet and His Fújì Costly International.
11. Fújì Commander Love Azeez Omowunmi and His Band.
12. Prince Eji Salami and His Fújì Organization.

Notes

Chapter 1

1. The only credible competitor for jùjú during my fieldwork was an Islamicized style called *fújì*. Fújì music, originally derived from music performed during the Ramadan fast, has yet to receive scholarly attention. In 1981 and 1982, fújì was growing in popularity, though still largely patronized only by Muslims.

According to a professional talking drummer from Ibadan, fújì has since overtaken jùjú in popularity. Scores of new fújì bands have popped up in Ibadan and other large Yoruba towns and have begun to compete with jùjú musicians on their own turf, winning over even Christian listeners. It is reported that aspiring fújì musicians hire a van, load their instruments, and drive the streets in search of celebrations without live music. The band manager jumps down and speaks to the host, offering the band's services for free. If the performance is successful, celebrants may offer the musicians cash, food, and drink. According to my informant, jùjú musicians in Ilẹṣa, a predominantly Christian town, have declared a ban on this practice, and on fújì music in general, within the town limits (Adebisi Adeleke, 1 Dec. 1988).

2. I wholeheartedly agree with the notion that ethnographers should address the articulation of local social and cultural processes with broader economic and political networks. In a review of interpretive and world system approaches, Marcus and Fischer suggest that

> experience, the personal, and feeling . . . refer to a domain of life that, while indeed structured, is also inherently social, in which dominant and emergent trends in global systems of political economy are complexly registered in language, emotions, and the imagination (Marcus and Fischer 1986:78).

3. Sources on southern African popular music include Andersson 1981; Clegg 1981; Coplan 1979, 1980, 1981b, 1985; Erlmann 1987, 1988; Hamm 1985; Kauffman 1972, 1980; Kubik 1971, 1974, 1980, 1981; Nurse 1964; Rycroft 1956, 1958, 1959, 1977; Vail 1983; and Zindi 1985. West Africanist publications include

Aig-Imoukhuede 1975; Alaja-Browne 1985; Ames 1970; Asante-Darko and Van Der Geest 1983; Bender 1983, 1984; Chernoff 1985; Collins 1976, 1977, 1978, 1985b; Collins and Richards 1982; Coplan 1978; Ekwueme 1977; Euba 1967, 1971; Keil and Keil 1977; Labinjoh 1982; Mensah 1966, 1970, 1971; Nketia 1955, 1957; Okagbare 1969; Omibiyi 1976, 1981; Smith 1962; Sprigge 1971; Thompson 1961; Vidal 1977; Ware 1970, 1978; C. Waterman 1982, 1985, 1988.

4. Central African sources include Bemba 1985; Fabian 1978; Kazadi 1973; Lonoh 1969; M.E.N./I.N.R.A.P. 1984; Matondo 1972; Mukuna 1980a, 1981; Rycroft 1961, 1962. East Africanist works include Kubik 1981; Low 1982; Martin 1980, 1982; Ranger 1975; Roberts 1968.

5. Much of the acculturation theory applied in studies of African urban musics—particularly the notion of syncretism—was first developed in Afro-Americanist anthropology; see, for example, Herskovits 1938; R. Waterman 1952; Merriam 1955; Hampton 1980.

6. For example, Alaja-Browne 1985; Bame 1985; Barber 1982; Bemba 1985; Collins and Richards 1982; Erlmann 1987; Jeyifọ 1984.

7. These ideas were adumbrated by Alan P. Merriam in his oft-cited "feedback model" of musical practice (1964). Intrerestingly, the processes that dynamize Merriam's sound-behavior-concept model—perception and learning—are among the least developed areas of ethnomusicological research.

8. See, for example, Griaule 1965; Turnbull 1962; Zahan 1963; Blacking 1971; Zemp 1971; Merriam 1973; C. Adams 1979; Wachsmann 1980:150–51; Riesman 1986:109–10.

9. Yoruba musicians, for example, suggest that the ideal performance generates *ètò* (good order, orderly arrangement) in sound; thus, outstanding musicians may be given the informal title *Bàbá Ètò,* or "father of good order." Popular musical styles are called "systems," and each band strives to define its own distinctive, organically unified "sound." Musicians may *dàlù* (mix) musical elements or styles; however, an *àdàlù* (mixture), like the mixture of corn and beans which carries the name (Abrahams 1981:125), does not necessarily exhibit good internal order. The term *dàpọ̀* (to unite things, cooperate, form alliances, copulate), on the other hand, suggests the controlled fusion of musical elements.

10. A popular joke recounts the experience of a Nigerian diplomat attending a dinner reception in England. As he picks up a bone and cracks it with his teeth, the mortified hostess sniffs, "What do you feed *dogs* in your country?" "Cheese and biscuit!" comes the sardonic reply.

11. *Alakara O Fe Keni Keji Odin,* Olumo Records ORPS 125, 1981.

12. *Ikilo,* Leader Records LRCLS 34, 1981; *Eni Tori Ele Ku,* Leader Records LRCLS 36, 1982.

13. The popular press provides a forum for the expression of musical taste, pleas by musicians looking for sponsors, and analysis of new trends. The following column from an Ibadan-based tabloid discusses the neologism *alatika,* coined by fújì star Ayinla Kollington:

> The use of the word "Alatika" came first from the composition of Alhaj Ayinla Kollington. In that piece, Ayinla described himself as

"Baba Alatika"—meaning Alatika patron. Since then the word Alatika has become a popular slang among certain sections of the music public and especially Kollington's fans. The slang "Alatika" is mostly used in public places like beer parlours, 'ogogoro' [distilled palm-wine] and 'burukutu' [maize beer] brothels as well as motor parks and market places.

On the surface, "Alatika" seems to mean "Atiraka" or "Atapata dide"—meaning self-struggling and self-supporting respectively. But viewed deeper within the context of use, it runs counter to the meaning of the words "Atiraka" or "Atapata dide".

Essentially, the category of citizens that accepts the use of "Alatika" to describe themselves and their admirers is too known to need expatiation [i.e., they are undesirables].

Salawa Abeni, the Waka Queen described "alatika" in her latest elpee as satanic children. Children that are not shown beauty at home and who can hardly appreciate beauty elsewhere. She prays God not to give her "Alatika" as children. Rather she pleads with God to give her children like Sunny Ade, Ebenezer Obey, Barrister, and Adawa king Dele Abiodun.

To counter Salawa Abeni's prayer and disabuse the minds of her admirers and followers, Alhaj Kollington said "*Alatika ki i se ole, won npa'wo*" meaning *Alatika are not rogues, they make money.*

The question from this defence is: Is money-making the exclusive competence of alatikas or are we to understand that being an alatika and a money-maker is the totality of human decency? And, even then, making money from what source is another question.

Another columnist, writing in *The Weekly Scene,* contended that:

"Alatika", for those of you who do not understand Yoruba, means "Omo-alata"—the pepper-seller. These are comparable with [women that] the people from Bendel Ibo precisely from Ubulu-Ubulu call "Ikpoti" of 1968.

Those girls are just too funny because they dress gorgeously and still maintain their social status quo when it comes to the case of moving with their counterparts, who are motor touts [rough, lower-class men]. That is because they regard it as a sin to move with the more-educated ones. That is why it is not surprising to see them moving with their tout husbands. If there is any unfortunate man who has the misfortune to run into those girls, he will be disgraced.

14. *Işe Logun Işe/No More War,* Siky Oluyole Records SKOLP 019, 1982.

Chapter 2

1. The northern orientation of wàkà music is indicated by its etymological derivation from the Hausa *wak'a,* a generic term for "song" or "poem" (Ames and

King 1971:135). *Péréséké,* like most Yoruba names for musical instruments, is an onomatopoeic term. It predicates a metaphoric connection on the basis of a perceptual similarity between the sound produced by the tin cymbals and the tinkling noise made by metalsmiths, many of whom were Muslims.

2. One of the earliest gramophone recordings of Lagosian music is entitled *Orin Kerikeri,* performed by Saka Adesina Lawani Jeje (Odeon A248501, recorded in Lagos in 1929 or 1930; *The Lagos Daily News* 21 Aug. 1931).

3. Other Afro-American immigrants in Lagos included members of the West Indian Regiment, which was barracked at Ebute-Metta on the adjacent mainland; successful merchants such as P. H. Williams, born in Trinidad in 1872, and brought to Lagos at the age of five; Antigua-born John Ambleston, who lived in Sierra Leone and worked in the Obossi gold mines of the Gold Coast before joining the Lagos Public Works Department, which he left to start a woodworking business; and entrepreneur J. C. Vaughn, born in Camden, South Carolina (Macmillan 1968:108, 114, 115).

4. The upward mobility of Nigerians serving in the colonial civil service during the 1920s and 1930s was for the most part limited to Class II of the Division of Public Offices, at a maximum annual salary of 300 pounds, well below the amount paid to most white colonial officials.

5. A similar drum, called *bandiri,* is found among the Hausa of northern Nigeria, and is a recent introduction into the worship activities of an Islamic sect, the K'adriyya (Ames and King 1971:13).

6. The first commercial recording of sákárà (Odeon A 248505), by Abibus Oluwa and his group, featured a praise song for Herbert Macaulay and Tijani Oluwa, important figures in the nationalist movement (*The Lagos Daily News,* 21 Aug. 1931).

7. Sámbà drums are today still made by carpenters and not by specialized instrument makers.

8. The phrase *àwon àsàyòn òrò* means "choice or select words." The term *esa,* translated by Alaja-Browne as "a meaningful whole," is unknown to me. A more likely term (perhaps a dialectical variant) is *ese,* used to describe an orderly row of things or persons, a neatly planted yam field, or a well-organized unit of verbal expression (e.g., a verse of poetry, a written paragraph; see Abrahams 1981:196).

9. *West African Pilot,* 24, 25 July 1942; 1 Jan., 30 Nov., 4, 7, 24, 31 Dec. 1943; 1, 5, 6, 8, 28 Jan., 25 May, 10 June, 19, 21, 29, 31 Dec. 1944; 6, 15 Jan. 1945.

10. A photograph of "Scottie," dressed in a striped jacket and holding a guitar, appeared in the *West African Pilot* (19 Dec. 1944, p. 4), with a caption reading "Well-known business man and a prominent member of the Agarawu Club. He was present at the memorial service held in the Ebenezer Baptist Church in memory of the late Dr. J. C. Vaughn last Sunday."

11. In reference to the origins of Ghanaian syncretic guitar styles, Coplan (1978:101–2) writes:

> Akan youngsters who were used to the music of the *seprewa* [a traditional Akan lute] found little difficulty in picking up the guitar instead,

and they readily learned the two-finger style of the Kru sailors. Kwame Asare, popularly known as Sam, claims to have learned the basis of the two-finger style known as *dagomba* from a Kru sailor. Robert Sprigge contends that it was the technical problem of working out Akan melodies in two-finger style that accounts for the particular form of "Yaa Amponsah" (still considered the prototype of the standard or "mainline" highlife rhythm and melody) and other early highlife melodies.

12. For example, "Oba Folagbade of Ijebu-Ode" (Odeon A 248000, recorded ca. 1929); "Oba Oludaiye of Ute via Owo" (Odeon A 248001), "Oba Oshemawe" (HMV JZ 3, recorded ca. 1935) and "Oba Gbelegbuwa" (HMV JZ 4).

13. The titles of Denge's earliest recorded songs also reflect a dual concern with social change and cultural continuity: e.g., "Frugality Pa Wonda" ("Frugality Changed Them") [Odeon A 248000], and "Iya Ni Wura" ("Mother is Gold") [Odeon A 248001].

14. Macmillan's [1920] 1968 *Red Book of West Africa* provides information on urban mercantile activities, including short biographies of African shopkeepers.

Chapter 3

1. One exception to this generalization is found among eastern Yoruba groups such as the Ekiti and Ijẹṣa, whose polyphonic choral style sometimes involves singing in parallel seconds (Euba 1967). This regional style did not influence jùjú until the 1950s, when musicians from these areas began to record.

2. See Alaja-Browne 1985:122–23 for transcriptions of three variants of the Johnnie Walker pattern, as performed by Tunde King.

3. King recounts, "We used to sing Hymnal Companion in school, and I must listen. If they start singing, and you don't know it, they can say, "Alhaji-Man! You don't know!" So I was playing it."

4. By the mid-1930s, King required a small amount several weeks in advance to reserve a given night, and generally charged five or ten shillings (about U.S. $1.20–$2.40) as a flat fee. During the course of performance the hosts and other guests would "dash" him and other members of his band; on a good night they might net ten or twenty pounds ($40–$50.00). One informant recalled a performance at which a woman dashed King a gold bracelet worth fifty pounds (about $250.00) while he was singing her praises (Keil 1966–67:362).

5. Tunde King has stated that Wisiki and Godini were the actual names of Joluwe's children (Alaja-Browne 1985:160). Given the importance of double entendres in the palmwine tradition, I suspect that these were nicknames based upon whiskey and Gordon's gin, symbols of urban sophistication and high status. Another interpretation which makes sense within the expressive framework of palmwine and early jùjú music is that Joluwe was an accomplished bon vivant. From this perspective, the phrase "father of whiskey, father of gin" may be read as a satirical variant of a traditional Yoruba praise formula.

6. A good example is provided by the early recordings of Tunde King. King recounts that his group was recorded by a German engineer at Forrester Hall on

Odunlami Street. The engineer was hired by representatives of a French trading company, who also suggested changes to enhance King's popularity among Europeans and Westernized Africans. These included the addition of a violin, played by Mr. Hacquert, a Saro merchant whose store offered a variety of Western stringed instruments and a keyboard instrument called a Dulcetone, which was given to King by the French merchants, "just to make the music full," and to advertise their wares. The Dulcetone was played on King's recordings by Tunde Anthony, a Saro who worked for the French company providing the instrument.

On the recordings, the violin plays pedal tones derived from the tonic triad and, on two pieces incorporating influences from the Islamicized style sákárà, imitates the role of the one-stringed gòjé fiddle, an instrument adopted from the Hausa [cassette example 11]. The Dulcetone also plays pedal tones, triadic chords, and, on several examples, a single-pitch rhythmic pattern related to a 12-pulse "timeline" pattern used in traditional percussion music throughout the Guinea Coast area. It is clear that King made a valiant attempt to fit the imported instruments into familiar musical roles. Nevertheless, the Dulcetone and violin appear not to have been added to the group in live performances. Despite the widespread influence of the Parlophone discs, which helped to establish jùjú style, the violin and available keyboard instruments were not adopted by other groups in any context. These European instruments appear to have been rejected by jùjú musicians for two reasons: first, the Dulcetone was not sufficiently portable; and second, the effect of both instruments, reminiscent of European chamber music, appears not to have appealed to the core audience for jùjú. They never appeared again in jùjú music, despite their prominence on the first recordings of the style.

Chapter 4

1. The first àgídìgbo hit record was also the first disc released on the Yoruba-owned Jofabro label: Jofabro JF1, recorded around 1952, included the songs "Egbe Rio Lindo" and a praise song for label owner Josy Ọlajoyegbe. The Rio Lindo Orchestra also recorded on Decca (e.g., "Bosi Corner," WA.3063/KWA.8145); while the Rosey Mambo Orchestra recorded for HMV (e.g., JZ 5689, released in 1954 or 1955).

2. Writing in the early 1960s, Sklar noted that:

Action Group leaders have cemented their relationships with the traditional leaders through the acquisition of honorary chieftaincy titles, a normal procedure for successful men in Yorubaland. Thus Mr. Awolowo [leader of the Action Group] became Chief Awolowo in October 1954, following his accession to the Premiership of the Western Region. . . . Action Group ideals and policies are propogated at an annual Chiefs Conference under the Presidency of the Oni of Ife; the conference maintains regular liason with the Premier and ministers of the regional government by means of a standing committee, called the Chiefs Council (Sklar 1963:234).

3. Badejọ's record store was located at 142 Broad Street in the Lagos business district (*West African Pilot,* 26 Feb. 1943). The earliest Badejọ discs were the BS series, beginning in 1947. The later BA series started in the early 1950s.

4. By the 1950s some discs were once again being manufactured in Germany, an important center for the production of commercial recordings sold in Nigeria before the Second World War. A number of the early Badejọ discs, for example, were made in Germany. Other discs were manufactured in the Union of South Africa (e.g., later Jofabro discs such as JS 8002, by Theophilus Iwalokun).

5. The railroad, like commercial shipping, exerted a pervasive influence on the development of jùjú music. The railroads may be usefully envisaged as inland extensions of the Atlantic shipping lanes connecting Nigeria to the outside world. Both systems were perceived as conduits for cultural influence and sociospatial mobility.

6. J. O. Oyeṣiku and His Rainbow Quintette recorded with Philips; J. O. Araba recorded first with Philips and then switched to Deccá in the mid-1960s, changing the name of his band to The Afro-Skiffle Group, at the suggestion of a British recording engineer. The original personnel of Oyeṣiku's group was: J. O. Oyeṣiku, guitar; K. O. Nikoi, doubling mandolin and kazoo; Miller Rose, sámbà; "Minister," side drum; and Brother Poti, àgídìgbo. Araba's Rhythm Blues included Araba on guitar; Fatayi ("Rolling Dollar") Layiwọla on àgídìgbo; Ọlaṣeeni Tẹjuoso on side drum; and Edward Faṣaye on maracas.

7. The 1950s and 1960s were the Golden Age of Nigerian highlife music, a pan-Anglophone West African urban tradition whose progenitors in prewar Lagos included the Calabar Brass Band and Ezekiel Akpata's Lishabi Mills Orchestra. The popularity of highlife in Lagos was intensified by the return of Bobby Benson from England in 1947. Benson established a reputation immediately upon his arrival by introducing various new instruments and "show business" production values. The earliest recordings made by Bobby's Jam Session Orchestra include highlife tunes, Latin American dance styles—including calypsos ("Calypso Minor One" Senafone FAO 1143) and sambas ("Maladidamu," Senafone FAO 1144)—and a few experiments with jazz ("Be Bop Jump at 4," Badejo BS 232). Almost all of the successful highlife bandleaders of the 1950s and 1960s were at one time members of Benson's band, including Victor Ọlaiya, Roy Chicago, Bill Friday, Eddie Okonta, Cardinal Jim Rex Lawson, and Fẹla Ransome-Kuti.

8. As Lagos journalist Segun Bucknor phrased the matter: "such names as E. C. Arinze and Charles Iwegbue no longer featured on the scene; Zeal Onyia was in Germany . . . and those who stayed behind, like Agu Norris and Eric Onugha, did not consider the atmosphere conducive to a high profile" (Bucknor 1976:20).

9. The Green Spot Band included Lawrence Akinyẹle on supporting guitar, Tunde Alade on talking drum, Ademọla Balogun on double toy, Tajudeen Fadeyi on ṣẹkẹrẹ, Tunde Babalọla on maracas, Bello Ajileye on agogo, Folorunṣo Oni on clips, Jossy Daniel on ògìdo, and Tafa Alabi on àkúbà.

10. African Songs AS 26 (LPAS 8006A/B).

11. Sunny Ade's 1983 tour of the United States set off a brief burst of interest in jùjú music among popular music journalists. Various "readings" of jùjú were advanced by critics who enjoyed the music but could not decode the Yoruba texts. A number of these interpretations drew analogies between reggae and jùjú—one

critic musing that "Bob may have been forwarded so that Sunny could save the West with juju music" (Tate 1983:34)—and a few saw in jùjú music a model of similarities and differences between African and African-American cultures. In a cover story on Ade's tour for the 15 March 1983 issue of *Village Voice*, Greg Tate wrote:

> Sunny's cool isn't like any of the cools I've ever known. It's not the hipper-than-thou cool of the jazz set or the aggressively aloof cool of dreads or the yeah-fuck-with-me-cool of the B-Boys. Sunny's cool is a congenial cool, a secure, calm cool. The kind of cool I imagine Jonathan Jackson had when he walked into that Marin County courthouse and said, "I'm taking over now, gentlemen." The kind of cool that could walk into battle respecting an enemy as a man and still go heads up. And though the principal theme in Sunny's lyrics is said to be love, the words in his catchiest tune, the mesmerizing "Ja Funme" [sic], mean, "my head shall fight for me." Onstage in "Synchro System" the Chairman tells folk if they want to dance to juju music keep everything from the waist up still and everything from the waist down in a slow grind. Like the P-funk, juju music is about keeping a cool nead and a hot body in motion. . . .
>
> In the lobby of the band's hotel in New Haven I meet this slim, dark young brother named Brian who works there as a luggage carrier. Brian's cool on the gig is about becoming a cipher, a blur, a peripheral vision that melts into the surroundings—the cool of a man whose optic nerves constantly remind him you best watch your ass up in here buddy. Shaped by common blood but different histories, Sunny and Brian share a presence. The difference is that where Sunny's cool comes from being a Yoruba prince, Brian's is all about trying to survive in white America (Tate 1983:35).

Chapter 5

1. See, for example, Akintoye 1971; Awe 1973; Biobaku 1957; Johnson 1921; Law 1970.

2. See Lloyd 1962, 1971; Lloyd, Mabogunje, and Awe 1967; Eades 1980.

3. My attempts to carry out a comprehensive census of band boys in Ibadan was complicated by a number of factors: the intermittent and part-time nature of musical employment; the movement of personnel from one group to another; and the expansion and contraction of groups in response to economic factors.

4. Talking drummers in Ibadan jùjú groups included two sets of brothers brought up in traditional drummers' compounds: two from Oṣogbo, and three from Ogbomọṣọ. Two of the Ogbomọṣọ brothers were talking drummers, the other a bass guitarist.

5. Such fictive kinsmen, often addressed by the bandleader as àbúrò ("younger sibling"), are frequently not consanguines, but individuals from the band captain's home community.

6. However, even in Yoruba groups that place more emphasis upon patrilineal transmission of skills, the craft system allowed for a great deal of variation. For

example, access to training might descend to a male individual consanguineally linked to a craft-specialized *agbolé* (patrilineal compound) via a "daughter of the compound," particularly if the individual in question could be determined, by demonstration of innate talent or divination, to have "craft blood" in him. Another widespread exception to craft group exclusivity was the *ìwòfà* or debt-peonage relationship, in which children were pawned by their parents for service in another compound, where they might learn a specialized craft (Krapf-Askari 1969:86). These alternative means of attachment to craft lineages may also have provided models for the predominantly non-kin based organization of modern urban craft groups.

7. This is one of the essential differences between highlife and jùjú groups cited by older musicians: as one prominent Ibadan jùjú captain put it, "In highlife they base on salary basic. In jùjú we do as we like."

8. The *èsúsú* is "one of the economic institutions of the Yoruba of Nigeria, [having] elements which resemble a credit union, an insurance scheme and a savings club, but it is distinct from all of these. The *èsúsú* is a fund to which a group of individuals make fixed contributions of money at fixed intervals; the total amount contributed by the entire group is assigned to each of the members in rotation" (Bascom 1952:63).

9. One jùjú band that I observed varied from a minimum of seven players at a small hotel in the Oke-Ado section of Ibadan (captain; one chorus vocalist; ògìdo, àkúbà, and sámbà drummers; a sèkèrè player; and an àdàmòn drummer) to ten at a wedding ceremony in a rural village near Ile-Ifè (captain; three chorus vocalists; ògìdo, àkúbà, sámbà, and double toy; sèkèrè; and one àdàmòn drummer) to a maximum of thirteen at a Christian birthday party in Oke-Ado (captain; four chorus vocalists, two of whom played sèkèrè and jùjú; bass guitarist; ògìdo, àkúbà, sámbà, and double toy drummers; a sèkèrè player; and two àdàmòn drummers).

10. I have little information regarding the number of active jùjú hotels in the vast area of post-1970 expansion. A couple of hotels in the elite Ring Road area were experimenting with live music on a sporadic basis. In the northern neighborhood in which I lived (Agbowo), there were no regular venues for live jùjú performance, though at least one local hotel (managed by a woman from midwestern Nigeria) had featured the band of jùjú captain Michael Robinson during the late 1970s. While the number of small drinking establishments and hotels has more or less kept pace with the growth of new neighborhoods at the margins of the city, the number of regular venues for jùjú performance has not.

11. While many of the hundreds of beer parlors and hotels in Ibadan offer electronically mass-reproduced popular music, only a small minority use live musical performance to attract patrons. Keil noted the existence of some twenty hotel venues for live jùjú performance in October of 1966, with perhaps a half-dozen of these forming a regular core. Fifteen years later, during a period of economic retrenchment, the total number of hotels with regular live jùjú music was around fifteen, though the number of core venues remained stable. While the population and area of the city had expanded greatly, the total amount of activity on the Ibadan jùjú club scene was more or less static.

12. Following is the schedule for the Independence Hotel in Oke-Bola during the summer of 1979:

Monday: Daniel Ajayi Owaduge and his Glorious Band
Tuesday: King Bayo Owo-Ọla and his International Brothers
Wednesday: Uncle Toye Ajagun and his Olumo Sound
Thursday: Captain Jide Ojo and his Yankee System
Friday: "Open night" (sometimes a band; irregular)
Saturday: "Disco" (recorded music)
Sunday: Closed

This schedule, at one of the most popular jùjú hotels in Ibadan, included both of the bands regularly placed in the first rank by my informants, one second-rank group, and one third-rank group. By January 1982, Owaduge (the weakest of the bands by general consent) had been replaced on Monday nights by Josy Ọla; Toye Ajagun, the most successful leader, had dropped out of the club scene entirely; and Bayo Owo-Ọla and Jide Ojo continued to reserve Tuesdays and Thursdays, respectively. Thus, though some of the specific faces changed, the general pattern remained the same over a two-and-a-half year period, with the top and bottom-ranked groups being displaced.

13. There is a growing practice among the elite of hiring a video cameraman to document important ceremonies, including the wedding, naming ceremony, or funeral itself, subsequent processions and activities, and the party afterwards. One very wealthy celebrant in Surulere, Lagos reported that she had hired one crew to document her father's funeral procession in their home village (₦800 = $1200), and another to document the subsequent celebration in Lagos (₦1000 = $1500). She received three copies of the videotapes; the cameraman-producer generally keeps master copies of all ceremonies recorded, so that celebrants may also purchase dubs (about ₦30 [$45] each; blank tapes sold for about ₦15 [$22.50] retail in Lagos at the time). Video documentation is actually only one aspect of the multimedia preservation of ceremonial activities for later reproduction. There are, in addition, at least two free-lance polaroid cameramen at any large urban ceremony—usually reputed to be non-Yoruba immigrants—and individual celebrants may make cassette recordings of the official proceedings and music.

14. Fear of armed robbers is one motivation for celebrants to stay at an àríyá until daybreak. According to Nigerian newspaper reports, the lavish displays of wealth at elite ceremonies were regarded by police officials as a primary cause for the marked increase in armed nocturnal attacks on motorists during the late 1970s and early 1980s. One of the informants cited in this chapter was, in fact, murdered at night by armed thugs in Lagos several months after I spoke with him.

Chapter 6

1. One is sometimes warned in such situations to avoid accepting food or drink from a stranger; fear of attack via poison or oògùn (magical medicine) is most acute in situations of conflict over resources, which the Yoruba recognize as potentially riven with jealousy and rivalry.

2. The distribution of Yoruba terminology for drum types is very complicated. The term àdàmọ̀n is used by Ibadan-based musicians; in other areas similar

drums used in jùjú music are called *gángan*. The term *àdàmòn* may be used in some areas to refer to a hierarchical position within a "family" of drums rather than a specific type of drum (personal communication, Andrew Frankel).

3. At a very large àríyá, the presence of more than one band maximizes cash flow opportunities.

4. See Agawu 1988 for a penetrating assessment of the tone/tune "problem" in northern Ewe performance.

5. The personnel of the Olúmọ Soundmakers was:

Ọlatoye Ajagunjeun, captain
Joshua Alao, solo guitarist
Tunde Peters, tenor guitar
Nicholas Kọlawọle Oyeṣiku, tenor guitar
Michael Dare Adedokun, bass guitar
Samuel Adedokun, senior àdàmòn drum
Adesọji Adewọle, junior àdàmòn drum
Anthony Adeleye, àkúbà (conga)
Oladipupọ Oguntunwaṣe, ògìdo (bass conga)
Bisi Johnson, double toy (bongos)
John Akanmu, vocalist
Ayinde Lasisi, vocalist
Samuel Ọmọwọle, treble vocalist
Taofiki Idowu "Chapiro," treble vocalist
Yisau Ṣoyinka, bass vocalist
Anthony Ademọla Abayọmi Ṣoluade, band manager

Chapter 7

1. A common way of asking how things are "going" (to use the English idiom) is ṣé ńkọn yí?, "Are things rolling?"

2. See, for example, McAllester 1954; Merriam 1967; Zemp 1971; Blacking 1973; Robertson-DeCarbo 1977; Nettl 1978b; Chernoff 1979; Ellingson 1979; Keil 1979; Neuman 1980; Feld 1982; Sakata 1983; Roseman 1984; Peña 1985; Seeger 1987; Nettl 1989.

3. Fẹla's life history is recounted in various publications (Darnton 1977; Moore 1982; Collins 1985b; Grass 1986; Graham 1988:62–65). He was born in Abẹokuta in 1938, son of the Reverend I. O. Ransome-Kuti, a primary principal and music teacher, and Funmilayọ Ransome-Kuti, a political activist and leader of the powerful Nigerian Women's Union. Informants generally suggest that creativity flows in his "blood"; from his father came the musical talent, from his mother, the radical politics. Fẹla began his professional career with Yoruba highlife star Victor Ọlaiya, and studied music theory and trumpet at Trinity College in London. When he returned to Lagos, he had developed a style he called "highlife-jazz." By the time of Charles Keil's 1966 popularity poll in *Spear Magazine*, Fẹla was regarded as the leading "jazz" musician in Nigeria.

1966 also saw the arrival of Geraldo Pino, a James Brown imitator from

Sierra Leone, who, according to Fẹla, "was tearing Lagos to pieces. . . . After that motherfucking Pino tore up the scene, there wasn't shit I could do in Lagos" (Berman 1985:63). Fẹla incorporated aspects of James Brown's music into his new Afro-beat style. In 1969, he went to the United States, and met Sandra Isidore, a Black Panther, who introduced Fẹla to the writings of Malcolm X, Nikki Giovanni, and Angela Davis. The experience transformed him. He returned to Lagos, changed the name of the band to Africa '70—Nigeria, he has said, was a colonial fiction—and began writing more explicitly political songs.

Glossary of Yoruba Terms

àdàmọ̀n. Small hourglass-shaped pressure drum ("talking drum") used in jùjú groups. This term is common in Ibadan; similar drums are referred to as *gángan, àpàlà,* etc.

Afro-beat. Popular music combining elements of dance band highlife, jazz, and Afro-American dance music of the 1960s and 1970s. Afro-beat is associated with Fẹla Anikulapo-Kuti, who pioneered the style around 1970. Lyrics are generally in pidgin English and emphasize political issues, social inequities, neo-colonialism.

agídìgbo. Large four- or five-key bass lamellaphone, used in a variety of popular musics, including palmwine and jùjú music (1950s). Also the name of a popular dance music style of the late 1940s and 1950s which strongly influenced postwar jùjú music. The major figure in agídìgbo music (also called *mambo*) was Adeolu Akinsanya.

agogo. Single- or double-flanged iron bell, used in many Yoruba popular musics. Often used to play a repetitive asymmetrical time line that orients other players.

Àgùdà. Afro-Brazilian repatriate; Roman Catholic (also called *Amaro*).

àkúbà. Single-headed hand-beaten drum based on Afro-Cuban conga prototype. Used in many Yoruba popular music styles.

àpàlà. Yoruba social dance and praise music played by ensembles made up of small pressure drums, bass lamellaphone, and various idiophones and conga drums. Pioneered in the late 1930s by professional talking drummers in response to the popularity of sákárà music. Now on the wane, àpàlà is mostly performed and patronized by Yoruba Muslims. The major stars were the late Alaji Haruna Iṣọla of Ijẹbu-Igbo and the late Alaji Ayinla Ọmọwura of Abẹokuta.

àríyá. Neotraditional celebration; lavish outdoor parties following important events in an individual's life (e.g., naming ceremonies, weddings, house warmings, business launchings, funerals).

aṣíkò. Yoruba-language popular music of the 1920s and 1930s. Associated with Christianity and Western influence, aṣíkò songs were accompanied on sámbà frame drums and a scraped carpenter's saw. The rapid tempos and samba-influenced rhythms of aṣíkò were an important factor in early jùjú music.

double toy. Bongo drums, based upon Afro-Cuban prototype and played with sticks.

dùndún. Large hourglass-shaped pressure drum ("talking drum"). Used in various popular styles, although not as widely as smaller types of pressure drum.

elé. The solo part of a call-and-response song (derived from the verb *lé*, "to drive something away or into something else").

ègbè. The fixed choral response in a call-and-response song (derived from the verb *gbè*, "to support or protect someone").

ẹgbẹ́. Organized group of people; general term for voluntary associations, occupational guilds, musical ensembles, etc.

Èkó. Yoruba word for Lagos.

fújì. Yoruba popular music derived from wẹ́rẹ́ or ajísáàrì, music played by ambulatory groups of young men to wake Muslims during the Ramadan fasting period. Part of a cluster of Islamicized styles (e.g., sákárà, àpàlà, wákà), fújì music became popular in the early 1970s, and by the mid-1980s had surpassed jùjú music in general popularity among Yoruba audiences. The superstars of fújì music are Alhaji Sikiru Ayinde Barrister and Alhaji Ayinla Kollington.

highlife. Generic term for a cluster of Anglophone West African popular musics. The two major highlife types, both of which appear to have crystallized in the Gold Coast (Ghana) during the early twentieth century, are (1) guitar band highlife, generally featuring one or two guitars added to a social dance drumming group; and (2) dance band highlife, a more Westernized style modeled on ballroom dance bands, with varying degrees of influence from West African traditions, Latin American dance music, and jazz.

ìjìnlẹ̀ẹ̀. Traditional; indigenous; literally "deeply-grounded" (compound of *jin*, "to be deep" and *ilẹ̀*, "ground").

jazz drums. Trap set. Used in many contemporary Yoruba styles (e.g., jùjú, fújì, Afro-beat).

jùjú. A Yoruba popular music. Evolved from palmwine guitar music in Lagos in the early 1930s. Early jùjú was performed by trios and quartets consisting of banjo, tambourine (jùjú), and ṣèkèrè, and was associated with Christians. The founder of the style, and the first to record it was Tunde King; other important early figures included Akanbi Wright, Ayinde Bakare, and Ojo Babajide. After World War II jùjú ensembles expanded—the most important addition being the Yoruba "talking drum"—and electronic amplification was introduced. Major figures in postwar jùjú include Ayinde Bakare, Ojogẹ Daniel, and Akanbi Ege (1940s–1950s); I. K. Dairo and Tunde Nightengale (1960s); and Chief Commander Ebenezer Obey and King Sunny Ade (1970s–1980s).

ògìdo. Single-headed hand-beaten drum, also refered to as "bass drum." Based upon Afro-Cuban conga drum prototype.

òrìṣà. Yoruba deities. Although the Yoruba are predominantly Christian or Muslim, many individuals maintain some level of commitment to traditional beliefs, particularly in crisis situations. Òrìṣà who continue to play important roles in contemporary life include Ṣàngó, god of thunder; Ifá, god of divination; and Ògún, god of war and iron (and thus blacksmiths, hunters, taxi and lorry drivers, and surgeons).

ọba. Yoruba sacred king.

ọmọ. Child; people. Thus *ọmọ Èkó* refers to the "indigenous" people of Lagos, *ọmọ Ìbàdàn* to natives of Ibadan.

palmwine. A beverage consisting of the slightly fermented sap of a palm tree; also a generic term for a type of urban West African small-group performance. Palmwine performances were centered on a singer, who offered philosophical commentary on current events and the travails of urban life. Instrumental accompaniment drew upon a wide range of materials—for example, African songs and chordophone techniques, Afro-American guitar styles and tunings, Christian hymns, Hawaiian guitar records—and were generally comprised of repetitive melodic-harmonic grounds played on lamellaphone, guitar, mandolin, or concertina. Accompanying instruments might include a frame drum, a bottle struck with a nail, match boxes, or a table top.

sákárà. Islamicized praise song/social dance music. Probably developed in northern Yorubaland in late nineteenth or early twentieth century, played in Lagos by 1914. Ensembles include gòjé, a monochord bowed lute, and sákárà, circular, peg-fastened ceramic frame drums (also called ọrùn'ṣà, "potneck"). Both instruments diffused from Northern Nigeria and are associated with the Islamic kingdoms of the Hausa and Nupe. The major stars of sákárà music have been Abibus Oluwa (1930s), Ojo Ọlawale (1940s), and S. Aka, Ojindo, and the late Yesufu Ọlatunji (1950s-1970s).

sámbà. Square wooden frame drum, associated with syncretic Christianity. Reputedly introduced to Yorubaland by Afro-Brazilian repatriates. Similar drums, often called gumbe, are found along the West African coast (e.g., Accra, Freetown) and in the West Indies (e.g., Jamaica).

Sàró. Sierra Leonean repatriate.

wákà. Islamicized Yoruba praise song/social dance style, usually sung by women. The Yoruba word is derived from the Hausa *wak'a,* a generic term for song or poem. Probably became popular in Yorubaland in the late nineteenth century. Early wákà groups included péréṣéké, pounded tin discs with metal rings attached. Contemporary groups have been strongly influenced by other popular styles, especially fújì, and include a variety of drums and idiophones. Important figures include Majarọ Acagba (1920s—1930s), Batile Alake (1950s–1960s), and Salawa Abeni (1970s–1980s).

wọ́rọ́. Generic term for a cluster of 12/8 social dance rhythms, often used in Yoruba popular music.

Bibliography

Abrahams, R. C. 1981. *Dictionary of modern Yoruba.* London: Hodder and Stoughton.

Abumere, S. I. 1982. Residential differentiation in Ibadan: Some sketches of an explanation. In *Ibadan Region,* ed. M. O. Filani, 225–46. Ibadan: Department of Geography, University of Ibadan.

Adams, Charles R. 1979. Aurality and consciousness: Basotho production of significance. In *Essays in humanistic anthropology,* ed. B. T. Grindal and D. M. Warren, 303–25. Washington: University Press of America.

Adams, Richard N. 1975. *Energy and structure: A theory of social power.* Austin: University of Texas Press.

Adedeji, J. A. 1969. The Alarinjo theatre: A study of Yoruba theatrical art from its earliest beginnings to the present times. Ph.D. diss., University of Ibadan.

———. 1973. The church and the emergence of the Nigerian Theatre: 1915–1945. *Journal of the Historical Society of Nigeria* 6(4):387–96.

Aderibigbe, A. B. 1975. Early history of Lagos to about 1850. In *Lagos: The development of an African city,* ed. A. B. Aderibigbe, 1–26. Lagos: Longman Nigeria.

Adewoye, 'Dupe. 1982. Stop it! Salawa's child is mine. *The Entertainer* 107 (September):1.

Adorno, Theodore. 1941. On popular music. *Studies in Philosophy of Social Science* 9:17–48. New York: Institute of Social Research.

Agawu, V. Kofi. 1988. Tone and tune: The evidence for northern Ewe music. *Africa* 58(2):127–46.

Aig-Imoukhuede, Frank. 1975. Contemporary culture. In *Lagos: The development of an African city,* ed. A. B. Aderibigbe, 197–226. Lagos: Longman Nigeria.

Ajala, Bisi. 1988. Immaturity of Nigerian musicians. *Sunday Concord,* 7 February, 12, 14.

Ajibero, Matthew I. 1978. Yoruba music on gramophone records: A comprehensive annotated discography of Chief Commander Ebenezer Obey's juju music. Senior thesis, Amadu Bello University.

Ake, Claude, 1978. *Revolutionary pressures in Africa.* London: Zed Press.

Akinbode, Gbolahan S. 1980. Exploiter or the exploited? The musician in the Nigerian recording industry. Senior paper, University of Lagos.

Akinsemoyin, Kunle. 1969. The daring "Caratas." *Lagos Weekend,* 3 Jan., 6.

Akintoye, Steven. 1971. *Revolution and power politics in Yorubaland, 1840–1893.* London: Longman.

Alaja-Browne, Afolabi. 1985. Juju music: A study of its social history and style. Ph.D. diss., University of Pittsburgh.

Ames, David W. 1970. Urban Hausa music. *African Urban Notes* 5(4):19–24.

Ames, David W., and Anthony King. 1971. *Glossary of Hausa music and its social contexts.* Evanston: Northwestern University Press.

Anderson, Benedict. 1983. *Imagined communities: Reflections on the origin and spread of nationalism.* London: Verso.

Andersson, Muff. 1981. *Music in the mix: The story of South African popular music.* London: Ravan Press.

Areola, O. 1982. The spatial growth of Ibadan city and its impact on the rural hinterland. In *Ibadan Region,* ed. M. O. Filani, 66–78. Ibadan: Department of Geography, University of Ibadan.

Armstrong, Robert Plant. 1971. *The affecting presence: An essay in humanistic anthropology.* Urbana: University of Illinois Press.

Aronson, Dan R. 1978. *The city is our farm: Seven migrant Ijebu families.* Cambridge, MA: Schenkman.

Asad, Talal. 1972. Market model, class structure, and consent: A reconsideration of Swat political organisation. *Man,* n.s. 7:74–94.

———, ed. 1973. *Anthropology and the colonial encounter.* New York: Humanities Press.

Asante-Darko, Nimrod, and Sjaak Van Der Geest. 1983. Male chauvinism: Men and women in Ghanaian highlife songs. In *Female and male in West Africa,* ed. C. Oppong. London: George Allen and Unwin.

Awe, Bolanle. 1973. Militarism and economic development in nineteenth-century Yoruba country. *Journal of African History* 14(1):65–77.

Baker, Pauline H. 1974. *Urbanization and political change: The politics of Lagos, 1917–1967.* Berkeley and Los Angeles: University of California Press.

Bame, K. N. 1985. *Come to laugh: African traditional theatre in Ghana.* New York: Lilian Barber Press.

Barber, Karin. 1981. How man makes God in West Africa: Yoruba attitudes towards the *orisa. Africa* 51(3):724–45.

———. 1982. Popular reactions to the petro-Naira. *Journal of Modern African Studies* 20(3):43–50.

———. 1984. Yoruba *oriki* and deconstructive criticism. *Research in African Literatures* 15(4):497–518.

———. 1987. Popular arts in Africa. *African Studies Review* 30(3):1–78.

Barnes, Sandra T. 1974. Becoming a Lagosian. Ph.D. diss., University of Wisconsin, Madison.

———. 1980. *Ogun: An old god for a new age.* Occasional Papers in Social Change no. 3. Philadelphia: ISHI.

Baron, Robert. 1976. Syncretism and ideology: Latin New York salsa musicians. *Western Folklore* 35(1):209–25.

Barth, Fredrik. 1966. *Models of social organization.* R. A. I. Occasional Paper no. 23. London: Royal Anthropological Institute.

Bascom, William R. 1951. Social status, wealth, and individual differences among the Yoruba. *American Anthropologist* 53(4):490–505.

———. 1952. The *esusu:* A credit institution of the Yoruba. *Journal of the Royal Anthropological Institute* 82(1):63–69.

———. 1955. Urbanization among the Yoruba. *The American Journal of Sociology* 60:446–54.

———. 1969a. *The Yoruba of southwestern Nigeria.* New York: Holt, Rinehart and Winston.

———. 1969b. *Ifa divination: Communication between men and gods in West Africa.* Bloomington: Indiana University Press.

Becker, Judith, and Alton Becker. 1981. A musical icon: power and meaning in Javanese gamelan music. In *The sign in music and literature,* ed. W. Steiner, 203–15. Austin: University of Texas Press.

Beer, Christopher. 1976. *The politics of peasant groups in western Nigeria.* Ibadan: University of Ibadan Press.

Béhague, Gerard. 1980. Afro-Brazilian folk music traditions. In *The new Grove dictionary of music and musicians,* ed. S. Sadie, vol. 2:240–44. London: Macmillan.

Belasco, Bernard I. 1980. *The entrepreneur as culture hero: Preadaptations in Nigerian economic development.* New York: Praeger.

Bemba, Sylvain. 1985. 50 ans de musique du Congo-Zaire. Paris: Présence Africaine.

Bender, Wolfgang. 1983. *Waka, Sakara, Apala, Fuji: islamische beeinflusste Musik der Yoruba in Nigeria und Benin.* Kommentierte Kataloge zur afrikanischen Musik no. 2. Bayreuth: Iwalewa.

———. 1984. *Songs by Ebenezer Calender in Krio and English.* Song texts of African popular music no. 2. Bayreuth: Iwalewa.

Bergman, Billy. 1985. *Goodtime kings: Emerging African pop.* New York: Quill.

Berry, Sara S. 1985. *Fathers work for their sons.* Berkeley and Los Angeles: University of California Press.

Biobaku, Saburi O. 1957. *The Egba and their neighbours 1841–1872.* Oxford: Clarendon Press.

Blacking, John. 1969. The value of music in human experience. *Yearbook of the International Folk Music Council* 1:33–71.

———. 1971. Deep and surface structures in Venda music. *Yearbook of the International Folk Music Council* 3:91–108.

———. 1973. *How musical is man?* Seattle: University of Washington Press.

———. 1977. Some problems of theory and method in the study of musical change. *Yearbook of the International Folk Music Council* 9:1–26.

Blum, Joseph. 1978. Problems of salsa research. *Ethnomusicology* 22(1):137–49.

Blum, Stephen. 1975. Towards a social history of musicological technique. *Ethnomusicology* 19(2):207–31.

Boas, Franz. 1932. The aims of anthropological research. *Science* n.s. 76:605–13.

Bohlman, Philip. 1988. *The study of folk music in the modern world.* Bloomington: Indiana University Press.

Bourdieu, Pierre. 1977. *Outline of a theory of practice.* Trans. R. Nice. Cambridge: Cambridge University Press.

Brown, S. H. 1964. A history of the people of Lagos, 1852–1936. Ph.D. diss., Northwestern University.

Bucknor, Segun. 1976. The big battle: Pop vs. juju. *Drum Magazine* Sept., 20.

Callaway, Archibald. 1967. From traditional crafts to modern industries. In *The city of Ibadan,* ed. P. C. Lloyd, Akin Mabogunje, and Bolanle Awe, 153–72. Cambridge: Cambridge University Press.

Chernoff, John Miller. 1979. *African rhythm and African sensibility: Aesthetics and social action in African musical idioms.* Chicago: University of Chicago Press.

———. 1985. Africa come back: the popular music of West Africa. In *Repercussions,* ed. G. Haydon and D. Marks, 152–78. London: Century.

Clark, Ebun. 1979. *Hubert Ogunde: The making of Nigerian theatre.* London: Oxford University Press.

Clegg, Johnnie. 1981. The music of Zulu immigrant workers in Johannesburg. International Library of African Music, Grahamstown. Typescript.

Cohen, Abner. 1974. *Two-dimensional man: An essay on the anthropology of power and symbolism in complex society.* Berkeley and Los Angeles: University of California Press.

Cohen, Robin. 1976. From peasants to workers in Africa. In *The political economy of contemporary Africa,* ed. P. C. W. Gutkind and I. Wallerstein, 155–68. Beverly Hills: Sage Publications.

Cole, Patrick D. 1975. *Modern and traditional elites in the politics of Lagos.* Cambridge: Cambridge University Press.

Collins, E. J. 1976. Ghanaian highlife. *African Arts* 10(1):62–68.

———. 1977. Post-war popular band music in West Africa. *African Arts* 10(3):53–60.

———. 1978. Sixty years of West African popular music. *West Africa* 16:2041–4.

———. 1985a. *African pop roots.* London: W. Foulsham.

———. 1985b. *Musicmakers of West Africa.* Washington: Three Continents Press.

Collins, John, and Paul Richards. 1982. Popular music in West Africa: Suggestions for an interpretive framework. In *Popular music perspectives,* ed. D. Horn and P. Tagg, 111–41. Goetburg and Exeter: International Association for the Study of Popular Music.

Comaroff, Jean. 1985. *Body of power, spirit of resistance.* Chicago: University of Chicago Press.

Coplan, David. 1978. Go to my town, Cape Coast! The social history of Ghanaian highlife. In *Eight urban musical cultures,* ed. B. Nettl, 96–114. Urbana: University of Illinois Press.

———. 1979. The African musician and the development of the Johannesburg entertainment industry: 1900–1960. *Journal of Southern African Studies* 5(2):134–64.

———. 1980. Marabi culture: continuity and transformation in African music in Johannesburg, 1920–1940. *African Urban Studies* 6:49–75.

———. 1981a. Popular music. In *The Cambridge encyclopedia of Africa,* ed. M. Crowder and R. Oliver 446–50. Cambridge: Cambridge University Press.

———. 1981b. The emergence of African working-class music in Johannesburg. In *Discourses in ethnomusicology* 2, ed. C. Cord, Bloomington: Indiana University.

———. 1982. The urbanization of African music: Some theoretical observations. *Popular Music* 2:113–29.

———. 1985. *In township tonight! South Africa's black city music and theatre.* New York: Longmans.

Crocker, J. Christopher. 1977. The social functions of rhetorical forms. In *The social use of metaphor: essays in the anthropology of rhetoric*, ed. J. D. Sapir and J. C. Crocker, 33–66. Philadelphia: University of Pennsylvania Press.

Crowder, Michael. 1978. *The Story of Nigeria.* 4th ed. London: Faber and Faber.

Da Cunha, Manuela Carneiro. 1985. *Negros, estrangeiros: os escravos linertos e sua volta à Africa.* Sao Paulo: Editora Brasiliense.

Daramola, Dapo. 1967. O wa n 'be. *Drum Magazine*, July.

Darnton, John. 1977. Nigeria's dissident superstar. *New York Times Magazine*, 24 July, 10–12, 22–24, 26, 28.

Delano, Issac. [1937] 1973. *The soul of Nigeria.* Nendeln: Kraus Reprints.

Denzer, Larry. 1982. Wallace-Johnson and the Sierra Leone labor crisis of 1939. *African Studies Review* 25 (2–3): 159–72.

Eades, J. S. 1980. *The Yoruba today.* Cambridge: Cambridge University Press.

Echeruo, Michael. 1977. *Victorian Lagos: Aspects of nineteenth century Lagosian life.* London: Macmillan.

Ekekwe, Eme N. 1983–84. Notes on oil and contemporary urban culture in Nigeria. *African Urban Studies* 17:19–29.

Ekwueme, Lazarus E. N. 1977. Blackie na Joseph: the sociological implications of a contemporary Igbo popular song. *Nigerian Music* 1:39–65.

Ellingson, Ter. 1979. The Mandala of sound: concepts and sound structures in Tibetan ritual music. Ph.D. dissertation, University of Wisconsin.

Erlmann, Veit. 1987. African music in Durban, 1913–1939. Typescript.

———. 1988. "A feeling of prejudice": Orpheus M. McAdoo and the Virginia Jubilee Singers in South Africa 1890–1898. *Journal of Southern African Studies* 14(3):331–50.

Euba, Akin. 1967. Multiple pitch lines in Yoruba choral music. *Journal of the International Folk Music Council* 19:66–71.

———. 1971. Islamic musical culture among the Yoruba: A preliminary survey. In *Essays on Music and History in Africa*, ed. K. Wachsman, 171–84. Evanston: Northwestern University Press.

———. 1975. The interrelationship of poetry and music in Yoruba tradition. In *Yoruba oral tradition: Poetry in music, dance and drama*, ed. W. Abimbola, 471–87. Ife: Department of African Languages and Literature, University of Ife.

Fabian, Johannes. 1978. Popular culture in Africa: Findings and conjectures. *Africa* 48(4):315–34.

Fadipẹ, N. A. 1970. *The sociology of the Yoruba.* Ibadan: Ibadan University Press.

Feld, Steven. 1982. *Sound and sentiment: Birds, weeping, poetics, and song in Kaluli expression.* Philadelphia: University of Pennsylvania Press.

———. 1984. Sound structure as social structure. *Ethnomusicology* 28(3):383–409.

Fernandez, James W. 1974. The mission of metaphor in expressive culture. *Current Anthropology* 15(2):119–45.

Frey, Roger. 1954. Brazzaville, capitale de l'Afrique Equatoriale. *Encyclopedie mensuelle d'outre-mer*, 48–49.

Gbadamosi, G. O. 1975. Patterns and developments in Lagos religious history. In *Lagos: The development of an African city*, ed. A. B. Aderibigbe, 173–96. Lagos: Longman Nigeria.

Geertz, Clifford. 1973a. Deep play: Notes on the Balinese cockfight. In *The interpretation of cultures*, 412–53. New York: Basic Books.

———. 1973b. Ritual and social change: A Javanese example. In *The interpretation of cultures*, 142–69. New York: Basic Books.

Genovese, Eugene. 1976. *Roll, Jordan, roll: The world the slaves made.* New York: Vintage Books.

Giddens, Anthony. 1984. *The constitution of society.* Berkeley and Los Angeles: University of California Press.

Goffman, Erving. 1959. *The presentation of self in everyday life.* Garden City: Doubleday|Anchor.

Goody, Jack. 1982. *Cooking, cuisine and class: A study in comparative sociology.* Cambridge: Cambridge University Press.

Graf, William D. 1988. *The Nigerian state: Political economy, state class and political system in the post-colonial era.* Portsmouth, NH: Heinemann.

Graham, Ronnie. 1988. *The Da Capo guide to contemporary African music.* New York: Da Capo.

Grass, Randall. 1986. Fela Anikulapo-Kuti: The art of an Afrobeat rebel. *The Drama Review* 30:131–48.

Great Britain. Colonial Office. 1946, 1947, 1955. *Annual report on Nigeria.* London: HMSO.

Green, L. 1974. Migration, urbanisation and national development in Nigeria. In *Modern migrations in West Africa*, ed. S. Amin, London: Oxford University Press.

Gronow, Pekka. 1981. The record industry comes to the Orient. *Ethnomusicology* 25(2):251–84.

Gutkind, P. C. W. 1974. *The emergent African urban proletariat.* Centre for Developing Areas Studies. Occasional Papers no. 8, Montreal: McGill University.

———. 1975. The view from below: political consciousness of the urban poor in Ibadan. *Cahiers d'Etudes Africaines* 57:5–36.

Hall, Edward T. 1984. *The dance of life: The other dimension of time.* Garden City, NY: Anchor Press|Doubleday.

Hall, Stuart, J. Clarke, T. Jefferson, and B. Roberts, eds. 1976. *Resistance through rituals.* London: Hutchinson.

Hamm, Charles. 1985. Rock n' roll in a very strange society. *Popular Music* 5:159–74.

Hampton, Barbara L. 1980. A revised analytical approach to musical processes in urban Africa. *African Urban Studies* 6:1–16.

Hannerz, Ulf. 1980. *Exploring the city: Inquiries toward an urban anthropology.* New York: Columbia University Press.

Hebdige, Dick. 1979. *Subculture: The meaning of style.* London: Methuen.

Herskovits, Melville J. 1938. *Acculturation: The study of culture contact.* New York: J. J. Augustine.

———. [1945] 1966. Problem, method and theory in Afroamerican studies. In *The New World Negro.* Bloomington: Indiana University Press.

Hobsbawm, Eric, and Terence Ranger, eds. 1983. *The Invention of tradition.* Cambridge: Cambridge University Press.

Hopkins, Anthony B. 1966. The Lagos strike of 1897: An exploration in Nigerian labour history. *Past and Present* 35:133–55.

Houlberg, Marilyn. 1983. The texture of change: Yoruba cultural responses to new media. *Cultural Survival Quarterly* 7(2):14–16.

Hughes, Arnold, and Robin Cohen. 1979. An emerging Nigerian working-class: The Lagos experience. In *African labour history,* ed. P. Gutkind, R. Cohen, and J. Copans, 31–55. London: Sage Publications.

Imoagene, Oshomha. 1976. *Social mobility in emergent society: A study of the new elite in Western Nigeria.* Canberra: Department of Demography, The Australian National University.

International Labour Organization. 1982. *Nigeria: First things first.* Addis Ababa: International Labour Organization.

Irvine, Judith T., and J. David Sapir. 1976. Musical style and social change among the Kujamaat Diola. *Ethnomusicology* 20(1):67–86.

Jeyifo, Abiodun, 1984. *The Yoruba popular travelling theatre of Nigeria.* Lagos: Nigeria Magazine Publications.

Johnson, Samuel. 1921. *The history of the Yoruba.* Lagos: Church Missionary Society.

Kanahele, George S. 1979. *Hawaiian music and musicians: An illustrated history.* Honolulu: University of Hawaii Press.

Kapferer, Bruce. 1974. Introduction: transactional models reconsidered. In *Transaction and meaning: Directions in the anthropology of exchange and symbolic behavior,* ed. B. Kapferer, 1–22. Philadelphia: ISHI.

Katz, Ruth. 1970. Mannerism and cultural change: an ethnomusicological example. *Current Anthropology* 2(4–5):465–75.

Kauffman, Robert. 1972. Shona urban music and the problem of acculturation. *Yearbook of the International Folk Music Council* 4:47–56.

———. 1980. Tradition and innovation in the urban music of Zimbabwe. *African Urban Studies* 6:41–48.

Kazadi, P. C. 1973. Trends of nineteenth and twentieth century music in Congo-Zaire. In *Musikkulturen Asiens, Afrikas und Ozeaniens im 19 Jahrhundert,* 267–83. Regensburg: Gustav Bosse Verlag.

Keil, Angeliki, and Charles Keil. 1977. In pursuit of polka happiness. *Cultural Correspondence* 5:5–11, 74. Reprinted in *Musical Traditions* 2 (1984):6–11.

Keil, Charles. 1966–67. Field notes on Yoruba popular music, Lagos and Ibadan, Nigeria. Handwritten papers and notebooks.

———. 1969. The evolution of juju. Paper presented at the annual meeting of the African Studies Association. Los Angeles.

———. 1979. *Tiv song: The sociology of art in a classless society.* Chicago: University of Chicago Press.

———. 1984. Response to Feld and Roseman: symposium on comparative sociomusicology. *Ethnomusicology* 28(3):446–9.

———. 1985. People's music comparatively: style and stereotype, class and hegemony. *Dialectical Anthropology* 10:119–30.

———. 1986. Participatory discrepancies and the power of music. Paper presented at the 85th annual meeting of the American Anthropological Association. Philadelphia.

Killam, G. D. 1968. *Africa in English fiction, 1874–1939.* Ibadan: University of Ibadan Press.

King, Anthony V. 1961. *Yoruba sacred music from Ekiti.* Ibadan: University of Ibadan Press.

Kinney, Esi S., ed. 1970. Special issue on African urban music. *African Urban Notes* 5.

Koetting, James. 1970. Analysis and notation of West African drum ensemble music. *Selected Reports in Ethnomusicology* 1(3):116–46.

Koll, M. 1969. *Crafts and cooperation in Western Nigeria.* Freiburg: Bergstraesser Institute.

Kopytoff, Jean Herskovits. 1965. *A preface to modern Nigeria: The "Sierra Leoneans" in Yoruba, 1830–1890.* Madison: University of Wisconsin Press.

Krapf-Askari, Eva. 1969. *Yoruba towns and cities: An enquiry into the nature of urban social phenomena.* Oxford: Clarendon Press.

Kubik, Gerhard. 1971. Die Verarbeitung von Kwela, Jazz und Pop in der modernen musik von Malawi. *Jazzforschung* 3–4.

———. 1974. *The Kachamba Brothers' Band.* Zambian Papers 9. Manchester.

———. 1980. Donald Kachamba's montage recordings: Aspects of urban music history in Malawi. *African Urban Studies* 6:89–122.

———. 1981. Neo-traditional popular music in East Africa since 1945. *Popular Music* 1:83–104.

Kuper, Adam. 1975. *Anthropologists and anthropology: The British School, 1922–1972.* New York: Pica Press.

Labinjoh, Justin. 1982. Fela Anikulapo-Kuti: Protest music and social processes in Nigerian. *Journal of Black Studies* 13(1).

La Fontaine, Jean. 1970. *City politics: A study of Leopoldville, 1962–63.* Cambridge: Cambridge University Press.

Laitin, David. 1986. *Hegemony and culture: Politics and religious change among the Yoruba.* Chicago: University of Chicago Press.

Lakoff, George, and Mark Johnson. 1980. *Metaphors We Live By.* Chicago: University of Chicago Press.

Langer, Susanne K. 1957. *Philosophy in a new key: A study in the symbolism of reason, rite, and art.* 3d ed. Cambridge: Harvard University Press.

Laotan, A. B. 1943. *The torch bearers or the old Brazilian colony in Lagos.* Lagos: Ife-Olu Printers.

Laoye I, Timi of Ede. 1959. Yoruba drums. *Odu* 7:5–14.

Law, Robin C. 1970. The chronology of the Yoruba wars of the early nineteenth century: A reconsideration. *Journal of the Historical Society of Nigeria* 5(2):211–22.

—————. 1973. The heritage of Oduduwa: Traditional history and political propoganda among the Yoruba. *Journal of African History* 14(2):207–27.

—————. 1977. *The Oyo Empire, c. 1600–c. 1836.* Oxford: Clarendon Press.

Leach, Edmund. 1976. *Culture and communication.* New York: Cambridge University Press.

Lévi-Strauss, Claude. 1963. *Structural anthropology.* New York: Basic Books.

Little, Kenneth. 1970. *West African urbanization: A study of voluntary associations in social change.* Cambridge: Cambridge University Press.

Lloyd, Peter C. 1953. Craft organization in Yoruba towns. *Africa* 23(1):30–4.

—————. 1962. *Yoruba land law.* London: Oxford University Press.

—————. 1966. Agnatic and cognatic descent among the Yoruba. *Man,* n.s. 1(4):484–500.

—————. 1967. Introduction. In *The city of Ibadan,* ed. P. C. Lloyd, A. Mabogunje, and B. Awe. 1–10. Ibadan: University of Ibadan Press.

—————. 1970. Ondo descent. *Man,* n.s. 5(2):310–12.

—————. 1971. *The political development of Yoruba kingdoms in the eighteenth and nineteenth centuries.* London: Royal Anthropological Institute.

—————. 1973. The Yoruba: An urban people? In *Urban anthropology: Cross-cultural studies of urbanization,* ed. A. Southall, New York: Oxford University Press.

—————. 1974. *Power and independence: Urban Africans' perception of social inequality.* London: Routledge and Kegan Paul.

Lloyd, P. C., Akin Mabogunje, and Bolanle Awe, eds. 1967. *The city of Ibadan.* Ibadan: Ibadan University Press.

Lomax, Alan. 1962. Song structure and social structure. *Ethnology* 1(4):425–51.

Lonoh, Major. 1969. *Essai de commentaire sur la musique congolaise moderne.* Kinshasa: Imprimerie St. Paul.

Low, John. 1982. A history of Kenyan guitar music: 1945–1980. *African Music* 6(2):17–36.

M.E.N./I.N.R.A.P. 1984. *La Chanson Congolaise.* Paris: Editions Fernand Nathan.

Mabogunje, A. L. 1967. The morphology of Ibadan. In *The city of Ibadan,* ed. P. C. Lloyd, Akin Mabogunje, and Bolanle Awe, 35–56. Cambridge: Cambridge University Press.

—————. 1969. *Urbanization in Nigeria.* New York: Africana Publishing Corporation.

Macherey, Pierre. 1978. *A theory of literary production.* Trans. G. Wall. London: Routledge and Kegan Paul.

Mackay, Ian. 1964. *Broadcasting in Nigeria.* Ibadan: Ibadan University Press.

Macmillan, Allister. [1920] 1968. *The red book of West Africa.* London: Frank Cass.

Mann, Kristin. 1985. *Marrying well: Marriage, status and social change among the educated elite in colonial Lagos.* Cambridge: Cambridge University Press.

Manuel, Peter. 1988. *Popular musics of the non-western world.* New York, Oxford: Oxford University Press.

Marcus, Geroge E., and Michael M. J. Fischer. 1986. *Anthropology as cultural critique: An experimental moment in the human sciences.* Chicago: University of Chicago Press.

Marre, Jeremy, and Hannah Charlton. 1985. *Beats of the heart: Popular music of the world.* London: Pluto Press.

Martin, Steven H. 1980. Music in urban East Africa: A study of the development of urban jazz in Dar es Salaam. Ph.D. diss., University of Washington.

———. 1982. Music in urban East Africa: Five genres in Dar es Salaam. *Journal of African Studies* 9(3).

Matondo, Kanza. 1972. *La musique zairoise moderne: Situation actuelle et perspectives d'avenir.* Kinshasa: Conservatoire National de Musique et d'Art Dramatique.

Mayer, Philip. 1961. *Townsmen or tribesmen: Conservatism and the process of urbanization in a South African city.* Cape Town: Oxford University Press.

McAllester, David P. 1954. *Enemy Way Music.* Papers of the Peabody Museum of American Archaeology and Ethnology 41(3).

McGrath, Joseph E. and Janice R. Kelly. 1986. Time and human interaction: Toward a social psychology of time. New York: The Guilford Press.

Mensah, Atta. 1966. The impact of Western music on the musical traditions of Ghana. *Composer* 19:19–22.

———. 1970. Song texts as reflectors of external influence. *African Urban Notes* 5(4):42–51.

———. 1971. Jazz: the round trip. *Jazzforschung* 3–4.

Merriam, Alan P. 1955. The use of music in the study of a problem of acculturation. *American Anthropologist* 57:28–34.

———. 1964. *The anthropology of music.* Evanston: Northwestern University Press.

———. 1967. *Ethnomusicology of the Flathead Indians.* Chicago: Aldine Press.

———. 1973. The Bala musician. In *The traditional artist in African societies,* ed. W. D'Azevedo, 250–81. Bloomington: Indiana University Press.

———. 1982. African musical rhythm and concepts of time-reckoniong. In *African music in perspective,* 443–61. New York: Garland Publishing.

Mitchell, J. Clyde. 1956. *The Kalela Dance.* Rhodes-Livingstone Papers no. 27. Manchester: Manchester University Press.

Moore, Carlos. 1982. *Fela, Fela, this bitch of a life.* London: Allison and Busby.

Morton-Williams, Peter. 1973. An outline of the cosmology and cult organization of the Oyo Yoruba. In *Peoples and Cultures of Africa,* ed. E. Skinner, 654–77. Garden City, NY: Doubleday, Natural History Press.

Mukuna, Kazadi wa. 1980a. The origin of Zairean modern music: a socioeconomic aspect. *African Urban Studies* 6:31–9.

———. 1981. The origin of Zaire modern music: result of a socio-economic process. *Jazzforschung* 13:139–50.

———, ed. 1980b. Special issue on African urban music. *African Urban Studies* 6.

Mustapha, Oyebamiji. 1975. A literary appraisal of Sakara: a Yoruba traditional form of music. In *Yoruba oral tradition: Poetry in music, dance and drama*, ed. W. Abimbola, 517–49. Ife: Department of African Languages and Literatures, University of Ife.

Neisser, Ulric. 1976. Cognition and reality: Principles of cognitive psychology. San Francisco: W. H. Freeman.

Nettl, Bruno. 1978a. Some aspects of the history of world music in the twentieth century: Questions, problems, and concepts. *Ethnomusicology* 22(1):123–36.

———. 1978b. Musical values and social values: Symbols in Iran. *Journal of the Steward Anthropological Society* 10(1):123.

———. 1983. *The study of ethnomusicology: Twenty-nine issues and concepts.* Urbana: University of Illinois Press.

———. 1985. *The western impact on world music: Change, adaptation, and survival.* New York: Schirmer.

———. 1989. *Blackfoot musical thought: comparative perspectives.* Kent, OH: Kent State University Press.

———, ed. 1978c. *Eight urban musical cultures: Tradition and change.* Urbana: University of Illinois Press.

Neuman, Daniel M. 1980. *The life of music in North India: The organization of an artistic tradition.* Detroit: Wayne State University Press.

Nisbet, Robert A. 1969. *Social change and history: Aspects of the western theory of development.* New York: Oxford University Press.

Nketia, J. H. Kwabena. 1955. The gramophone and contemporary African music in the Gold Coast. West African Institute of Social and Economic Research. *Proceedings* 5:191–201.

———. 1957. Modern trends in Ghana music. *African Music* 1(4):13–17.

Nurse, George T. 1964. Popular songs and national identity in Malawi. *African Music* 3(3):101–6.

Ojo, G. J. Afolabi. 1966. *Yoruba culture: A geographical analysis.* Ibadan: University of Ibadan Press.

Ojo, Olasebikan. 1978. Sakara music as a literary form. Senior honors thesis, University of Ibadan.

Okagbere, B. C. 1969. *The Songs of I. K. Dairo.* Lagos: Nigerian National Press.

Okediji, Oladejo O. 1978. On voluntary associations as an adaptive mechanism in West African urbanization: Another perspective. In *The processes of urbanism: A multidisciplinary approach*, ed. J. Aschenbrenner and L. R. Collins, 195–222. The Hague: Mouton.

Okonjo, C. 1967. Stranger communities: the Western Ibo. In *The city of Ibadan*, ed. P. C. Lloyd, Akin Mabogunje, and Bolanle Awe, 97–116. Cambridge: Cambridge University Press.

Olabode, Afolabi. 1974. Àpàlà Songs in Yorùbá Land. Senior honors Paper, University of Ibadan.

Olinto, Antonio. 1970. *The water house* (A casa da agua). Trans. D. Heapy. London: Rex Collings.

Olusanya, G. O. 1973. *The Second World War and politics in Nigeria 1939–1953.* London: Evans Brothers.

Omibiyi, Mosunmola. 1976. Interaction between African and Afro-American music. *International Congress of Americanists* 62:597–604.

———. 1981. Popular music in Nigeria. *Jazzforschung* 13:151–72.

Onimole, M. O. 1949. Ju-Orchestra. *Nigeria Magazine* 32:88.

Osoba, Segun. 1978. The deepening crisis of the Nigerian national bourgeoisie. *Review of African Political Economy* 13:63–77.

Oven. *See* Van Oven.

Paine, Robert. 1974. *Second thoughts about Barth's models.* London: Royal Anthropological Institute.

Peace, Adrian. 1974. Industrial protest in Nigeria. In *Sociology and development,* ed. E. DeKadt and G. Williams, 141–67. London: Tavistock.

Peel, J. D. Y. 1968. *Aladura: A religious movement among the Yoruba.* London: Oxford University Press.

———. 1984. Making history: The past in the Ijesha present. *Man,* n.s. 19:111–32.

Peña, Manuel. 1985. *The Texas-Mexican conjunto: History of a working-class music.* Austin: University of Texas Press.

Post, Kenneth W., and George Jenkins. 1973. *The price of liberty.* Cambridge: Cambridge University Press.

Ranger, Terence O. 1975. *Dance and society in eastern Africa,* 1890–1970. London: Heinemann.

Read, Sir Herbert. 1952. *English prose style.* New York: Pantheon Books.

Riesman, Paul. 1986. The person and the life-cycle in African social life and thought. *African Studies Review* 29(2):71–138.

Roberts, John Storm. 1968. Popular music in Kenya. *African Music* 4(2):53–55.

———. 1972. *Black music of two worlds.* New York: Praeger.

Robertson-DeCarbo, Carol. 1977. Tayil as category and communication among the Argentine Mapuche. *Yearbook of the International Folk Music Council* 8:35–52.

Roseman, Marina. 1984. The social structuring of sound: The Temiar of peninsular Malaysia. *Ethnomusicology* 28(3):411–45.

Rycroft, David. 1956. Melodic imports and exports: a byproduct of recording in South Africa. *Bulletin of the British Institute of Recorded Sound* 1.

———. 1958. The new "town" music of southern Africa. *Recorded Folk Music* 1.

———. 1959. African music in Johannesburg: African and non-African features. *Journal of the International Folk Music Council* 11:25–30.

———. 1961. The guitar improvisations of Mwenda Jean Bosco, Part 1. *African Music* 2(4):81–98.

———. 1962. The guitar improvisations of Mwenda Jean Bosco, Part 2. *African Music* 3(1):86–102.

———. 1977. Evidence of stylistic continuity in Zulu "town" music. In *Essays for a humanist: An offering to Klaus Wachsman,* 216–60. New York: Town House Press.

Sahlins, Marshall. 1976. *Culture and practical reason.* Chicago: University of Chicago Press.

———. 1981. *Historical metaphors and mythical realities: Structure in the early history of the Sandwich Islands kingdom.* Association for Social Anthropology in Oceania, Special Publication Series 1. Ann Arbor: University of Michigan Press.

Sakata, Hiromi Lorraine. 1983. *Music in the mind: The concepts of music and musician in Afghanistan.* Kent, OH: Kent State University Press.

Sapir, J. David, and J. Christopher Crocker, eds. 1977. *The social use of metaphor: Essays on the anthropology of rhetoric.* Philadelphia: University of Pennsylvania Press.

Schafer, R. Murray. 1980. *The tuning of the world: Toward a theory of soundscape design.* Philadelphia: University of Pennsylvania Press.

Schutz, Alfred. [1951] 1977. Making music together: A study in social relationship. In *Symbolic Anthropology,* ed. J. L. Dolgin, D. S. Kemnitzer, and D. M. Schneider, 106–19. New York: Columbia University Press.

Schwab, William B. 1955. Kinship and lineage among the Yoruba. *Africa* 25(4):352–74.

Seeger, Anthony. 1987. *Why Suyá sing: A musical anthropology of an Amazonian people.* Cambridge: Cambridge University Press.

Shepherd, John. 1982. A theoretical model for the sociomusicological analysis of popular musics. *Popular Music* 2:145–78.

Sklar, Richard L. 1963. *Nigerian political parties: Power in an emergent African nation.* Princeton: Princeton University Press.

Smith, Edna M. 1962. Popular music in West Africa. *African Music* 3(1):11–17.

Sprigge, Robert. 1971. The Ghanaian highlife: notation and sources. *Music in Ghana* 2:70–94.

Stapleton, Chris, and Chris May. 1987. *African all-stars: The pop music of a continent.* London: Quartet Books.

Stevens, Christopher. 1984. *The political economy of Nigeria.* London: The Economist.

Stone, Ruth M. 1985. In search of time in African music. *Music Theory Spectrum* 7:139–48.

Szwed, John F. 1970. Afro-American musical adaptation. In *Afro-American anthropology: Contemporary perspectives,* ed. N. E. Whitten, Jr., and J. Szwed, 219–28. New York: The Free Press.

Tate, Greg. 1983. Are you ready for Juju? *Village Voice,* 15 Mar. 1983, 1, 34–5, 81.

Thieme, Darius. 1967. Style in Yoruba music. *Ibadan,* June, 33–39.

———. 1969. A descriptive catalog of Yoruba musical instruments. Ph.D. diss., Catholic University of America.

Thompson, Robert Farris. 1961. Highlife in Nigeria. *Saturday Review* 44, 26 Aug. 34–35.

———. 1966. An aesthetic of the cool: West African dance. *African Forum* 2(2):85–102.

———. 1971. *Black gods and kings: Yoruba art at UCLA.* Bloomington: Indiana University Press.

———. 1974. *African art in motion.* Berkeley and Los Angeles: University of California Press.

Titon, Jeff. 1977. *Early downhome blues: A musical and cultural analysis.* Urbana: University of Illinois Press.

Turino, Thomas. 1989. The coherence of social style and musical creation among the Aymara in southern Peru. *Ethnomusicology* 33(1):1–30.

Turnbull, Colin. 1962. *The forest people.* New York: Simon and Schuster.

Turner, H. W. 1967. *African Independent Church* 2 vols. London: Oxford University Press.

Turner, Terisa. 1985. Petroleum, recession and the internationalization of class struggle in Nigeria. Labour, Capital and Society 18(1):000–000.

Turner, Victor. 1974. *Dramas, fields, and metaphors.* Ithaca: Cornell University Press.

Udo, R. K. 1982. Ibadan in its regional setting. In *Ibadan region,* ed. M. O. Filani, 1–15. Ibadan: Geography Department, University of Ibadan.

Vail, Leroy, and Landeg White. 1983. Forms of resistance: songs and perceptions of power in colonial Mozambique. *The American Historical Review* 88(4):883–919.

Van Oven, Cootje. 1980. Sierra Leone. In *The new Grove dictionary of music and musicians* vol. 17: 302–4. London: Macmillan.

Vidal, Tunji. 1977. Traditions and history in Yoruba music. *Nigerian Music Review* 1:66–92.

———. 1983. Two decades of juju music among the Yoruba people. Typescript. Ife: Department of Music, University of Ife.

Wachsmann, Klaus. 1980. Africa. In *The new Grove dictionary of music and musicians,* Vol. 1: 144–53. London: Macmillan.

Ware, Naomi. 1970. Popular musicians in Freetown. *African Urban Notes* 5(4):11–18.

———. 1978. Popular music and African identity in Freetown, Sierra Leone. In *Eight urban musical cultures: tradition and change,* ed. B. Nettl, 296–320. Urbana: University of Illinois Press.

Waterman, Christopher A. 1982. "I'm a leader, not a boss": Popular music and social identity in Ibadan, Nigeria. *Ethnomusicology* 26(1):59–72.

———. 1985. Juju. In *The Western impact on world music: Change, adaptation, and survival,* ed. Bruno Nettl, 87–90. New York: Schirmer Books.

———. 1988. Aṣíkò, sákárà and palmwine: popular music and social identity in inter-War Lagos, Nigeria. *Urban Anthropology* 17(2–3):229–58.

Waterman, Peter. 1976. Conservatism amongst Nigerian workers. In Nigeria: Economy and society, ed. G. Williams, London: Rex Collings.

Waterman, Richard A. 1952. African influence on the music of the Americas. In *Acculuration in the Americas,* Vol. 2. Proceedings of the 29th International Congress of Americanists, ed. S. Tax, 207–18. Chicago: University of Chicago Press.

———. 1963. On flogging a dead horse: lessons learned from the Africanisms controversy. *Ethnomusicology* 7(2):83–87.

Watts, Michael, and Paul Lubeck. 1983. The popular classes and the Oil Boom: A political economy of rural and urban poverty. In *The political economy of Nigeria,* ed. I. W. Zartman, 105–44. New York: Praeger.

Westermarck, Edward. 1926. *Ritual and belief in Morocco*. 2 vols. London: Macmillan.

Whitten, Norman E., Jr. 1970. Personal networks and musical contexts in the Pacific lowlands of Colombia and Ecuador. In *Afro-American anthropology: Contemporary perspectives*, ed. N.E. Whitten, Jr., and J. Szwed, 203–17. New York: Free Press.

Williams, Gavin. 1976. Nigeria: A political economy. In *Nigeria: Economy and society*, ed. G. Williams, 11–54. London: Rex Collings.

Williams, Raymond. 1977. *Marxism and literature*. Oxford: Oxford University Press.

Young, Crawford. 1982. *Ideology and development in Africa*. New Haven: Yale University Press.

Zahan, Dominique. 1963. *La dialectique du verbe chez les Bambara*. Paris: Mouton.

Zemp, Hugo. 1971. *Musique Dan: La musique dans la pensée et la vie sociale d'une société africaine*. Paris: Mouton.

Zindi, Fred. 1985. *Roots rocking in Zimbabwe*. Harare: Mambo Press.

Index